Australia's OUTBACK

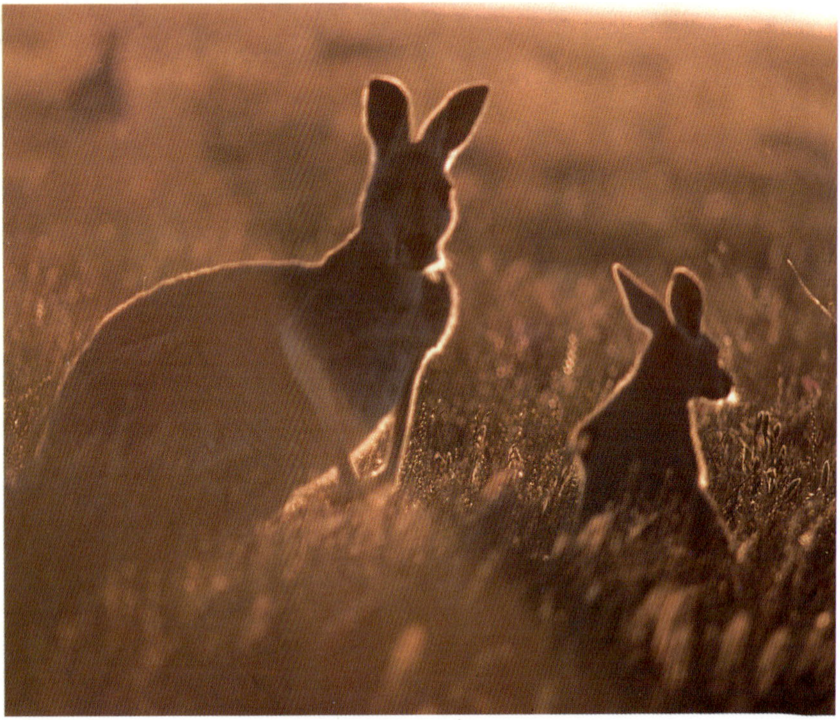

ENVIRONMENTAL FIELD GUIDE

Australia's OUTBACK

Frank Haddon

SIMON & SCHUSTER
AUSTRALIA

PHOTO CREDITS

Murray Fagg, page 71; G.A. Hoye/NPIAW, page 182; A.Y. Pepper/NPIAW, page 171, bottom; P.E. Roberts, page 179; J.D. Waterhouse, page 59; Babs & Bert Wells/NPIAW, page 118.
Background cover photograph by Jonathan Chester/Extreme Images

THE ENVIRONMENTAL FIELD GUIDE TO AUSTRALIA'S OUTBACK

First published in Australasia in 1992 by
Simon & Schuster Australia
20 Barcoo Street, East Roseville NSW 2069

A Paramount Communications Company
Sydney New York London Toronto Tokyo Singapore

© 1992 Text and photographs, Frank Haddon;
illustrations, Simon & Schuster Australia

All rights reserved. No part of this publication may be reproduced, stored in a retrieval system, or transmitted, in any form or by any means, electronic, mechanical, photocopying, recording or otherwise, without the prior permission of the publisher in writing.

National Library of Australia
Cataloguing in Publication data

Haddon, Frank, 1942–
　Environmental field guide to Australia's outback.

　Includes index.
　ISBN 0 7318 0008 7.

　　1. Botany – Australia. 2. Zoology – Australia. 3. Ecology – Australia. 4. Plants – Identification. 5. Animals – Identification. I. Title.

581.994

Project coordinated by Elizabeth Halley
Designed by Michelle Havenstein
Illustrated by Craig Webb
Typeset in Garamond and Futura by Asset Typesetting Pty Ltd
Printed in Hong Kong by South China Printing Company

Contents

Introduction 6

Roadside 11
Mammals 13
Birds 18
Reptiles and Amphibians 28
Insects 31
Plants 35

Farmland 46
Mammals 48
Birds 54
Reptiles and Amphibians 61
Insects 68
Plants 69

Rivers, Swamps, Billabongs and Lakes 73
Mammals 75
Birds 76
Reptiles and Amphibians 93
Fish and Crustaceans 96
Insects 102
Plants 103

Forests and Woodlands 110
Mammals 112
Birds 118
Reptiles and Amphibians 137
Insects 141
Plants 144

Scrubland and Shrubland 154
Mammals 156
Birds 165
Reptiles and Amphibians 180
Insects 184
Plants 185

Further Reading List 195
Index 197

Introduction

Ever since the first time I travelled in the outback, I have revelled in the wide open space, the tang of the dust, and the sense of being away from the pressures of everyday life. This book is an opportunity to share my delight in learning the names and characteristics of the extraordinary range of plants and animals we have in Australia and, more importantly, the interactions and inter-relationships that hold the whole wonderful web together.

I have had heated arguments with outback people about why snakes should be protected, and the cause and effect of removing any species from the natural system. It is not just because we should preserve the species for future generations, it is because they are a vital part of the controls and balances that keep an ecosystem viable.

A balanced ecosystem does not mean one which always has the same number of plant and animal species. There may be wild swings in numbers of species depending on the seasons or climatic conditions, but the forces of natural balance swing it back. Lake Eyre in southern central Australia, for instance, is usually a dry salt lake, but every few years it fills up with water and, when this occurs, there is an incredible increase in the waterbird population as huge numbers of birds arrive to feed and breed. Then, when the lake evaporates away in the burning heat of the inland sun, thousands of birds perish as their food source disappears. The pendulum has swung and the natural balance is maintained.

No part of the ecosystem of the outback can exist on its own. All parts are interlinked and dependent upon another, whether it be directly by providing food or shelter, or indirectly by displaying features that preserve the ecosystem, for instance, kangaroos do not breed during drought times.

The plants and animals isolated in Australia since the Ice Age have evolved in a unique fashion. Outback plants can cope with one of the harshest climates in the world by minimising water loss. Insect species adapted by developing mouthparts that can chew tough leaves, and digestive systems that can cope with aromatic but toxic oils such as eucalyptus. Bird evolution was also influenced by the nature of the plants, so that we have species like the malleefowl, whose very

INTRODUCTION

survival is tied to the preservation of its mallee habitat. Kangaroos are dependent upon the grasses and herbs that provide their food, but their long legs do little damage to the land or to the soil, compared to the sharp pointed hooves of sheep.

The Aboriginal people have been an established and influential part of the outback for over 40 000 years. Their use of fires, with the resulting green pick, affected the evolutionary pattern of plants and animals. After a fire, the plants produce new growth, which in turn attracts and feeds more animals for the Aborigines to hunt. Trees resistant to fire, like the eucalypt with its fire-tolerant bark, became widely established in Australia, as did animals that can survive bushfires and thrive on the green pick, like the burrowing wombat, and the fleet-footed kangaroo.

Early white settlement of the outback was based on the exploitation of the little grazing land that was available. The fragile nature of arid-land plants meant they could not cope with grazing by hardfooted animals like sheep and cattle, and many outback areas were devastated.

The introduction of the rabbit and other species such as cats, camels, donkeys and goats, has caused major disturbances to the web. The ramifications of the damage to the outback ecosystem caused by the rabbit are still being felt today, 130 years after its first release.

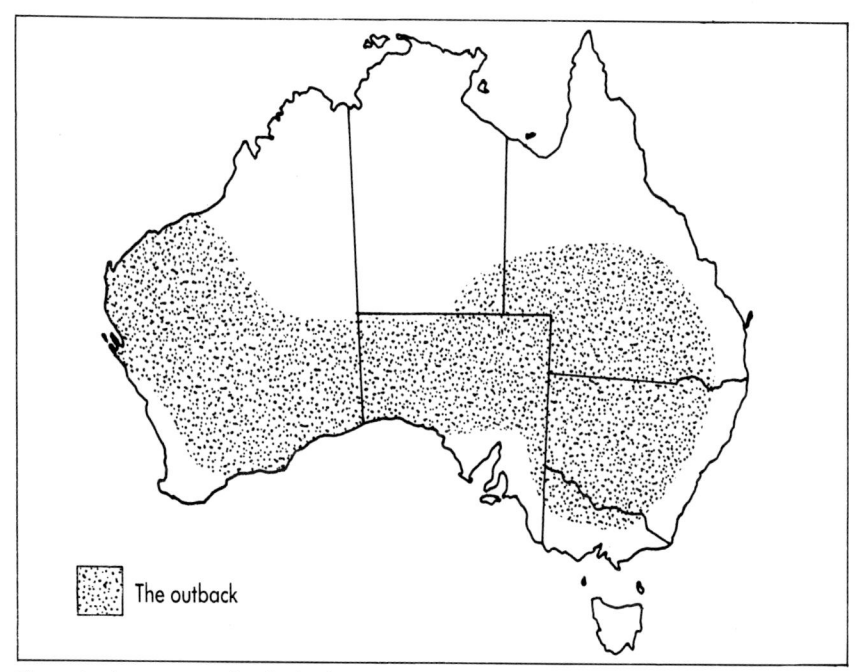

The outback area covered in this book

INTRODUCTION

Land management does not always sit well with short-term exploitation, but many of today's farmers and graziers have learnt from the mistakes of the past, and are well on the way to sustaining the natural ecosystem while continuing to make a reasonable living from it.

The outback requires understanding by all those who use it, be they farmers, miners or travellers. Outback travellers are often strangers in a hostile land. Even with bitumen roads and service stations out on the wide expanse of the open plains, the outback must never be taken lightly. These days it is possible to travel to wild and arid zones and have the convenience of airconditioned cars and motel accommodation, or even to fly to luxurious hotels and have five-star living in between walks through the spinifex and ghost gums. Nevertheless, every traveller should be aware of what can happen. Understanding the possible hazards and planning for each eventuality is essential.

Remoteness and the dangers associated with extremes of heat, must give you some pause for thought. Often you will be several hundred kilometres from the nearest medical help, or even the nearest habitation. The car traveller in the outback must always carry spare water and petrol, and in sufficient quantities. When you realise that an adult can consume between 6 and 8 litres of water a day in very hot weather, carrying a 1 litre soft drink bottle will not be much help if you are stranded for several days. You also need to know the approximate kilometres per litre of petrol (or diesel) used by your vehicle, to calculate a safe margin so that you do not run out of fuel.

Unfortunately, many people still rely upon the chance that if they run into trouble someone will be along in a short while. It is true that Australia's outback is now travelled more than ever before, and some parts have traffic over the roads and tracks in a fairly constant stream. Never rely on this at any time of the year, because that stream of traffic can completely disappear if a road is cut by a flash flood. There have been countless tales of stranded vehicles, left in an endless sea of floodwater, with desperate people waiting for help. Planning and forethought can prevent that desperation, even though it may not lessen the hazard.

Obviously it is essential that the vehicle to be used is thoroughly checked before and during any outback trip. A broken fanbelt can cripple a car as surely as a broken axle and, while it would be unrealistic to expect outback travellers to carry a full set of spares for their car, a good mechanic can tell you what it would be sensible to carry.

Of course, there is one answer to all of these hazards: only travel those roads that have inbuilt safety insurance, like emergency telephones or frequent towns and villages. You may see a road that

INTRODUCTION

you want to follow because it leads to a place you have heard about — and off you go. Before long you have left the security of the tar road and telephones, and you are a long way from the nearest fresh water or petrol station. Be prepared for such an eventuality.

Before you leave on your trip, know where you are going. This may sound unadventurous, but you will need to take maps, guide books for national parks, or other information sheets. Also contact your state National Parks And Wildlife service to obtain their code of practice for outback travellers, particularly that relating to protected species, farm stock and fences. Do your homework before you leave. Understand the distances you will have to travel in relation to time and fuel and be conscious of the nearest point where assistance would be available.

If you are going into very remote areas find out from the nearest police station, or better still from travellers who have recently returned from those areas, what the road conditions are like, and if your vehicle is suitable for the road you are going to travel. In some places it may even be advisable to inform the police where you are going just in case you do run into trouble.

Finally, know what the weather is going to be like. In the outback of Australia during the summer months (December, January and February) the temperature can exceed 45°C in the shade, and there is no shade. The outback heat in many months of the year is severe and totally debilitating, and simply cannot be ignored. Also be aware of those places that are likely to have winter or summer rain, or be affected by monsoon rains, as many roads in the outback are totally impassable after even the smallest amount of rain, even in four-wheel drives.

My wish is that, like me, you will want to get out of the car and take a look at that lizard you see crawling away, or to notice the roadside covered with flowers and want to know what they are. What was that funny-shaped lizard? And how can you tell if that bird circling overhead was really a wedge-tailed eagle? What were those beautifully concentric little cones dug into the fine red sand of the bush track? How come some years driving country roads in summer becomes a constant battle with hundreds of insects splattering on the windscreen?

I hope this book leads you to not just hear the beautiful call of a bird on a clear, crisp outback morning, but to track that bird down and find out something about it. This way I can share my love for the countryside of Australia and make you feel a kinship for it too. Once you feel you belong, you will come to understand more about the elements that make it so special and why it is essential for our own survival that we do not wantonly destroy it. Obviously it is important not to disturb the wildlife — to leave nothing but footprints and take nothing but photos. Some plants and animals are poisonous,

INTRODUCTION

and it is always best not to touch — you could damage them and they could damage you.

The book is divided into five chapters: 'Roadside', 'Farmland', 'Rivers, Swamps, Billabongs and Lakes', 'Forests and Woodlands' and 'Scrubland and Shrubland'. These are all artificial sections in the outback because animals and plants know no such boundaries. They are places where you are likely to see a species, but you are just as likely to see a rabbit or a hare on the roadside as on a farm. If you see a plant or an animal, and you do not know what it is called, turn to the chapter which corresponds with the place where you saw it. Species are grouped within each chapter into the following categories: 'Mammals', 'Birds', 'Reptiles and Amphibians', 'Fish and Crustaceans' and 'Plants'. You may have to look in another chapter if you don't find a particular plant or animal in the first chapter you look under. If you know the name of the species, the 'Index' at the back of this book will direct you to the page with information about that species. The divisions in the book are to make it easier for the road traveller, the day bushwalker, the camper or the casual visitor to quickly find an animal or plant, identify it, and come to know a little more about it.

This book does not pretend to be a scientific field guide, with keys and careful descriptions of the major features of the plants and animals. It is meant to be 'user friendly', something that can be flicked through or read at leisure, or used to very quickly find the name of a plant or animal. No book like this can hope to cover anything but a small percentage of the living things in an area, but it will guide you to know where the plant or animal fits in a broad group. If you wish to learn more I have included a 'Further Reading List' at the end of the book, and even these titles could be only a starting point to much more detailed investigation.

The species in the book are the ones most likely to be seen by the casual observer in the outback. Where there are several species of animal or plant that are very similar, usually only one or two have been given, for instance only a couple of the many species of honeyeaters are included, and likewise for daisies. More specific information, if required, will be easier to access from texts in the 'Further Reading List' once you recognise the group to which the plant or animal belongs.

Note: The sizes given for birds are the length from beak to toe, when the neck is stretched out in front and the legs out behind. Egg sizes are only included when they are particularly large or small.

CHAPTER ONE

Roadside

So much of the outback is now accessible by good roads that almost everyone can experience the special environment of the Australian 'bush'. Unfortunately, the distances are usually so great that all you want to do is get from place to place as quickly as possible. There is not a lot you can see when travelling at 100 kph.

Still, even at that speed there are animals and plants you will see near the road. When you stop for a drink at a roadside rest place, you are bound to see some of the animals and plants in this chapter.

It is quite usual to see a form of plant community growing along roadsides that is totally different from the farmland plants. As you drive, ride or walk, notice how farm fences not only form a boundary to keep farm animals in, they also form a boundary between distinct plant types.

Many outback roads were used as stock routes, taking sheep and cattle from the farm to the marketplace or to another farm. Since the

Roadside near Cobar, NSW

introduction of big transport trucks this practice has almost ceased, so that the grasses and other plants have been able to regenerate. In some places the old stock routes are the best places to find interesting and rare plants — ground orchids, for example, because the ground is no longer compacted around them.

You will notice along the side of many outback roads a wide drain called a 'table drain'. Obviously, this is to carry the water away from the road surface, serving as a catchment for any rain that falls. Water often lies in the table drain long after it has left all other areas around, which makes the drains excellent areas for the growth of plants. The plants then attract animals, particularly seed-loving birds and grass-eating kangaroos.

The grain spilled from trucks on the way to the silo provides easy pickings for birds such as galahs, that are attracted from kilometres around. You will see huge flocks of these beautiful grey and pink birds feeding on roadsides in the summer harvest season.

If you see a flock some distance ahead, sound your horn. It will not always make them fly out of your road, but it gives them a little chance. It is a very unpleasant experience for both the bird and the driver if a collision occurs.

Roads serve as 'larders' for many of the meat-eating animals. Dead animals are a common sight in the outback, from animals as large as red kangaroos to small frogs. Roads form unnatural barriers to the movement of many outback animals, and they have no protection from speeding cars.

On some memorable occasions you are sure to come across the sight of the majestic wedge-tailed eagle feeding on an animal that has been killed by a vehicle. It is an unhappy fate for the dead animal, but one that lets you see Australia's largest eagle at close range.

If you are driving at dusk or early evening, extreme care must be taken on many outback roads, as kangaroos can cross without warning. Reasonable speeds, excellent headlights, and someone to act as an assistant 'spotter' to help you see the animals, all help. The best answer is to avoid travelling those roads at night that have the 'Kangaroos Ahead' sign, but I know this is not always possible.

Mammals

BROWN HARE
Lepus capensis

LOCATION
Eastern Australia, from the central Queensland coast, inland through outback NSW, to west of Adelaide in South Australia.

HABITAT
Open, grassed areas that provide green feed and tussocks for shelter. You will not find it in burrows but sheltering under grass tussocks, moving out at night to feed. Often a hare will be 'flushed' out of the same 'form' (its nest), time and again, indicating that it lives in an established territory.

IDENTIFICATION
Colour Mottled grey-brown on top, with the colour depending on the thickness of the coat and the season; soft white underneath.
Size Average head and body length (male and female): 60 cm. Average tail length (male and female): 8 cm. Average weight (male and female): 4 kg.
Distinguishing features The hare looks like a large rabbit, but with a much longer body and larger ears. When you see it in the daytime it is usually alone (unlike rabbits), and is often seen as a speeding flash of brown as it sprints across an open paddock.

ENVIRONMENTAL NOTES
Status The hare was introduced to Australia in the 19th century for game hunting, particularly to provide 'coursing' for greyhounds and deerhounds. Like the rabbit, the hare escaped and multiplied, but never reached the horrific plague numbers soon achieved by the rabbit population. Occasionally, the hare has reached numbers large enough to severely damage crops. The main method of control has been shooting.
Feeding habits The hare eats pastures, any soft green crop and the bark of young trees.
Predators Feral cats and foxes prey on the hare, particularly the young ones as they attempt to hide in their forms. A young hare will also be taken by hawks and eagles. During the winter months the hare's fur becomes luxurious and there have been various times in Australia's history when hunting hares was quite profitable. This served as a reasonable method of control, but fashions change and demand for skins is now almost non-existent.
Reproduction A young hare is born with its eyes open and with fur, a necessity when the nest is virtually in the open, rather than in a burrow like a rabbit's. The doe can have up to 6 litters a year, with 5 young in each, though rarely would more than 1 or 2 leverets (young hares) survive to adulthood.

ROADSIDE

RABBIT
Oryctolagus cuniculus

LOCATION
Throughout Australia, with the exception of the tropical north.

HABITAT
Almost unlimited, from coastal dry eucalypt forests to sandy desert. The only limitation appears to be the availability of suitable plants for food. You are more likely to see a rabbit at dusk and after dark, but a rough indication of high populations can be gained if large numbers of rabbits are seen in the hot, daylight hours.

IDENTIFICATION
Colour The rabbit ranges in colour from soft grey, through ginger, black and white. Those from different climatic zones may show slightly different body structures and colouring. In times of plague, when numbers in a warren are huge, you might see coloured rabbits, often in company with many other rabbits sitting on the top of warrens.
Size Average head and body length (male and female): 39 cm. Average weight (male and female): 1.6 kg.
Distinguishing features The wild rabbit differs from the pet shop rabbit in that it is usually leaner in shape and the fur is less luxurious. It is a very appealing animal, with long upright ears and soft eyes, and I could become fond of the rabbit if it weren't for the damage it does to the environment.

ENVIRONMENTAL NOTES
Status The rabbit has spread to most of Australia since its introduction in Victoria in the 1860s. It was controlled to a degree in the late 1950s and early 1960s by myxomatosis, a disease spread by mosquitoes and introduced by humans to cull the rabbits, but rabbit numbers have again increased to plague proportion in some areas. The damage done by the rabbit is beyond calculation. Not only has it destroyed farming and grazing land, it has also ruined the habitat of dozens of species of native animals, such as the bilby (*Macrotis lagotis*).
Feeding habits The rabbit will feed on any green pick in a paddock, crops, tree bark — any plant material that is slightly succulent.
Predators Foxes, feral cats, eagles, hawks, snakes and goannas take some of these prolific breeders. People also shoot, trap, poison, fumigate and blow up a small percentage of the population. The rabbit is really only controlled by the availability of food. When food is eaten out the survivors will establish themselves elsewhere.
Reproduction The breeding capacity of the rabbit is amazing, hence the common expression to 'breed like rabbits'. The female can have her first litter at 3 months of age. She may have 5 litters a year, with an average of 5 young in each litter. It is a fascinating exercise to calculate the potential number of offspring produced in a year, starting with one pair of rabbits.

EASTERN GREY KANGAROO
Macropus giganteus

LOCATION
Eastern Australia, from the tropical north of Queensland to the southeast corner of South Australia.

HABITAT
Ranges from coastal forest to arid outback. The grey kangaroo is abundant over much of its range, particularly in conservation areas such as national parks. In times of good feed, or in conservation areas, you will see huge mobs of kangaroos, particularly in the evening when they come out to graze.

IDENTIFICATION
Colour A generally soft grey to charcoal-grey colour, with slightly darker colouring along the back and a black tip to the tail. The underbelly is a lighter grey.

Size A male eastern grey kangaroo can stand over 2 m tall when propped on its tail and back legs, and weigh up to 70 kg. The female is smaller and more delicate looking, being between 1.5 m and 1.8 m tall, and weighing about 30 kg.

Distinguishing features Apart from the grey colour you can identify the eastern grey kangaroo by the 'blocky' head shape. The large mature male has powerfully developed shoulders and forearms.

ENVIRONMENTAL NOTES
Status The eastern grey kangaroo has been assisted in its survival as a species by the changes to the environment made by farmers. A guaranteed supply of food and water all year round, even in times of drought, means that its biological clock allows it to breed freely. In the arid outback, the competition between the kangaroo and domestic stock for limited grazing has caused conservation authorities to permit controlled culling when kangaroo populations appear to be too large. The controversy regarding kangaroo management will continue for some time.

Feeding habits Unfortunately, it is the kangaroo's liking for farmers' pastures and crops that has caused problems. In a truly

---

Abandoned Joeys

Several times I have found a joey left abandoned by its mother, particularly if she has been harassed by dogs. The joey is often too small to fend for itself, and it stands pitifully helpless, or crouched under a bush. It has been suggested that the doe throws the joey out of her pouch to save the baby, or it may be that she is more likely to get away without its weight slowing her down. Whatever the reason, it is quite a deliberate act on the part of the mother.

'wild' situation the kangaroo feeds on native green plants — grasses and herbs — but if a farmer's lucerne or oat crop is available it will feed on that in preference.

Predators A young kangaroo is preyed upon by eagles and dingos but the adult has no natural enemies. This has caused problems and many schemes have been developed to 'manage' the wild kangaroo population, but no solution has been reached that satisfies all parties.

Reproduction The eastern grey kangaroo has the amazing ability to respond immediately to improved environmental conditions by holding an embryo 'in reserve', as it were, through a process called embryonic diapause. At birth the 2 cm long pink, blind, naked baby climbs from the mother's birth canal, through a jungle of fur to the pouch, where it attaches itself to a nipple. The female mates about 2 weeks after the birth of her incredibly tiny baby, but the fertilised embryo from that mating does not develop until the first 'joey' has left the pouch. Should the joey in the pouch die, the fertilised embryo will begin to develop immediately and be born about 30 days later. This means that, in good times, a doe can have a joey in the pouch, one about 18 months old with her as well, and an undeveloped embryo ready for development at the appropriate time. If conditions are poor, the embryo does not develop, thus ensuring a natural control method during times of drought.

WESTERN GREY KANGAROO
Macropus fuliginosus

LOCATION
From the outback of NSW and southern Queensland, through southern South Australia, to southern Western Australia.

HABITAT
Although western and eastern grey kangaroo populations do mix, the western grey is found in the more arid areas of southern Australia.

IDENTIFICATION
Colour A major difference between the western and eastern greys is that the western grey is browner in colour.
Size Male — head to tail: 2.3 m; tail: 1 m; weight: 54 kg. Female — head to tail: 1.7 m; tail: 0.8 m; weight: 28 kg.
Distinguishing features The western grey kangaroo is a strong-bodied kangaroo with large mule-like ears. Unlike other kangaroos (except for the eastern grey), its nose is covered with fine hairs. In the wild, a kangaroo that has not been shot at will stand up tall, with front paws dangling, to stare at you until it decides whether you are a danger. In national parks you can often approach within a few metres of a western grey.

ENVIRONMENTAL NOTES
Status As for the eastern grey kangaroo (see page 15).

MAMMALS

Feeding habits Very similar to that of the eastern grey kangaroo, although the western grey tends to live in the more arid areas where green feed is usually restricted to the edges of temporary and permanent waterways.

Predators As for the eastern grey kangaroo.

Reproduction For an animal to live in an area very prone to droughts it is essential that it has some biological mechanism that restricts breeding when food and water are limited. During times of drought the kangaroo population almost ceases to breed. However, unlike the eastern grey, the western grey can not have a dormant embryo waiting to develop when the joey leaves the pouch.

RED KANGAROO
Macropus rufus

LOCATION
All of outback Australia, with the exception of the tropical north and southwestern Western Australia.

HABITAT
The arid lands of the outback, particularly the open plains where scattered trees provide some shade. If any sight is typical of the outback, it is that of a mob of red kangaroos bounding across the open plains. Like all kangaroos, the red kangaroo tends to shelter in the heat of the day, moving out in the early evening to its favourite feeding spot. In the cooler weather, you may see mobs resting in the sunshine, watching the world through half-closed, sleepy eyes.

IDENTIFICATION
Colour The distinctive outback clay-red colour of the male is not always present, but it is sufficiently common for you to use as a good guide. The underside is whitish, unlike similar sized kangaroos. The female is usually a soft dove-grey colour.

Size A male red kangaroo can stand up to a height of 2 m when rearing back on its tail and hind legs. The male body length, without the tail, can be up to 1.4 m, and the female up to 1.1 m. In both male and female the tail length is about 1 m. It is the weight that shows the most difference between male and female, the male weighing up to 85 kg and the female less than half that at 35 kg.

Distinguishing features It is the face and head that will help you pick the red kangaroo. It has a long face, with a distinctive white stripe that runs from below the nostrils right up the side of the face. It has long pointed ears and a hairless muzzle.

ENVIRONMENTAL NOTES

Status As for the eastern grey kangaroo (see page 15). Despite arguments to the contrary, it appears that red kangaroo numbers are greater than prior to European settlement in 1788.

Feeding habits As for the eastern grey kangaroo. Mobs may move long distances to find the green grazing that is their preferred food.

Predators As for the eastern grey kangaroo.

Reproduction As for the eastern grey kangaroo.

Birds

EMU
Dromaius novaehollandiae

LOCATION
Most of mainland Australia, but very scattered in coastal areas.

HABITAT
From open timber country to the arid outback.

IDENTIFICATION
Colour From a distance the emu has a smoky-grey colour, and it is not until it is up close that the black or brown streaky markings through the feathers are evident. The skin of the neck and face is blue. The chick has brown-black stripes running from the front of its head to the back of its tail.

Size Both male and female are up to 1.85 m tall.

Distinguishing features The emu is Australia's largest bird, with long, strong legs, feathers that look like old roofing thatch, and a long neck. It has a deep rumbling call, sounding like the echoes of an empty drum rolling down a hill.

ENVIRONMENTAL NOTES

Status The emu was once much more numerous in coastal areas but it does not mix well with human habitation. In the more remote and arid areas its numbers seem to be on the increase, particularly in national parks and other sanctuaries.

Feeding habits It eats a variety of plant food, from grass to fruits, and also some

BIRDS

> **How to Attract an Emu**
>
> Emus have a curiosity that can be fatal. Aboriginal hunters used to bring emus close enough to their spears by waving an object in the air. You can do the same by waving a handkerchief out the window of a car, not for the purpose of making a meal out of the emu but for observing it more closely (but not too close for safety reasons).

insects. When an emu is kept captive in wildlife parks, it can become quite aggressive toward anyone who is giving food handouts, so don't become too friendly with a 'tame' emu. Its powerful legs and strong bill should be treated with the respect they deserve.

Predators An adult emu has no natural enemies, but the eggs and chicks are preyed upon by dingos, foxes, eagles and hawks, and goannas. An emu egg is a huge meal for an animal, but it is protected by a rock-hard shell. It must present a challenge to a hungry predator.

Reproduction The female lays up to 11 huge, dark green eggs in a 'scrape' (its nest) on the ground and then leaves them. An emu egg is 134 mm long and weighs 900 g. The male incubates the young and looks after the chicks for up to 18 months. It is common in the wild to see a family group with both parents accompanied by fluffy youngsters at various stages of growth.

STRAW-NECKED IBIS
Threskiornis spinicollis

LOCATION
Throughout Australia, with the exception of a small area in central eastern Western Australia.

HABITAT
Often seen in paddocks where irrigation is being carried out, the straw-necked ibis lives and feeds in large numbers in shallow areas around lakes, swamps and lagoons. It is sometimes found in tidal saltwater areas, but not usually. During times of flood, large flocks of sacred ibis and straw-necked ibis will be seen patrolling the water's edge.

IDENTIFICATION
Colour At first glance this ibis just seems to be black-backed, with a small amount of white front showing. On closer inspection, the black colour shows glossy lights and a bunch of straw-like, short, yellow feathers hang down from the front to dress up the bird.

Size Both male and female are up to 76 cm tall.

Distinguishing features This bird has the typical sickle-shaped bill of an ibis, a small head, longish slim neck and long legs with large feet.

ENVIRONMENTAL NOTES

Status The straw-necked ibis is tremendously important to the ecology of farmlands throughout Australia. It is attracted to areas where outbreaks of plague insects, such as locusts, occur, and the straw-necked ibis eats its own weight in these pests in a very short time. It would not be unusual to see hundreds of straw-necked ibis walking across a paddock in orderly fashion, feeding on insects as they go.

Feeding habits As well as feeding on insects, the straw-necked ibis eats small molluscs like snails, small crustaceans like yabbies, and frogs. It does not normally eat fish.

Predators The adult bird seems to have no natural predators and the young bird is usually protected by the swamp location of the nests. However, it is possible that some of the larger birds of prey may take chicks or even adults.

Reproduction It breeds in shallow areas around swamps, lakes and billabongs in huge, smelly noisy colonies, that flatten the branches of the trees and shrubs they nest in. It lays up to 5 white eggs.

BLACK-SHOULDERED KITE
Elanus notatus

LOCATION
Throughout Australia, with the exception of the central desert and southern Tasmania.

HABITAT
Widely varied, from eucalypt forest to open plains. You will see this beautiful member of the kite family most often perching on high branches at the roadside, or hovering 20 to 30 m above the ground.

IDENTIFICATION
Colour Up close this bird is the softest white underneath, with light grey wings outlined with an edging of black. From a distance it is a soft grey in colour.

Size Both male and female are up to 38 cm in length, with a wingspan of 90 cm.

Distinguishing features There are two birds that hover and are often seen in the outback. These are the black-shouldered kite and the Australian kestrel. Both birds have the amazing capacity to use swiftly flapping wings to hang in the air over one spot. The black-shouldered kite has distinctive, soft, grey plumage which makes it easy to identify.

ENVIRONMENTAL NOTES
Status It has been pleasing to see an increase in the number of this species of kite around suburban areas. In the outback the black-shouldered kite's numbers are determined by the availability of prey species. Following plagues of the house mouse, kites will be seen every few kilometres in the less arid areas of the outback.

Feeding habits It uses its hovering to

spot its prey of small mammals, reptiles and insects. When the prey is seen, it swoops down and grasps it in its hooked talons. If it is a small animal like a lizard, it is taken back to a favourite perch, torn apart and eaten. Animals with skins, like mice, are skinned before they are eaten, and the skin is dropped to the ground.

Predators The adult bird has no natural predators, but the young may be preyed upon by large birds and lizards.

Reproduction It builds a deep nest of sticks high up in a tall tree, and lays up to 5 brownish-white eggs.

BROWN FALCON
Falco berigora

LOCATION
Throughout Australia.

HABITAT
All areas apart from dense forest. You can usually identify this bird by where it is seen — sitting quietly on the crossbars of a telephone or electricity pole, or on a fencepost, by the roadside.

IDENTIFICATION
Colour Species tend to vary in colour, but the most predominant colour ranges from dull mahogany to sooty-brown.
Size Both male and female are 50 cm from head to tail, with a wingspan of 90 cm.
Distinguishing features The brown falcon is by far the most common dark-brown coloured hawk in Australia. Its slow flight away from its perch will help you recognise it.

ENVIRONMENTAL NOTES
Status Immediately after plagues of mice or locusts, brown falcon numbers show marked increases. This is because there is a rapid increase in the number of young that survive to adulthood. Unfortunately the large numbers of chicks that grow into adult falcons may not find sufficient food as the plague finishes. The brown falcon was shot indiscriminately as a killer of poultry and other small livestock, but most people now realise its value as an essential part of the ecological balance.
Feeding habits The brown falcon was often the notorious 'chicken hawk' that preyed on farmers' hens. With prey such as that it was not uncommon for the falcon to kill several hens in one attack, tearing their throats open and eating only the heart. It usually catches the prey by dropping from its perch and hooking the prey with its talons. It will also pursue prey on the ground, whether it be farmers' hens or grasshoppers.
Predators No natural predators.
Reproduction The brown falcon uses a stick nest, that it may or may not have built itself, in which it lays 2 to 4 buff-white eggs.

PEREGRINE FALCON
Falco peregrinus

LOCATION
Throughout Australia, but not really common anywhere.

HABITAT
Hilly country, particularly when associated with open woodland and rocky outcrops.

IDENTIFICATION
Colour Even at a distance the peregrine falcon's dark-blue to black back and creamy underside are visible. It also has a regular pattern of bands of speckles on the belly.
Size Both male and female are up to 50 cm tall, with a wingspan of 90 cm.
Distinguishing features It is usually seen sitting on the dead limb of a branch, or on top of a fencepost, with an alert posture and wide eyes.

ENVIRONMENTAL NOTES
Status Peregrine falcon populations have suffered from centuries of thoughtless hunting, and recently from the poisoning of their eggs by the pesticides used on crops. Also, not long ago it was common practice for farmers to shoot anything that looked like a hawk on the offchance it might harm their stock. It is only recently that people have come to realise that birds of prey like the peregrine falcon help to control the numbers of 'pest' species like galahs. The extraordinary speed and hunting ability of the peregrine falcon made it one of the most popular hunting birds in the 'sport' of falconry. For centuries, all around the world, peregrines were used to hunt ducks, rabbits and other small game.
Feeding habits A flock of feeding galahs that sees a peregrine falcon overhead flies screeching into the air. If the peregrine is hungry there is no way a small animal or bird can escape, as the falcon can dive at more than 300 kph. It strikes its prey in the air with its talons and, if it is a large bird, it will hold it hooked in its talons until reaching the ground.
Predators No natural predators.
Reproduction The peregrine falcon does not build a nest, preferring instead to lay 2 to 3 reddish-fawn eggs on a rock ledge, in a hollow tree or in another large bird's nest.

WEDGE-TAILED EAGLE
Aquila audax

LOCATION
Throughout Australia, but very scattered in areas of population.

HABITAT
From hilly, open woodland to plains. In the outback you are most likely to see the

BIRDS

soaring easily on its vast wingspan. Its tail has an unmistakable wedge shape, like a wide 'V'.

ENVIRONMENTAL NOTES
Status Not so long ago it would not have been unusual for you to see dead wedge-tailed eagles hanging on outback fences, having been shot by farmers accusing the bird of taking live lambs. Thankfully, this is now a rare practice, as educated farmers realise that the eagle benefits them by helping control pest animals like rabbits. As a result the wedge-tail's numbers are on the increase in many areas.

Feeding habits This eagle often feeds on carrion, more so in modern times when speeding vehicles kill animals on outback roads. The wedge-tail also takes live prey, ranging from rabbits to small kangaroos. It kills the prey with its hooked talons, which act like small, curved daggers that reach right into an animal's vital organs. Once the animal is down, the beak is used to cut and tear.

Predators The wedge-tail has no natural predators.

Reproduction The wedge-tail builds a huge nest of sticks, that may be added to year after year. It can be built right at the top of the tallest tree or, in the more remote and arid areas, on low branches that can bear its huge weight. Occasionally this bird will build on cliff ledges in inaccessible places. Up to 3 blotchy white eggs are laid.

wedge-tail in one of three places: on the road (feeding on animals killed by traffic), perching midway up dead trees, or soaring high on rising thermal air currents. Occasionally it will be seen sitting on a fencepost by the side of the road, waiting for the traffic to pass to return to its meal of carrion.

IDENTIFICATION
Colour Its general appearance is almost black, with splashes of golden yellow visible as it moves or flies.

Size Both male and female are about 1 m tall, with a wingspan of at least 2.5 m. Seen on the ground the wedge-tailed eagle is startlingly large.

Distinguishing features The wedge-tail is the largest of the eagles or hawks in Australia. In flight it is a majestic bird,

AUSTRALIAN KESTREL
Falco cenchroides

LOCATION
This bird can be found throughout Australia.

HABITAT
Open areas like savannah woodlands, and open forests. The kestrel is not just a bird of the outback, as you will often see it

ROADSIDE

in open grassland areas close to major centres of population.

IDENTIFICATION
Colour The Australian kestrel is fawn to tan above and pale cream underneath. Its other common name, nankeen kestrel, came from the soft fawn colour of a cloth from Asia, called 'nankeen'.
Size Both male and female are up to 35 cm from head to tail, with a wingspan of about 75 cm.
Distinguishing features You will see this bird hovering on rapidly beating wings over open paddocks and grassland. The kestrel is a delicate, almost fragile-looking bird.

ENVIRONMENTAL NOTES
Status Like many birds of prey, the kestrel population shows huge increases after plagues of mice or locusts. In normal times it would be usual to see one kestrel about every 5 km on an outback road. Immediately following plagues it is not unusual to see a kestrel every kilometre, or even more frequently.
Feeding habits The kestrel's size belies its fierce hunting ability. While it hovers about 20 m over the ground it waits for movement that shows a grasshopper or mouse. It then plummets down, catching its prey in hooked talons. If the prey is a mouse it will often take it to a high perch and skin it before eating. When catching food for its young it will take the whole animal back to the nest before skinning it. The Australian kestrel is an extremely valuable part of nature's control of over-population by 'pest' species.
Predators No natural predators.
Reproduction The nest is usually in the hollow of a tree or in the old nest of another bird, but I have seen birds with a precarious nest at the edge of a ledge on a church tower, and another in a narrow lip of metal at the top of a lighthouse. Three to 5 buff eggs are laid.

RICHARD'S PIPIT
Anthus novaeseelandiae

LOCATION
Throughout Australia, with the exception of wet, forested areas.

HABITAT
Any open grassland area, from beach dunes to alpine fields.

IDENTIFICATION
Colour The pipit is a drab little bird, being light brown, with scattered patches of darker brown.
Size Both male and female up to 19 cm.
Distinguishing features You will soon come to recognise its 'personality'. It peers

BIRDS

> **Pipit Plays Follow-the-leader**
> The little bird will scuttle along the road just in front of your car, turning to see if you are following, and then scampering off again. They often will not fly until the car is almost on top of them, and then they will only fly a short distance. My family and I followed a pipit for more than a kilometre along a single lane track in Willandra National Park in NSW. It did not want to go and we had nowhere to go except along the track, so we played follow-the-leader until it took pity on us and allowed us to overtake.

at you from the top of fenceposts or from the roadside as if to say 'want to come and play?'. It moves with light flickering movements over the ground, never really running away, just staying far enough ahead for you to want to follow it. When it stops, it performs a bobbing dance, with the whole body moving up and down on bending legs.

ENVIRONMENTAL NOTES
Status Very common, although rarely in large numbers in any one place. You will see this bird from seashore dunes to arid grasslands to alpine meadows.
Feeding habits The pipit likes to hunt for insects along the cleared road tracks, particularly when the pastures and roadsides are covered with high grass.
Predators Like all small ground birds, the pipit is easy prey for feral cats, although its alert behaviour and nimble footwork probably help it get away better than the other species can. The nest would also be preyed upon by small marsupials, rodents and lizards.
Reproduction The pipit builds a neat, cup-shaped, grass nest in a hollow in the ground, usually in the shelter of a grass tussock or rock, in which it lays 3 or 4 grey-white eggs.

COCKATIEL
Nymphicus hollandicus

LOCATION
The cockatiel is to be found throughout most of mainland Australia, with the exception of the southeast coast, Cape York and the southwest of Western Australia.

HABITAT
Open plains and grasslands, through to scattered woodlands and roadsides.

IDENTIFICATION
Colour Although predominantly grey in

colour, the cockatiel is still a very attractive bird, having a yellow face (bright yellow in the male) and a distinctive orange 'beauty spot' on the cheek.
Size Both male and female are up to 33 cm long.
Distinguishing features As you drive along, watch out for the wheeling flight of this smallish bird. The cockatiel has a head crest which is raised periodically both when perching and flying. It is not easy to see until it flies, as the soft grey colouring blends with the background.

ENVIRONMENTAL NOTES
Status There has been a noticeable increase in the numbers of the cockatiel in some areas of the outback, but it is hard to determine if this has been just a movement to follow food sources, or a general increase. It may be that you are more likely to see a cockatiel in an aviary than in the outback, as many are still kept in cages.
Feeding habits The cockatiel can often be seen in quite large flocks feeding along the roadside, particularly after floods have encouraged the growth of the seed plants that the bird feeds on. It sometimes feeds in small groups with the red-rumped parrot *(Psephotus haematonotus)*, moving over the ground picking up fallen seeds from harvested crops.
Predators Like all the parrot family, the cockatiel is harassed and attacked by many of the birds of prey. Its rapid dipping flight, flocking behaviour and the habit of wheeling close to the ground helps to escape predation. Like the galah, its eggs and young are taken by large lizards. Unfortunately, one of the main 'predators' of the cockatiel has been people. Its value and popularity as a cage bird has meant that eggs and young birds have been taken from nests by bird-fanciers. Recent huge increases in the penalties for the illegal trafficking of birds may lessen this form of predation.
Reproduction A hollow in a tree is used as a nest and 4 to 7 white eggs are laid.

GALAH
Cacatua roseicapilla

LOCATION
Widespread throughout Australia, with the exception of the far north and parts of the far south of South Australia and Western Australia.

HABITAT
Everything from the desert fringe to suburban gardens. The galah is often seen gathering to drink at dusk in huge flocks in the branches of dead trees.

IDENTIFICATION
Colour The galah is a beautiful bird, having a superb contrast of pink underneath and soft grey on top, with a white

cap to its head. Its pink colour stands out boldly and a flock of wheeling birds at sunset is an impressionist's painting in fluid motion. In Australia the galah has become such a common sight that we tend to accept it as part of the scene.

Size Both male and female are up to 38 cm from head to tail.

Distinguishing features Two main features make the galah stand out. One is the mass of colour that the huge flocks bring to the outback sky and the other is their incredibly raucous call. A mob of galahs screeching at each other in the treetops has all the musical beauty of fingernails on a blackboard.

ENVIRONMENTAL NOTES

Status The galah expanded its range with the clearing of land and the spread of cereal farming. In some areas it has become so numerous as to become a real menace to wheat farmers, as the birds attack the planted wheat seed, and scatter wheat left stored in the open as they eat it. Farmers no longer leave bagged wheat in the fields, but few wheat farmers have any love for the galah.

Feeding habits As well as wheat, it feeds on a wide variety of grains, including the seeds of native and introduced plants.

Predators The adult bird is taken on the wing by several of the medium-sized birds of prey, including peregrine falcons and some of the larger hawks. Young birds and eggs are taken from the nests by goannas, and the presence of any species of goanna in a nesting colony sends the birds into a screeching frenzy.

Reproduction The most common nesting place is in the hollow of a tree, often where a dead branch has broken off and left a cosy tunnel down its centre. It lays 2 to 5 white eggs.

Galahs Have Little Road Sense

During the wheat harvesting season you must take great care when travelling country roads, as countless flocks of galahs will be feeding at the edges of the road on spilled wheat. They have very little road sense and will wheel and fly as a mob straight into the windscreen of a speeding car. This is very distressing for the driver and does little for the well-being of the galah.

FAIRY MARTIN
Cecropis ariel

LOCATION
Throughout Australia, with the exception of the Cape York peninsula.

HABITAT
It is found in open country, but it needs access to water for making the mud nest.

IDENTIFICATION

Colour The fairy martin is distinctly two-toned, with white underneath and a black back. Up close, a russet fawn cap and white rump can be seen.
Size Both male and female are up to 13 cm long.
Distinguishing features It looks a little like the welcome swallow *(Hirundo neoxena)* that builds a cup-shaped mud nest, often under the eaves of houses. The fairy martin is smaller and lighter in colour.

ENVIRONMENTAL NOTES

Status The fairy martin is a very common bird in some localities. I have often seen these birds flying around and under road bridges over rivers and creeks, where their nests can be counted in the hundreds.
Feeding habits Its main food is insects, which it catches on the wing. You can often see the fairy martin 'hawking' over patches of water, either catching insects or drinking as it flies. It is a superb flier, and flickers over the water very much like a feathered bat.
Predators The inaccessibility of its nest and its flying skill makes it very difficult prey. However, the nest colonies are prone to attack by 'plagues' of blood-sucking parasites, such as lice.
Reproduction If you are walking near a road culvert or a bridge, you might discover a colony of fairy martins by the twittering call they give as they fly. It is worth investigating (at a suitable distance) a nesting colony of martins as you may be fortunate enough to see them building their nests. They laboriously carry in pellets of mud and build a bottle-shaped nest with a long entrance. Each pellet requires a flight to a suitable mud patch and then back to the nest, and each nest takes many pellets. The bird lays 4 or 5 freckled white eggs.

Reptiles and Amphibians

GOULD'S GOANNA
Varanus gouldii

LOCATION
All of the Australian mainland, but particularly the more arid inland.

HABITAT
From forest areas to the fringe of the desert.

IDENTIFICATION
Colour Gould's goanna tends to be speckled with yellow, or to have broken yellow bands on a black background.
Size It can grow to a length of over 1.5 m from head to tail.
Distinguishing features It has the typical

REPTILES AND AMPHIBIANS

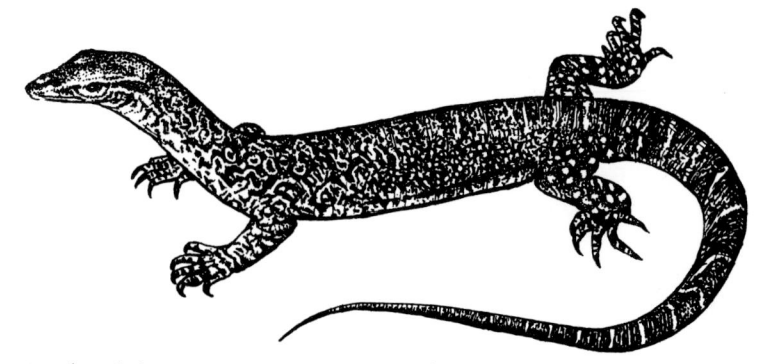

monitor lizard shape and structure, with a long head and tail, and strong legs and claws. Like all goannas, a startled Gould's goanna will rise up on its legs and race over the ground. The sudden burst of speed is usually enough to carry it away from danger, as it lives in areas where some sort of cover is near at hand. If you see Gould's goanna out in the open away from its hideaway, like on a roadway, it will often stop and pretend it's not there. Any move in its direction will cause it to become the greyhound of the outback.

ENVIRONMENTAL NOTES
Status The goanna plays an extremely valuable role in controlling the numbers of other species, such as snakes, rats, rabbits and mice. Gould's goanna either lives in hollow logs or a burrow it has dug for itself. It will also live in rabbit burrows, where it has a home and a ready supply of fresh food close by. It is relatively common throughout its range.

Feeding habits It will eat any mammal, bird or reptile small enough to be caught, and the eggs and young of many animals.

Predators The adult is a little too tough and fearsome a foe to be taken as prey, but young animals are preyed upon by birds like kookaburras and hawks.

Reproduction Gould's goanna is one of the egg-laying group of monitor lizards. It lays 5 to 10 eggs in a hole in the ground.

BEARDED DRAGON
Amphibolurus barbatus

LOCATION
Eastern and central Australia, but not southern Victoria or northern Queensland.

HABITAT
From forested areas to the arid outback. The most likely place to see a bearded dragon as you drive along is clinging on to the side of a fencepost, its colour merging in beautifully, but able to be seen because its head sticks up above the top of the post.

IDENTIFICATION
Colour Dark grey, with lighter speckles of colour in lines along the back and sides. As much of its survival depends upon not being seen, you will notice a colour difference in bearded dragons dependent upon the local habitat.

Size It can grow in length up to 70 cm, but the usual size is about 50 cm.

Distinguishing features The bearded dragon is wonderfully camouflaged, so it is is not always easy to spot one. But it

29

ROADSIDE

also has the habit of coming out onto roads, where you will soon pick the distinctive box-shaped head, rough body and general grey colouring. It is a fierce-looking lizard and, if disturbed, will swell up its throat, pushing out the spikes that give it its name. It opens its mouth wide, displaying the bright yellow interior, and puffs out its body to twice the size. If it is a large specimen, and all else fails, it will often charge the intruder, be it dog or human and, if the other animal runs away, the bearded dragon will chase after it. However, most of its displays are bluff, and it prefers to be left alone.

ENVIRONMENTAL NOTES
Status It is common to very common throughout its range, wherever there is suitable forest or woodland habitat. Some people keep dragons as pets, but this is not a good idea, as it is illegal in some states of Australia, and the animal is better off in the bush.

Feeding habits It preys on insects of all sizes, and a wide variety of other small animals, from worms to young birds.

Predators Being very tough and spiky, the adult lizard would be rather unpalatable, but the younger lizards are taken by kookaburras.

Reproduction The bearded dragon lays clutches of white, soft-skinned eggs about 2 cm long, often in piles of broken rocks. It usually lays up to 10 eggs, although much larger clutches have been recorded.

SHINGLE-BACK
Trachydosaurus rugosus

HABITAT
From dry, forest timber country to scrublands and semi-desert.

IDENTIFICATION
Colour Very dark mahogany-brown, through to dark, slaty charcoal-grey, the colour varying according to the location. The mahogany shingle-back tends to be in the red soil areas.

Size The fully grown adult is usually around 30 cm from head to tail, although some specimens can be half as big again.

Distinguishing features If you see an animal on or near the road that looks like a slowly moving piece of brown wood,

LOCATION
The southern and western mainland Australia; with the exception of coastal NSW, Victoria and the northern half of the mainland.

REPTILES AND AMPHIBIANS

> **Bearded Dragon Chases Man**
>
> When I was five I had the terrifying experience of seeing my father chased by a huge bearded dragon, hurtling over a paddock with the lizard mere centimetres from his heels. Apparently, the lizard had taken objection to having his favourite tree chopped down around him. Looking back, I am sad to say that the lizard had chased his last farmer once my father got his hand on a suitable weapon, but that gallant rush across the paddock by man and lizard left me with a very healthy respect for the biting end of reptiles.

it is probably a shingle-back. For an animal that looks like its head could be either end and with the outward appearance of a long pine cone, it may be strange to say it is a 'cute' animal, but it seems to me to have a very amiable nature, ambling along the road or moving on stumpy legs through the underbrush, apparently bothering nothing and not wanting to be bothered.

ENVIRONMENTAL NOTES

Status The shingle-back is very common in its range, and it is possible to see 10 in one day's travel on an outback road. Despite its unflustered and apparently harmless appearance, a shingle-back should not be handled, as it resents this and will give the handler a painful bite.

Feeding habits The shingle-back (or stumpy) has a wide-ranging diet, from fruit to snails, or any small animal slow enough to catch. One specimen I saw in the outback came back on its track to feed on an apple core dropped on the dusty road.

Predators The young would fall prey to hawks and kookaburras, as well as reptiles such as goannas.

Reproduction The shingle-back gives birth to 1 to 3 living young, each baby being almost half the length of the adult.

Insects

BAG-SHELTER MOTH
Ochrogaster contraria

LOCATION
Where suitable food trees are found.

HABITAT
The scrubland areas of the outback, particularly where the myall tree grows.

IDENTIFICATION
Size The nest size is up to 30 cm across; the fully grown caterpillar is approximately 3 cm long; and the adult moth has a wingspan of about 6 cm.

Colour The nest colour is dark brown-grey; the caterpillar is dark grey and covered with lighter long hairs; and the adult moth is speckled fawn to dark tan.

Distinguishing features Sometimes the hairy caterpillars are called 'procession'

ENVIRONMENTAL NOTES

Status The nests are a very common sight as you drive along outback roads, and sometimes it is evident that the caterpillars have almost eaten themselves out of house and home, as the acacias have been stripped of all their foliage.

Feeding habits The bag-shelter caterpillar, regardless of the particular species, is a voracious feeder on its 'host' plant. The damage that a procession of caterpillars can do to a medium-sized acacia has to be seen to be believed.

Predators Because of the covering of spines, the caterpillar is almost immune to predation, but some of the smaller cuckoos have adapted to cope with the irritating hairs (see page 121). The adult moth is preyed on by bats, reptiles, small mammals and birds such as fairy martins.

Reproduction The female moth lays her eggs on the leaves of a suitable host tree. The caterpillars congregate after hatching, forming into the 'bag-shelter' that becomes their fortress home. They pupate inside the bag of leaves, twigs, silk and spikes, and emerge as adults.

caterpillars because they play follow-the-leader in one long line. Your first experience of the bag-shelter moth will probably be seeing clumps of what appear to be birds' nests hanging in acacia trees. If you want to examine them, be very careful as the 'birds' nests' are actually the colonial cocoon of a group of caterpillars that will grow and change into the bag-shelter moth.

Don't Touch Bag-Shelter Moth Caterpillars

Warning: the caterpillars are equipped with fine hairs all over their bodies, and these are also in the silk from which the cocoon is made. The fine hairs will penetrate your skin and cause extreme irritation if you touch them.

YELLOW-WINGED LOCUST
Gastrimargus musicus

LOCATION
Throughout Australia.

HABITAT
Open country, particularly pastures and grassland. Most people would call this locust a grasshopper, as this is exactly what it does — hops vigorously amongst the grass.

IDENTIFICATION
Colour It is a very attractive insect, with

INSECTS

> **The Joys of a Locust Plague**
> The number of insects that fly in a locust plague is phenomenal. Visualise a car with a radiator grill so full of dead insects that the car overheats. Then try to imagine the smell of hundreds of squashed locusts being slowly boiled by the steaming radiator. These are some of the joys of driving through a locust plague.

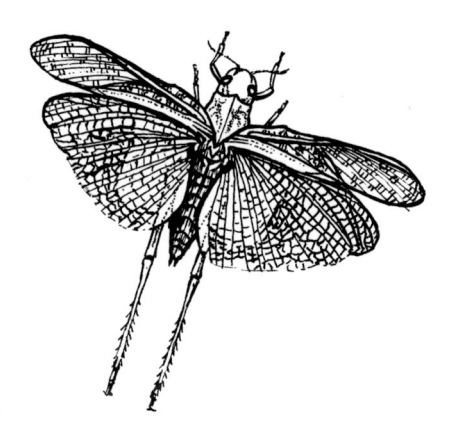

a bright-green body, sometimes with brown markings, and a bright-yellow flash on the wings as it flies.

Size The adult ranges in size from 3 cm to 5 cm (head and body length).

Distinguishing features As it flies it makes a clicking sound. There could be times when you are driving along outback roads that you run into a swarm of locusts that clatter onto your windscreen like living hail. If you catch one of these specimens, you will be able to distinguish the plague locust *(Chortoicetes terminifera)* from the yellow-winged locust thus: the plague locust has a black spot on the back wing.

ENVIRONMENTAL NOTES

Status Like its relative the plague locust, the yellow-winged locust occasionally appears in swarms, but mainly in the tropical north. Locust swarms do great economic damage to crops and pastures, and a great deal of skill, time and money is spent in predicting when a swarm will appear. Plagues occur following a period of weather that allows most of the young locusts from a succession of generations to survive. These congregate in huge groups, and biological and behavioural changes take place as the groups grow bigger. The bands of locusts then begin to move across the country, eating all the plant material in their path.

Feeding habits The locust feeds on a wide range of green plants, from native grasses and crops, to trees and shrubs. In times when populations are 'normal' the damage it does is minimal. During times of swarms the yellow-winged locust population can completely denude pasture and cropland.

Predators Like all insects, the locust has many predators. Birds of all shapes and sizes, from the tiny Richard's pipit to the straw-necked ibis happily feed on locusts. Some lizards and a few mammals, such as marsupial mice and foxes, also include locusts in their diet.

Reproduction A bare patch of ground with reasonably soft soil is chosen for mating and laying eggs. Mating occurs on the ground, then the female burrows down into the earth with her ovipositor (an organ at the end of her abdomen) and lays about 50 eggs at the bottom of the narrow hole.

TERMITES
Coptotermes spp. (and several others)

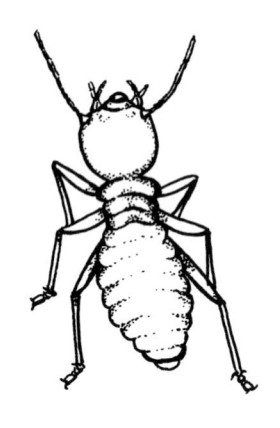

LOCATION
Throughout Australia.

HABITAT
Varied, from forest to native grassland.

IDENTIFICATION
Colour The worker termite inside the nest is a pale, creamy white, hence its name 'white ant'. The soldier ant is creamy, with a brown head. The winged male and female that swarm on warm summer evenings have light brown bodies with lighter underparts.
Size The worker and soldier are about 5 mm long, and the winged male and female about 8 mm long.
Distinguishing features You are unlikely to become very familiar with the appearance of a termite, as it tends to scurry away quickly if exposed to the light. If you are unlucky enough to have had termites in your home, you know how hard they try to stay hidden. They will build soil-covered tunnels to take them from their nest to a new food source, and this is often the only way people find out they have termites sharing their house. In the outback, you will soon come to recognise the termite's mounds. These vary in shape and colour depending on the part of the outback you are in, but basically they are cones or slabs of hard-packed earth and other materials. Inside these nests thousands of termites are teeming, from workers who digest the cellulose in wood and build the nests, to soldiers who guard against intrusion, to the queen, who is a living sack of eggs.

ENVIRONMENTAL NOTES
Status The termite is very common and very numerous. Unfortunately, we have lessened the natural control agents by the improperly planned clearing of forest land and the unwise use of pesticides.
Feeding habits The termite feeds on almost any dead and dry wood. Few timber species are resistant to its attack, and a colony of termites can turn a hardwood floor support into a tunnel-filled shell of timber in a frighteningly short space of time.
Predators There are some natural control agents for the termite. Echidnas dig into the nests and feast on the insects, as do numbats *(Myrmecobius fasciatus)*, and birds swoop in amongst the mating swarms, gorging on the moveable feast.
Reproduction You may witness the extraordinary mating flights of the male and female termites on a warm summer evening. Swarms of flying termites pour from nooks and crannies in trees and fenceposts. A male and female will find a suitable nest site, mate, and a new termite colony begins.

Plants

HOPBUSH
Dodonaea spp.

LOCATION
Throughout Australia.

HABITAT
Hopbush grows in a wide range of habitats. In the outback some species, such as the broad-leaf hopbush (*Dodonaea viscosa*) are often seen in large thickets growing right up to the road.

IDENTIFICATION
Colour The fruit ranges in colour from yellow-green to bright red, and the foliage is medium to dark green.
Size It is usually a bushy shrub, about 2 to 3 m high, with a variety of leaf shapes. The round fruit is about 1 cm wide.
Distinguishing features The fruit is the most distinctive feature for most species, as it has fleshy, coloured 'wings' around the seed. The bush gets its name from the slight resemblance the fruit has to the fruit of the domestic hop used in making beer. The domestic hop grows on long vines, not a bushy plant.

ENVIRONMENTAL NOTES
Status In the central west of NSW, huge areas of grazing land are covered by hopbush. If you can find a hill or ridge to use as a vantage point you will see hopbush growing for as far as the eye can see. It can be eaten by sheep without ill effects, but they do not appear to graze on it. An effective form of control has been a major project for some years for scientists from state and federal authorities. Methods such as controlled burning have been tried in various places.
Natural control agents The modification of the land for grazing has dispersed or destroyed many of the insects that would have controlled the spread of hopbush. Widespread use of chemicals has also had a telling effect. It is probable that the natural control mechanisms will re-establish themselves over time.
Reproduction The prolific production of winged fruit, which is dispersed on the wind, allows the hopbush to spread rapidly.

KANGAROO GRASS
Themeda australis

LOCATION
All Australian states.

HABITAT
A wide variety of soil types and locations,

IDENTIFICATION
Colour It is usually reddish brown in colour, with a red tinted flower head, that droops from the top of long stems.
Size Kangaroo grass grows in a dense tussock ranging from 60 to 150 cm high, and 25 cm across the base.
Distinguishing features Kangaroo grass is a tall grass that grows from a central dry brown tuft. The individual stems are so long that they curve over at the top.

ENVIRONMENTAL NOTES
Status Kangaroo grass was once one of the widespread native grasses found in almost every habitat, apart from rainforest. Domestic grazing animals, such as sheep, and rabbits, overgrazed the tussocks and wiped out the species in many areas.
Natural control agents Prior to white settlement in 1788, native grazing animals such as kangaroos.
Reproduction The dry seeds are dispersed by wind or carriage in the fur of animals.

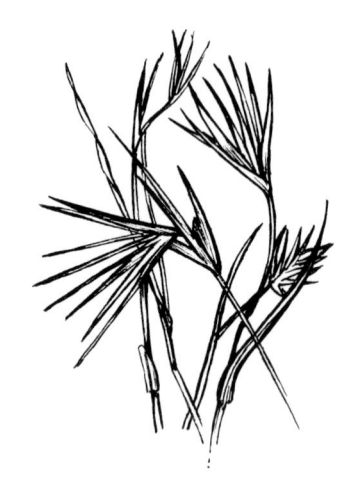

often dependent upon the amount of grazing that has taken place. One of the most likely places to find kangaroo grass in the outback is in the water run-off areas of sandy and rocky ridges, and along the table drains of roads. If the road has not been used as a stock route for some years, you are likely to see dense stands of kangaroo grass.

GOLDEN BILLY BUTTONS
Craspedia chrysantha

HABITAT
A wide variety of soil types, but often on grey soils that are subject to flooding.

IDENTIFICATION
Colour It has bright yellow, roundish flowers growing right at the end of the stem.
Size Plant is about 25 cm tall. Flowers are about 1 cm across.
Distinguishing features After rains in the outback, a mass of plants with flowers of all colours appear as if by magic. One of these is golden billy buttons. You are most

LOCATION
The semi-arid outback of NSW, Queensland, Victoria and South Australia.

PLANTS

likely to find masses of them growing from late winter to early spring.

ENVIRONMENTAL NOTES
Status Very prolific after rain.

Natural control agents Weather, and leaf-eating and flower-eating insects.
Reproduction The plants spread rapidly with the dispersal of many tiny tufted seeds.

DAISY
Brachycome spp.

LOCATION
A range of areas in mainland Australia.

HABITAT
Very varied, but often in sandy areas, roadsides, dry watercourses, and stony plains.

IDENTIFICATION
Colour The flowers have a yellow centre, and petals vary in colour from purple to white.
Size Plants vary in height from several centimetres to over a metre, depending on the species. Flowers of the *Brachycome* group are usually more than 2 cm wide.
Distinguishing features There is a bewildering array of daisy-like flowers in the outback and you would need to carry a detailed botanical 'key' to unlock the identity of each one. The *Brachycome* daisy tends to be more spindly than the compact bushes of the minnie daisy (see below).

ENVIRONMENTAL NOTES
Status Very common.
Natural control agents Weather conditions, and various leaf-eating and flower-eating insects.
Reproduction The flower heads produce many small seeds that may lie dormant in or on the soil until the rains come.

MINNIE DAISY
Minuria leptophylla

LOCATION
Throughout mainland Australia.

HABITAT
In the outback, on sandy red soils or in stony patches in most dry areas of the mainland states. Elsewhere, a wide variety of soil types, although it does better in sandy soils.

IDENTIFICATION
Colour A purple or white show when it blooms. The coloured parts are not the petals, the flower is actually only the

37

yellow centre.
Size It is a small daisy bush, rarely being more than 20 cm high. The flowers have the typical daisy shape, although they are only up to 2 cm wide.
Distinguishing features This neat and attractive daisy is one of the most common flowers you will see as you drive through the semi-arid outback. It grows in clumps along the roadsides and it will make you want to stop the car and take a closer look.

ENVIRONMENTAL NOTES
Status Species of this small daisy are grown as garden plants, as they are hardy and very colourful. In some parts of Australia people grow it as a 'lawn', giving the benefit of a green cover and a living carpet of little daisies.
Natural control agents Weather, and attacks by leaf-eating and flower-eating insects.
Reproduction The seeds are held in the true flower head at the centre of the coloured 'petals'. They are tiny, less than 2 mm long, and disperse out from the plant as the flower head dries.

KURRAJONG
Brachychiton populneus

HABITAT
Sandstone hills, and sandy soils where mallee eucalypts grow.

IDENTIFICATION
Colour Leaves are an attractive, dark glossy green. Black seed pods.
Size This tree can grow up to 20 m high. Pods are boat-shaped, about 5 cm long.
Distinguishing features It has a thick, almost luxurious growth. Kurrajong is a very popular street and shade tree, particularly in country towns, and it provides very welcome shade when you stop for lunch in a country park. The palatable nature of the leaves is the reason why a kurrajong in a sheep paddock always looks so neat — it has had all its lower branches trimmed off cleanly up to the

LOCATION
In scattered areas in NSW, Queensland, Victoria and the Northern Territory.

PLANTS

height a sheep can reach. Cattle also feed on the lower branches.

ENVIRONMENTAL NOTES
Status The good farmer carefully preserves the kurrajong, as it can mean life or death to the stock during severe droughts. The foliage is pruned off when required and used as stock feed.

Natural control agents Many leaf-eating insects enjoy the nutritious leaves of the kurrajong, and you will often find insect-chewed leaves and little nests of caterpillars in the tree.

Reproduction The boat-shaped fruit protect the seeds until they are ready to be dispersed. Both the fruits and the seeds are carried by downpours of rain to establish plants in areas away from the parent plant.

Kurrajongs Make a Mess

A word of warning: do not park your car under a kurrajong if there is any chance of rain. The pods contain a brown resinous substance that is almost impossible to remove from the duco of your car. Also, discourage children from handling any pods they may find on the ground, as the seeds are surrounded by yellow, hairlike bristles that can act as a severe skin irritant.

SILVER CASSIA
Cassia artemisioides

cypress pine. It prefers rocky ridges or broken areas along roadside cuttings. I have seen it growing as a lone, stunted bush on bare, sun-scorched rocky ridges, and also as a vigorous bush on red sandy plains in association with woodland plants.

LOCATION
All mainland states.

HABITAT
In association with a variety of forest trees like the eucalypts in the 'box' group, and

IDENTIFICATION
Colour Whitish silvery-green leaves; flowers buttercup yellow.
Size Up to 2 m high and often as wide.
Distinguishing features Many gardeners will be familiar with the bright yellow-flowered cassias that grow like weeds in higher rainfall areas. This dryland cassia is much more subdued in both its flower and leaf colouring. It shows the silvery-grey fine leaves that assist with conserva-

tion of water, and a tough, bushy outward appearance. It has a mass of bright-yellow flowers in winter and spring.

ENVIRONMENTAL NOTES
Status Prolific to the point of becoming a weed in some parts of its growing area. In parts of western NSW species of hopbush and silver cassia have combined to form almost impenetrable scrublands.
Natural control agents In natural circumstances, its own very short life span would tend to control it. However, given a series of favourable seasons it can grow and spread quickly, until the next round of prolonged drought conditions puts the brake on its spread.
Reproduction Like the acacias, cassias have a pod-shaped fruit containing the seeds. The number and viability of the seeds is the method that allows cassias to spread quickly.

BIMBLE BOX
Eucalyptus populnea

Distinguishing features You will find it one of the easiest eucalypts to identify at a distance, as it has a glistening appearance. Most outback trees are characteristically dull greyish-blue in colour, and the bimble box stands out from the rest.

ENVIRONMENTAL NOTES
Status Bimble box was once a common tree in the woodland and savannah areas of its range. Now you are much more likely only to see it growing along the roadside, rather than on farmlands. This eucalypt does not extend far into the more arid zones of the outback because of its liking for water. As the rainfall decreases so do the number of bimble box. The provision of table drains on the roads have made a form of local catchment for water, and are another reason why tall and healthy bimble box are often seen beside the road.
Natural control agents Leaf-eating and leaf-mining insects and their larvae.
Reproduction Like all eucalypts, bimble box has a small cup-shaped or urn-shaped fruit containing many small seeds. When dry the fine seeds are dispersed a short distance from the parent tree.

LOCATION
Scattered through some of the western areas of NSW and Queensland.

HABITAT
Very varied, but usually on red sandy-clay loams, in medium to low rainfall areas, and in association with other woodland plants such as grey box.

IDENTIFICATION
Colour Dark green, glossy leaves that appear to glisten. The bark is dark.
Size Up to 20 m tall.

PLANTS

MYALL
Acacia pendula

the other acacias (wattles) but it does not make the brave and bold show seen by wattles in wetter areas.

Size It grows up to 10 m tall, but its branches hang down in a willow-like fashion.

Distinguishing features You have two main guides to identification for the myall — one is its half-open umbrella shape and another is the bag-moth caterpillar 'cocoons' that it often contains.

ENVIRONMENTAL NOTES

Status Myall is a very common species of acacia in the eastern outback, and will be seen as isolated roadside trees, clinging to a piece of protected land between the farm fence and the road, and also as thickets on flood plains. Like the mulga, the myall is used by the Aborigines for a variety of purposes, including working its highly decorative wood into boomerangs.

Natural control agents The larvae of bag-shelter moths.

Reproduction Acacias produce seeds in pea-like fruit. When dried the pods spread open, scattering sturdy seed. Many species of acacia have the ability to establish themselves very quickly in a suitable area.

LOCATION
The semi-arid zones of NSW, Queensland and Victoria.

HABITAT
From the cropping areas of the eastern outback, to the river flood plains of the west. Heavy clay soils are preferred.

IDENTIFICATION
Colour Myall has the grey colouring typical of many Australian trees and shrubs. It has yellow flowers, like most of

WHITE CYPRESS PINE
Callitris columellaris

LOCATION
All mainland states.

HABITAT
Follows the red sandy ridges of low rainfall areas. These ridges may run for many kilometres. Often seen on red, rocky hillsides.

IDENTIFICATION
Colour White cypress pine is a dark foliaged tree.

41

ROADSIDE

Size The tree is up to 20 m tall. The fruit is a very hard cone about 2 cm long.
Distinguishing features This tree makes up extensive forests in some parts of the outback, but you should be careful not to confuse it with the commercially planted pines such as radiata pine *(Pinus radiata)*. Commercial plantations can usually be identified by the more orderly planting of trees of all one size. Cypress pine does not have the typical shape of a Christmas tree that the plantation pines have.

ENVIRONMENTAL NOTES
Status In some areas, such as the Pillaga State Forest in NSW, cypress pine grows in sufficient quantities to be milled commercially. In other parts of the outback it has shown such vigorous growth to have become a nuisance, forming almost inpenetrable thickets. Farmers probably bless the presence of cypress pine on their property while it stays in manageable amounts. It is an easily sawn timber with a straight grain that makes excellent round fenceposts and gateposts. It can also be split easily while green, and it has been used for 'slab' walls for farm buildings in some areas, in preference to the much harder ironbark. Cypress pine does not last as long in the ground as the harder eucalypt but it takes a lot less effort to work with it.

Many floors in Australia are made from cypress pine, as it has a wonderful pattern of knots and variety of yellow and orange colours when stained and polished.
Natural control agents Because of the resin contained in its leaves and timber, it has few natural enemies.
Reproduction The cones contain winged seeds that are dispersed over a wide area.

DARLING PEA
Swainsona spp.

LOCATION
NSW, Queensland, Victoria and South Australia.

HABITAT
A wide variety of soil and climatic conditions throughout the outback. Often in clayey soils in scrubland and open plains, and along roadsides.

IDENTIFICATION
Colour The flowers vary in colour from orange through to the deepest purple.
Size Usually less than 60 cm in height, but it can be a rambling vine that covers an area of up to 2 m across.
Distinguishing features Throughout the outback you will find this plant or vine with its flowers that are very similar in

PLANTS

shape to the flower of the garden pea. They are usually carried on a straggly vine or small bush.

ENVIRONMENTAL NOTES
Status The 'Darling' part of the common name is not any form of endearment, but refers to the location around which it is common in NSW. An interesting aspect of some species of *Swainsona* is the effect that they can have on grazing animals. Animals can become 'addicted' to eating the plant, and eat it in preference to others. The result is that they become 'pea-struck', and will fall ill and do very poorly.
Natural control agents As many of the *Swainsona* peas contain toxins, any animal that feeds on them would need to have immunity to survive. It is likely that each specific species has it own natural insect enemies that act as agents of control.
Reproduction Darling pea has pod-like fruit, allowing it to produce and protect many sturdy seeds before they are released to spread the plant.

WILD MELON
Cucumis and *Citrullus* spp.

LOCATION
All mainland states.

HABITAT
Roadsides, sandy areas, old sheep yards, along the walls of farm dams. Light to medium clay loam soils, particularly in areas where moisture is retained after rain. In some seasons following heavy rains, clusters of green and yellow fruit will collect in roadside table drains and in the run-off from farm dams.

IDENTIFICATION
Colour Green fruit with various patterns of yellow or white.
Size Fruit varies according to species.
Distinguishing features The wild melon grows on long, straggling vines, often seen draped down the side of a sandy road cutting. The incredibly bitter-tasting fruit of the wild watermelon (*Citrullus colocynthis*) is whitish, striped, round, and about the size of a softball. Depending on your location, you may find camel melons (*Citrullus lanatus*) with fruit shaped more like a watermelon, or paddy melons (*Cucumis myriocarpus*), with small, hairy fruit.

ENVIRONMENTAL NOTES

Status Very widespread to the point of being a pest in pasture and cropping areas. The tough vines become entangled with harvesting machinery and cause costly waste of time and damage to equipment.

Natural control agents Although birds will be seen eating the seeds of any fruit that has been smashed open, the bitter taste and possible chance of poisoning would prevent most other animals from feeding on the fleshy fruit.

Reproduction Seeds from previous crops are retained in the soil until suitable moist conditions occur. Vines that grow in roads, drains and dam spillways have their seeds carried to new locations after every downpour.

ROLY-POLY
Salsola kali

day. You will see piled against the fences the skeletons of round, dry, twiggy bushes. These are the roly-polys, or tumbleweeds, as they are called in the American West. While it is alive, this species is a small bush, rounded in shape. When it dies, this round shape makes it roll over the ground as the wind drives it along.

ENVIRONMENTAL NOTES

Status There are several species of plants that have the same habit of being tumbled along by the wind. Following very good seasons huge numbers of these plants are piled up aginst fences, thus becoming a form of dam for the dust and sand that is also carried by the wind. Whole fences can be covered by the mixture of roly-poly and sand, making them virtually useless as fences, as the stock can walk over them.

Natural control agents Leaf-eating insects.

Reproduction An advantage of being tumbled along by the wind is the spreading of seeds. As the plant dies and dries out, its winged seeds can be carried away by the wind or, if the wind is strong enough, the whole plant comes out of the ground, tumbling along, spreading seeds as it goes.

LOCATION
In all Australian mainland states.

HABITAT
A wide range of soils and plant types, in a variety of areas, but very common in places where the soil has been disturbed, as around sheds and homesteads.

IDENTIFICATION
Colour Dense bright-green foliage on spindly grey twigs.
Size Up to 70 cm tall.
Distinguishing features As you drive, look along the fence lines after a windy

PLANTS

WILD HOP
Acetosa vesicaria

IDENTIFICATION
Colour Wild hop has bright green leaves on the lower part of the stem, and a brush-shaped mass of pinkish purple 'fruits' at the top. The colour is not from the tiny flower, but from the 'wings' of the fruit.
Size Plant grows up to 75 cm tall.
Distinguishing features If you drive through parts of the outback in early summer, following heavy winter rains, you will see whole hillsides of this pinkish, purple flower. On rocky soil it will not have the lush appearance and large fruiting head, but close examination will show it is the same plant.

ENVIRONMENTAL NOTES
Status At first glance it looks like an introduced weed, as the growth is so lush and has none of the usual appearance of native wildflowers. Your first instincts would be right, as this plant was probably introduced from the Mediterranean area. It is a very common species in some seasons following good winter rains.
Natural control agents Rainfall, and insects and other small animals that feed on the rich, green growth.
Reproduction As the winged fruits dry they carry the seed to spread the plant over a wide area.

LOCATION
NSW, Queensland, South Australia and Western Australia.

HABITAT
From rocky ridges and roadsides, to sand dunes, and dry creekbeds, where water is only present after infrequent rains. You will find wild hop not only in the areas along the road where water has collected, and in pockets in roadside cuttings, but also as struggling, individual plants on barren, rocky hillsides.

CHAPTER TWO

Farmland

The outback of Australia became desirable farming and grazing land soon after the European settlement of Australia in 1788. Graziers began to move their stock onto land almost before explorers returned from their travels, and in many outback areas the explorers actually were graziers.

Mobs of sheep moved ever further into the scrublands and shrublands of the dry country, and cattle grazed in the areas where a supply of water was a little better assured. All grazing was tied to water for stock and so the first flocks and herds were based around permanent rivers and creeks. Then settlers discovered the apparently endless supply of underground water from the great artesian basin, and windmills were used to pump water to dams, or earth tanks. The result was more water for stock, but also more water for wildlife, and many species flourished.

The nature of the countryside was changed by the removal of huge tracts of forest and woodland. Graziers found they could increase the

Outback farmland plains, western NSW

carrying capacity of their land by killing the trees, and the easiest expedient was to 'ringbark' living trees. This consisted of cutting right through the bark in a continuous ring, right round the tree, causing its death in a very short while.

The result was a greater area suitable for grazing and improved pastures, but a loss of habitat for a wide range of birds, mammals, insects and reptiles.

A recent result of the use of land for farming has been the accumulation in the environment of chemicals such as fertilisers and pesticides. Happily, since the 1970s there has been an increasing realisation that the indiscriminate use of any farm chemical has little short-term benefit and disastrous long-term consequences. While it is obvious that farm production would suffer if no chemicals were used, it is also obvious that all farmers will have to understand what the future environmental outcomes will be for any chemical they use.

Rabbits were brought to Australia for 'sport', part of an English tradition to bring as much of the 'old country' to the colony as possible. A few rabbits escaped from a farm in Victoria in the 1860s and, by the end of the century, rabbits had a foothold over a huge area of Australia. The damage they caused is almost unimaginable, as they ate everything green, destroyed huge areas with their warrens, and drove native animals from their natural habitats and into extinction.

The animals that suffered most were the small mammals as the grass tussocks and low bushes like saltbush were destroyed. The combination of overstocking, rabbits and droughts decimated areas of Australia to the point where they have never recovered.

The arid outback is a fragile land, and newspapers of the 1860s carried stories of the damage being done through overstocking. This is an unhappy tradition that continues to this day, where graziers increase the number of stock on a property in the good years, so that when the inevitable droughts come, the land has been stripped bare.

Many widespread and valuable bushes such as saltbush were almost destroyed over huge areas of the outback, as the sheep fed their hungry way through scrubland. Native grasses and herbs were eaten off to the ground, never to recover, the land became open to the savage, drying westerly winds, and whole areas became dust bowls.

The 'battle' between the farmer and grazier and the natural environment will continue until each is given a chance to exist in a way that does as little damage as possible to the other. This will mean that the agriculturalists will have to modify some of their practices, just as there will have to be some modification of the natural system. Unless this happens there will be no winners, just losers, and all of us will be poorer in many ways.

Mammals

FERAL CAT
Felis catus

LOCATION
Throughout Australia.

HABITAT
There seems to be no limiting factor to the establishment of cat populations in any habitat, apart from, obviously, the availability of food.

IDENTIFICATION
Colour Widely varied, as with domestic cats, but usually tabby-grey with dark markings, or black-and-white.
Size Head and body length — male: up to 62 cm; female: up to 56 cm. Tail — male: up to 34 cm; female: up to 32 cm. Weight — male: up to 7 kg; female: up to 5 kg.
Distinguishing features It is not sufficient to say that the feral cat is just a domestic cat gone wild, since it evolves to adapt to its habitat. Within two generations, the cat begins to change shape, becoming blockier, heavier, with a squarer head, and a fierceness that is alien to the 'house' cat.

ENVIRONMENTAL NOTES
Status The feral cat is responsible for the loss of many small native animals (mammals, birds, reptiles and amphibians). Many domestic cats are casual killers, more from instinctive behaviour than from hunger, but the feral cat is an incredibly efficient and voracious predator.
  The original source of all feral cats is domestic strays, either dumped deliberately by the owners, or bush wanderers that stay bush. The return to the wild favours those cats that are stronger, fiercer and better camouflaged, and thus the feral cat appears. There seems to be no recorded information of successfully returning a feral cat to the domestic fold — once the fierceness is aroused in the species it appears irreversible. The male feral cat will kill any male domestic cat anywhere near its territory.
Feeding habits Although you will find the feral cat living in rabbit burrows and taking rabbits as food, it is more likely to prey upon native animals that are easier to catch.
Predators Like the fox, the feral cat is at the top of its food chain. The adult feral cat has no predators.
Reproduction Exactly as for domestic cats. Strangely, many female feral cats come into sheds or barns to have their litter, returning to the wild once the kittens are able to walk.

HORSE (including the Brumby)
Equus caballus

LOCATION
Mainly the outback of Queensland, through to northern South Australia and up into the Northern Territory.

HABITAT
The fringes of the desert region, through the grassland and shrub areas of the arid zone, its presence governed by the availability of water.

IDENTIFICATION
Colour Usually bay (light brown) or chestnut (reddish brown).
Size Both male and female: up to 170 cm high.
Distinguishing features You can distinguish the wild horse, or brumby as it is called, from domestic animals gone stray by its blockier shape and generally rougher appearance. The difference is only slight, as many wild horses are caught and 'broken' to the saddle.

ENVIRONMENTAL NOTES
Status Horses ran wild from the time when the first European colonists brought them to Australia in the late 1700s. Since then, the wild population has moved away from centres of settlement and established itself in central and northern Australia and the Snowy Mountains.

When the wild horse population reaches a certain point it begins to have a devastating effect by its grazing of pasture land and muddying of waterholes. This devastation is increased during times of drought, when large mobs of horses collect around a small amount of water, churning it to a sticky mud that becomes a death trap for the weaker individuals.

The control or elimination of the wild horse brings fierce debate. On one side are the graziers, who see their limited grazing and water supplies being destroyed by the horses and, on the other, the large contingent of horse lovers. Somewhere in the middle are the conservationists, who may or may not see a place in the Australian outback for the horse, depending upon their personal point of view.

Feeding habits As for domestic horses.
Predators Some foals may be taken by dingos, but the adult is far too large to be preyed upon.
Reproduction As for domestic horses.

FOX
Vulpes vulpes

LOCATION
Throughout the Australian mainland, with the exception of the tropical north.

HABITAT
Incredibly varied, from above the snow line of the Snowy Mountains in eastern Australia, to the dry and harsh centre of the continent.

IDENTIFICATION
Colour The predominant colour of the fox is a brown, rusty-red, shot through with flecks of grey. If you see a healthy

FARMLAND

fox in full coat in winter, it is like a flash of flame as it flickers through the undergrowth.

Size Head and body length — male: up to 74 cm; female: up to 67 cm. Tail — both male and female: about 44 cm. Weight — male: up to 9 kg; female: up to 7 kg.

Distinguishing features When compared to dingos or large breeds of dogs, the fox is a slight and delicate creature. A fully grown male fox will weigh less than 9 kg, compared to the 20 kg of a fully grown dingo or medium-sized domestic dog.

ENVIRONMENTAL NOTES

Status The fox was introduced to Australia for the 'hunt', where, as in England, a procession of beagles and red-coated riders pursued a fox till its death. Sufficient foxes escaped the hunters to establish a very successful population on the Australian mainland.

Apart from any population control caused by shortage of food, the fox is also prone to a form of mange, a fungal skin disease. It can cause them to totally lose all fur, with death resulting from infection or exposure. Aside from starvation and disease, there is little else to control the numbers of this cunning (but appealing) night-time predator.

Feeding habits The fox has an amazing capacity to adapt to available food, catching and eating everything from grasshoppers to frogs, rabbits and domestic chickens. It has also shown an incredible ability to make use of the scraps left by people. Normally the fox stays right away from human habitation, but there are exceptions: one population of foxes in the Snowy Mountains has become proficient at raiding garbage bins.

Predators The adult fox is at the top of the food chain and has no natural predators, though small cubs may be taken by goannas or large snakes.

Reproduction The fox breeds in burrows, or sometimes in the middle of dense lignum thickets. It may dig its own burrow or cohabitate with rabbits in a warren system. It usually has more than 4 young, but rarely more than 2 survive to adulthood.

Fox Antics

I once watched a fox perform the most extraordinary antics — it would stand perfectly still, head slightly turned to one side, then take huge springing leaps into the air, landing with all four feet on a tussock of grass. It was catching grasshoppers! The spring onto the tussock made the grasshoppers fly into the air and then the fox attempted to take them in full flight. I was too far away to see how successful it was but I hoped it caught enough to replace the energy it used in catching them.

FERAL PIG
Sus scrofa

LOCATION
All of outback Queensland and NSW, into the Northern Territory and the north of Western Australia.

HABITAT
The major limiting factors in the spread of the feral pig appear to be distance from human settlement, proximity of a reliable water supply, and forest, scrub or swamp thickets to provide shelter.

IDENTIFICATION
Colour Colours vary greatly, but 'characteristic' colours are jet black, gingery-orange, or a piebald mixture of the two.
Size Head and body length — male: up to 155 cm; female: up to 130 cm. Tail — male and female: 30 cm. Weight — male: up to 115 kg; female: up to 70 kg.
Distinguishing features The feral pig is leaner and tougher than its domestic cousins. If you see a big, black, wild boar in the wild it bears little resemblance to the soft, fat baconers winning prizes at an agricultural show. The feral boar is a slab-sided, round-shouldered, long-snouted animal that, one could say, seems to bear a grudge against the world.

ENVIRONMENTAL NOTES
Status There are accounts of feral pigs from the first days of European settlement in 1788, when domestic pigs were escaping from farms around Sydney, NSW, until the middle of the 20th century. But it is in the swamps and scrublands of eastern Australia that the populations of feral pig are found today.
Feeding habits It is a coarse eater, tearing up large areas of crops and pastures to get the plants that make up most of its food. It is in direct competition with domestic stock, damaging as much as it eats, and fouling up the access to dams and waterholes.

It does not confine its diet to plants, as it is an omnivore, like us. It will feed on the carrion flesh of dead lambs, and there is evidence that the feral pig kills lambs, and lambing ewes. Its predation upon native species is also frighteningly high, taking everything from amphibians to emu eggs and chicks.
Predators Some piglets may be taken by very brave foxes, dingos or large hawks and eagles, but the adult pigs have no natural predators.
Reproduction As for domestic pigs.

FARMLAND

HOUSE MOUSE
Mus musculus

LOCATION
Throughout Australia.

HABITAT
Anywhere food is available.

IDENTIFICATION
Colour Varies from a soft grey, to a greyish-brown, to dark grey on top, with a lighter colour underneath.
Size The house mouse is less than 20 cm in total length, with tail and body 10 cm each. It weighs up to 25 g.
Distinguishing features It has a small face with a short nose and small ears, compared to many native Australian mice.

ENVIRONMENTAL NOTES
Status The house mouse is one of the most widely distributed mammals in the world. It is able to cope with an incredible range of environments and live on a wide array of foods.

In Australia, you will find the house mouse a long way from houses. It is particularly common in the cereal grain-growing areas of the outback, but it can also occur in enormous numbers in the arid and desert areas.

Plagues of mice occur regularly throughout Australia, where uncountable numbers invade every sort of dwelling and anything representing shelter. Fortunately, the plagues are usually short-lived, and the huge numbers of mice disappear almost as suddenly as they appeared.

The destruction caused to cereal crops, and by competition, to native species, has yet to be fully assessed. There is one group of species that benefits from the recurring plagues — the smaller birds of prey. You will find a marked increase of these birds during and immediately after plagues.
Feeding habits It can feed on almost anything edible, and even sometimes eats the indigestible plastic coatings on electric wires.
Predators In a natural system it has almost everything preying on it, from introduced cane-toads *(Bufo marinus)* to dingos. Living as it does in the lap of luxury in human habitation, it is protected from much of this predation. Its supposed

---

Tales of Horror of Mice Plagues

Anyone who has lived in the outback can tell you gruesome tales of horror of mice plagues. The mice can take up residence in any space available — the insulation around stoves, inside refrigerator motors, in clothing, in cupboards ... If they happen to die while living there the stench, for such a small body, is incredible.

arch-enemy, the cat, finds catching small birds and lizards easier prey than the lightning-fast mouse.
Reproduction The house mouse has an unbelievable capacity to reproduce. It reaches sexual maturity at about 2 months of age, the young are born about 3 weeks after mating takes place, with at least 8 in the litter, and the female can become pregnant immediately after giving birth. This means that every month she can have a litter, and 2 months after that her female offspring will be old enough to have a litter, and so on.

LITTLE RED FLYING-FOX
Pteropus scapulatus

LOCATION
Tropical and eastern Australia.

HABITAT
Largely determined by the presence of the wide variety of eucalypt blossoms that are its food.

IDENTIFICATION
Colour Pale reddish-brown all over, with a beautiful, soft, russet-yellow fur on the head and shoulders.
Size Head and body length — both male and female: up to 24 cm. Weight — both male and female: up to 0.6 kg.
Distinguishing features The flying-fox is usually seen as a black, flapping shape against the night sky. You can distinguish it from a bird by its size and the loud, distinctive flapping sound of its wings. It is also a very noisy feeder, and yells and squabbles as it moves around its food tree. The word 'fox' in its name may give you a wrong impression. It is a bat, not a fox, its name coming from its fox-like facial features.

ENVIRONMENTAL NOTES
Status Although blamed for destruction of fruit crops, the preferred food of the little red flying-fox is eucalypt blossoms, and it only raids orchards when its natural food is not available. The flying-fox is an attractive-looking animal, living in huge, smelly noisy colonies. It spends a great deal of its time arguing over roosting places in its daytime camp or squabbling over food at night.
Feeding habits As evening approaches the flying-fox leaves its daytime camp and heads out to the blossom trees. Its incredibly acute sense of smell seems to be the major method by which it finds its food, although it may be that scouting parties lead others to food sources.
Predators The adult flying-fox has few, if any, predators, mainly because of the inaccessible nature of its roosting places. Young flying-foxes that fall out of the roosting tree could become prey for

FARMLAND

prowling goannas.
Reproduction The baby flying-fox is born high in the treetops, while its mother hangs upside-down. She has to catch the baby in her wings as it is born, else it will plummet to the earth and perish. She then hugs it to her breast so that it can begin suckling. The baby remains clinging to its mother for a short while, but soon learns to hang around by itself.

Birds

BANDED LAPWING
Vanellus tricolor

general, or 'plovers' as they are also called, tend to have two main characteristics — they like open areas and they defend their nests with screeching cries and whirling flights. Many city dwellers will know the masked lapwing *(Vanellus miles)*, also known as spurwing plover. The banded lapwing has much shorter legs than its relative and thus is unable to easily negotiate long grass or the improved pasture of farmlands. It also does not appear to be so dependent on being near water, so it is able to live more easily in the arid and bare outback. If you are camping where groundcover is sparse, it is likely that you will hear the screeching cries of the banded lapwing in the stillness of the night.

LOCATION
The central and southern portion of Australia.

HABITAT
Dry, open grassland areas with a minimum of cover, occasionally near water.

IDENTIFICATION
Colour You can identify the banded lapwing by its white throat and bold black bib. Up close you will be able to see the red dot above its nose.
Size Both male and female are up to 28 cm long.
Distinguishing features Lapwings in

ENVIRONMENTAL NOTES
Status This is a reasonably common bird in those areas where the habitat is suitable. You are more likely to see a solitary bird or pairs than big flocks.
Feeding habits It takes small animals like insects, and also feeds on many different kinds of seed.
Predators The vigorous defence of the nest put up by the parent bird is enough to deter even the most determined predator. I have seen a very persistent fox eventually being driven away by the

harrowing divebombing of lapwings. It was definitely a case of 'sour plovers'.

Reproduction Not only does the lapwing defend its nest by literally hair-raising flights, it also performs the 'broken wing' trick. The lapwing nest is just a scrape in the ground, very vulnerable to predators, and so the nesting bird will pretend to have a broken wing. It lurches over the ground in a heartrending fashion until it lures the intruder far enough away from the nest and then it leaps into the air with a triumphant shriek, usually to return to its nest by a roundabout route.

CRESTED PIGEON
Ocyphaps lophotes

Distinguishing features The head crest on the crested pigeon immediately identifies it and separates it from the feral pigeon *(Columbia livia)* and the spotted turtle-dove *(Streptopelia chinensis)*. Whether living in the sparse grass and scrubland of the outback, or in the green luxury of a coastal garden, the crested pigeon always gives me the impression of alertness. It is watchful, and ready to spring into flight at the slightest alarm. It takes off with a loud clatter of wings, to fly a short distance before settling again.

LOCATION
Throughout mainland Australia, with the exception of tropical Queensland and the Northern Territory.

HABITAT
Widely variable, from suburban lawns to arid scrubland, but always somewhere near fresh water. The crested pigeon particularly likes scattered woodland, interspersed with the seed plants that are its food.

IDENTIFICATION
Colour It is generally dove-grey in colour, with a small irridescent bronze flash at the back of the wing.
Size Both male and female are up to 36 cm long.

ENVIRONMENTAL NOTES
Status In the 1960s you could almost mark the beginning of the outback by the point at which you began to see the galah and the crested pigeon. Now both these species are common in many coastal areas of Australia. It is less than 30 years since the crested pigeon was predominantly a bird of the dry inland of Australia. In the space of a human generation it has moved to many coastal areas and into a wide range of climatic zones. This has been brought about by two major factors — the clearing of dense forests to create open areas of grassland for human habitation, and the migration of the species away from inland droughts.

Feeding habits An extraordinarily wide variety of plant seeds, including many that

FARMLAND

are considered to be pest species, like Paterson's curse *(Echium plantagineum)*.
Predators It is taken in the air by large hawks and falcons, and on the ground by cats and foxes. Its nest is also robbed by cats. I have often found the scattered nest and shattered egg-shells of a crested pigeon under the low trees where it had its nest. Almost always the bark of the tree was torn by the claws of a climbing cat.

Reproduction A very flimsy nest of crossed twigs is constructed in shrubs and thickets, usually about 3 m from the ground. Two or 3 eggs are laid on this precarious place and the female settles over them to hatch them. Once she has begun to sit, she is very loath to move and will stay until you come within a metre or so of her, hoping that her camouflage will hide her.

STUBBLE QUAIL
Coturnix pectoralis

LOCATION
Queensland, NSW, Victoria, eastern South Australia and southwestern Western Australia.

HABITAT
Cereal crops such as wheat and oats, grasslands, low scrub country with a thick covering of grass.

IDENTIFICATION
Colour Mainly shades of brown, but streaked with lighter points of colour.
Size It is a small, plump bird, with the female slightly larger than the male, but both are about 19 cm long.
Distinguishing features The first sight you will usually get of a stubble quail is a brown flash as a small bird bursts out from underfoot, with a startling whirring of wings. There is often no warning, as the quail will stay hidden until the last minute before bursting into flight.

It is most unusual to see a stubble quail in the wild unless it has been flushed from cover. Very rarely you may see a small family group moving quickly from one grass clump to another. The capacity to hide protects them from most predation and their sudden flight is another line of defence. The stubble quail's flight only lasts for about 50 m, before it literally drops to the ground, to disappear again.

ENVIRONMENTAL NOTES
Status The stubble quail has benefited from the clearing of land for cereal crops and grasslands. This has provided it with a very suitable habitat, where food and shelter is plentiful.
Feeding habits It feeds on a variety of seeds, including those left from the harvesting of grain crops. During times when the crops have been harvested and

there is no stubble in the fields, the quail will move out into tussock grass areas or scrubby woodland with grass cover.
Predators The quail is very prone to predation by a wide range of reptiles, mammals and birds. Snakes seek out the nest hidden away in the grass, as do a variety of lizards. The adult bird is caught on the ground by foxes and feral cats, and occasionally is taken in the air by hawks, falcons, and harriers. It makes a delicious meal for any animal quick enough to catch it.
Reproduction A scrape is made in the ground, then it is lined with grass, and 5 to 11 brownish-yellow eggs, 30 mm long, with camouflage smudges, are laid in the nest.

BLACK KITE
Milvus migrans

mon name, the 'fork-tailed kite', describes the V-shaped dip in the tail. You will usually see it in groups, soaring on rising air currents over its favourite feeding places. Like all kites, the black kite is master of the air. It soars effortlessly, using its forked tail as a rudder as it rises.

ENVIRONMENTAL NOTES
Status Because of the large numbers often found over country airfields this bird has been some cause for concern due to the danger it may cause to planes using the field. It is not clear why it is common over the airfields, but it is most likely that the hot flat surface creates the thermal air currents that the kite uses to rise high in the air.
Feeding habits It is not only a scavenger; it also eats many small animals. It can be seen in large numbers in times of outbreaks of locusts, or when a plague of mice occurs.

The black kite is attracted to grass fires not only because the rising heat causes thermal air currents, but because the fire disturbs small animals, like mice or grasshoppers. The kite swoops and weaves in amongst the smoke as it hunts. A wisp of smoke in the air will often attract many birds to the area.

LOCATION
All of inland mainland Australia.

HABITAT
Often seen over open spaces like country airfields. It is also common over grass fires, or any areas where it can scavenge, like rubbish tips and slaughter yards.

IDENTIFICATION
Colour From a distance this bird will look almost black, hence its name, but it is actually very dark brown in colour.
Size Both male and female are up to 55 cm long, with a wingspan of 1.2 m.
Distinguishing features Another com-

Predators Being a fierce predator, the kite has little need to worry about being preyed upon.

Reproduction It builds a flat nest of sticks, often along a watercourse, in which it lays 2 or 3 blotchy brown eggs.

AUSTRALIAN MAGPIE
Gymnorhina tibicen

LOCATION
Throughout Australia, with the exception of the central desert area of Western Australia.

HABITAT
Any area of open forest or woodland.

IDENTIFICATION
Colour The magpie is a large, bold, black-and-white bird.
Size Both male and female are up to 44 cm long.
Distinguishing features It is easily distinguished from other large black birds by the greater amount of white that it shows at all times, not just when it flies. If you are observant you will notice that magpies from different parts of Australia have different amounts of white on their bodies.

ENVIRONMENTAL NOTES
Status The magpie fits in very well with human habitation. It is seen everywhere from suburban yards to remote corners of the outback. It is such a familiar sight that many people do not realise that it is a marvellous songster. Its early-morning carolling is matched by few other birds, with the possible exception of the butcherbird. It is a wonderful throaty sound, full of melody and variety, and is given by the birds throughout the day, particularly when feeding on the ground.
Feeding habits The magpie feeds on a wide variety of small animals, as well as some plant material, not being fussy which type.
Predators I have never known any animal prey upon the magpie, either as an adult or as a chick.
Reproduction It sometimes causes havoc

BIRDS

when nesting because of its habit of 'divebombing' passers-by. This is a territorial defence mechanism, not only aimed at us but also cats, dogs, goannas or any large animal. It is an instinctual reaction by the magpie, a behaviour over which it has no control, and one which human residents have to learn to cope with.

AUSTRALIAN MAGPIE-LARK
Grallina cyanoleuca

LOCATION
Throughout the mainland of Australia, except for the driest desert areas.

HABITAT
Almost everywhere in its range, except for the thickest forests and waterless deserts.

IDENTIFICATION
Colour It has a mixture of black and white colouring, with more white than black. It has a bold black stripe running around its eyes and under the throat to form a bib.
Size Both male and female are up to 30 cm long.
Distinguishing features The magpie-lark is more commonly known as the 'pee-wee' from the call that it makes. It is a very neat bird, smaller and slimmer than the better-known Australian magpie. The magpie-lark is a ground forager and spends a great deal of the day walking briskly over open areas of ground, zig-zagging and bobbing as it goes, looking for any insect silly enough to be in the open. It is very common in suburban parks and gardens, although less common where cats are allowed to wander at will.

ENVIRONMENTAL NOTES
Status Very common throughout its range.
Feeding habits It spends a large part of each day wandering across open ground, picking up insects and other small animals as it goes.

Predators It is an incredibly watchful bird, and I have seen many a frustrated cat attempting to sneak up on a feeding magpie-lark, only to be caught in the act while some distance away. The magpie-lark uses very strong bird language towards any animal that tries to prey upon it, but this does not always drive off goannas that climb the trees to rob its nest.
Reproduction This bird has yet another common name by which you might know it — the 'mudlark' — so called because it builds a bowl-shaped nest out of mud. During the nesting season both members of the pair will fly from a suitable mud spot carrying a small amount of mud in their bills, to deposit it on the gradually growing nest bowl. The nest is often placed out along an overhanging branch 10 to 20 m from the ground.

LITTLE CROW
Corvus bennetti

LOCATION
Inland mainland Australia, from outback NSW and Queensland to the Western Australian coast.

HABITAT
Very varied, from inland watercourses to the garbage dumps in inland towns.

IDENTIFICATION
Colour Glossy black with white circles around the eyes.
Size Both male and female are up to 48 cm long.
Distinguishing features Two species of birds — ravens and crows — are so similar that it takes an expert to distinguish them. The little crow and the Australian raven (*Corvus coronoides*) are both large, glossy black birds with distinctive white rings around the eyes. They both tend to feed on any available food, from fruit to carrion, and their call is basically similar, although the raven has a distinctive call sounding like a baby crying. The only major difference is that the little crow is shorter by some 6 cm. In the outback, the little crow often gathers in mobs to fly high on thermal air currents, diving out of the formation to zoom back to earth.

ENVIRONMENTAL NOTES
Status The crow and the raven are blamed for killing and eating young lambs. While it cannot be argued that they eat dead lambs, controversy still rages concerning whether they actually kill them. The crow will gather at the carcass of any dead animal, using its strong bill to tear away morsels.
Feeding habits It feeds on carrion, fruit, small animals, eggs, rubbish on rubbish tips — almost anything edible.
Predators The crow is at the top of its food chain and is too big and powerful a bird to be prey for another animal.
Reproduction Where suitable trees are not available, the little crow will build its nest on the crossbars of telephone and electricity poles. As you drive along country roads, look out for untidy clumps of sticks on the tops of poles, and you might see the head of a little crow peering over the top.

MANED DUCK
Chenonetta jubata

LOCATION
Eastern Australia (not Cape York) and western Western Australia but not central or northern Australia.

HABITAT
Widely scattered, from coastal farmlands to inland farm dams, and any timbered areas near water.

IDENTIFICATION
Colour A very handsome bird, with a small head and short beak, and a soft grey colouring. The male has a chocolate-brown head, while the female has a white stripe above and below the eyes.
Size Both male and female are up to 50 cm tall.
Distinguishing features The maned duck has a soft, haunting cry that is one of the most common night-time sounds you can hear if you are camping around billabongs and swamps in the outback. It tends to call more often at night than other waterbirds, and the sound is totally unlike the harsh quack of other ducks.

ENVIRONMENTAL NOTES
Status You will often see the maned duck walking over paddocks, feeding on the green pick in the wetter areas. It is by far the most common duck on farm dams, and many birds breed in close vicinity to the dams.
Feeding habits In some farming areas the maned duck was regarded as a pest because it eats grass and soft, green crop plants such as rice. Fortunately, control measures have not made any marked difference in the spread and survival of the maned duck population.
Predators The adult duck is taken by large birds of prey like the peregrine falcon, and night-prowling foxes. The ducklings are taken from nest holes by goannas.
Reproduction Its breeding behaviour is fascinating as it has a nest high up in the hollow of a tree. When the ducklings are old enough to swim and feed themselves they are either tipped out of the nest, or voluntarily leave, to fall on the ground below. They then pick themselves up and head off with the parents to the nearest food supply.

Reptiles and Amphibians

GREEN TREE FROG
Litoria caerulea

LOCATION
Central and northern NSW, Queensland, the northern half of the Northern Territory and the north of Western Australia.

HABITAT
In a variety of places, usually associated with water, and very often in farm buildings and other structures, such as water tanks.

IDENTIFICATION
Colour It is a beautiful bright green on top, sometimes patterned with some white dots. Underneath it is white. It has bright black eyes that sometimes peer

FARMLAND

down at you from the roof rafters of outside toilets.
Size Both male and female are 10 cm long (head and body length).
Distinguishing features The green tree frog is very common around houses on farms in the eastern and northern parts of the mainland. The first you may know of its presence is the deep croak that comes echoing out of a gutter downpipe, or from the cool area around a water trough.

Some people believe that the green tree frog is a predictor of rain. Sometimes as much as 24 hours before rain comes the frog will begin to give its deep croak, and this is most common in the summertime following a long dry spell. Perhaps its senses allow it to feel a change in atmospheric conditions long before the weather forecaster would be able to know anything about it.

ENVIRONMENTAL NOTES
Status The green tree frog is very common throughout its range, but is dependent upon a clean and reliable source of water in which to breed.
Feeding habits It plays a vital role in the control of populations of a wide range of small animals, from insects to mammals like baby mice.
Predators One reason that the green tree frog is not as common in the suburban areas is that many fall victim to domestic cats. The frog is no match for cats. In the wild it is eaten by snakes and waterbirds.
Reproduction The green tree frog lays its eggs in a frothy sago-like mass around the edge of clean, still water. The eggs hatch into tadpoles, which change over time from water-breathing young to air-breathing adult frogs.

CARPET PYTHON AND DIAMOND PYTHON
Morelia spilotes

LOCATION
All of mainland Australia, with the exception of southern Victoria and a narrow strip along the Great Dividing Range in NSW.

HABITAT
From coastal sand dunes, through wet forest areas, to the central desert.

IDENTIFICATION
Colour The main colouration is dark, often blackish-olive, with speckles and varied shapes of a yellow-fawn.
Size Carpet pythons of over 3.5 m are not unusual and at this length they can have a girth of about 32 cm. This makes them very capable of swallowing an animal as large as a small wallaby in one meal.

REPTILES AND AMPHIBIANS

Distinguishing features The diamond python and carpet python are so closely related that they can inter-breed, producing a snake with a confusion of colours. They are similar enough in general shape and colouring for the following description to assist you.

They are very large snakes, although by no means the largest of the python group in Australia. You will recognise them partly by the size and partly by the colouring, although this shows a wide variety throughout Australia. The head is shaped like a small, round-nosed shovel, often as large across as the back of an adult human hand.

ENVIRONMENTAL NOTES
Status Carpet and diamond pythons are fairly common throughout their range, and many set up 'home territories' where they will live for many years, growing to be very large snakes. Many farmers keep carpet pythons in their sheds and barns to control rats and mice, and they become accepted as part of the farm stock.

They are not harmful to humans unless interfered with, then they can give a nasty, but not venomous, bite.

Feeding habits They will feed on any animal small enough to be caught and swallowed. For a large python a fully grown rabbit makes a good meal, leaving a telltale bump in the snake until the rabbit is digested.

Predators Small snakes are fed upon by other snakes, large lizards and birds such as kookaburras. As they grow they become too powerful for any animal to attack them.

Reproduction The diamond and carpet pythons lay anywhere between 35 and 50 eggs, each egg being a little smaller than a hen egg. The pythons are known to coil around the eggs for a period of time to promote incubation. When the young hatch they are up to 40 cm long.

MYALL SNAKE
Suta suta

LOCATION
The outback areas of NSW, Queensland, South Australia and the Northern Territory.

HABITAT
A variety of places, from saltbush country and woodland to dry, stony ridges.

IDENTIFICATION
Colour Its colouring is fairly distinctive, being reddish-fawn on top, with a dark fawn colouring on its head. The underside is creamy-yellow.

Size It is not a large snake, rarely exceeding 70 cm in length.

63

FARMLAND

Distinguishing features The myall snake's other common name of 'curl snake' gives a clue to the way it holds its body when in a defensive pose. It curls its body back, ready to spring forward. If you see one in this pose, be warned, it is preparing to defend itself.

ENVIRONMENTAL NOTES
Status The myall snake is nocturnal and hides away during the day under timber on the ground, or other suitable cover. It is fairly common throughout its range in the central outback. Although it is venomous it is not regarded as dangerous to people, but its bite is extremely painful.
Feeding habits During warm nights it hunts over the ground looking for small animals, like lizards, to take as prey.
Predators Kookaburras, hawks and falcons, other snakes and large lizards.
Reproduction The myall snake gives birth to living young.

TESSELLATED GECKO
Diplodactylus tessellatus

IDENTIFICATION
Colour The tessellated gecko gets its name from the colour patterns it has on its back. The background colour is grey to brown and the pattern can be evenly scattered, like a pattern on a carpet, or in blotchings and white dots.
Size Usually less than 10 cm, from nose to tip of tail.
Distinguishing features You can recognise the gecko by the very large eyes in comparison to the rest of its body, and a tail that ranges from just thick, to fat, to so fat that it resembles a leaf, and is half as big as the body. The fat tail is a food storage reserve for hard times.

The gecko has two strange characteristics that you would not notice in casual observation. Because the eyes have no lids it uses its large flat tongue to keep its eyes clean, and its feet are equipped with

LOCATION
Outback NSW, Queensland, South Australia and the Northern Territory.

HABITAT
A ground-dwelling species of gecko that lives in leaf litter, fallen timber and cracks in the ground during the day.

gripping pads that enable it to walk on slippery surfaces, such as glass.

ENVIRONMENTAL NOTES
Status The gecko is a small fascinating lizard found throughout the world, particularly in tropical areas. In tropical areas the gecko often 'adopts' a house, sharing the indoors with the human owners and catching insects that are attracted into the building.
Feeding habits Insects are caught at night as it forages over open areas in the woodland and scrubland country it prefers.
Predators Night-hunting animals like owls seek out the gecko, as do feral cats.
Reproduction The gecko lays 1 or 2 eggs in cracks in the ground or among the forest litter.

WESTERN BLUE-TONGUED LIZARD
Tiliqua occipitalis

LOCATION
Western NSW, northwestern Victoria, southern and central South Australia, and southern Western Australia.

HABITAT
Dry areas, such as in mallee and tussock grass, and into the desert zones.

IDENTIFICATION
Colour The western blue-tongue has bold dark-brown stripes across its yellow-brown body.
Size Up to 50 cm long from head to tail.
Distinguishing features The blue-tongued lizard is a large member of a group of smooth-skinned lizards called skinks. Skinks can range in size from the 10 cm common garden skink (*Leiolopisma guichenoti*), to the size of the blue-tongue. You will be able to identify the western blue-tongue by its smooth skin and colouration. Also, if it becomes annoyed it will let you know how it got its name by flashing its bright violet-blue tongue at you. The blue-tongue tries to bluff its enemies by swelling out its body so that it appears bigger than it really is.

ENVIRONMENTAL NOTES
Status The blue-tongue is completely harmless and very beneficial, as it plays a role in controlling outbreaks of pest species. You should watch it but not handle it, as its fragile rib cage is easily damaged.
Feeding habits It feeds on a wide range of small animals, from other lizards to snails. It also takes the eggs of ground-dwelling birds. The eastern blue-tongued lizard (*Tiliqua scincoides*) is particularly valuable in suburban gardens, as it controls snails.
Predators Young lizards are taken by birds, other lizards and snakes. The fully grown adult is fairly safe from predation.
Reproduction It gives birth to living young, about 10 being the average born at one time.

YELLOW-FACED WHIP SNAKE
Demansia psammophis

LOCATION
Mainland Australia, with the exception of the northwestern tropical zone.

HABITAT
Widely varied, from coastal forests to the arid inland. The yellow-faced whip snake is sometimes found in farm gardens, particularly if there is a fishpond or similar area that attracts small frogs. The snake will 'camp' in vegetation surrounding such areas and hunt out the small frogs that live there.

IDENTIFICATION
Colour It is generally a drab, olive-brown colour, with the last third of its body being a lighter shade.

Size The yellow-faced whip snake is small, usually less than 60 cm long.

Distinguishing features It is a slim snake that moves very quickly. It has the capacity to spring a short distance if disturbed from its hiding place. If you are able to observe one closely you will see the yellowish patch near the eyes that gives it its common name. Although it is venomous, it is usually so slim, with a correspondingly small head, that it would be unlikely to bite an animal as large as a human, unless actually handled. The same rule applies for all venomous snakes: be aware, observe where you are walking or putting your hands, and leave all snakes to their own devices.

ENVIRONMENTAL NOTES
Status Common in suitable habitat, although large numbers are eaten by cats.
Feeding habits Frogs, lizards and small snakes form most of its diet.
Predators Like many small snakes, the yellow-faced whip snake is taken by feral cats. It is also eaten by other snakes, predatory birds and large lizards.
Reproduction The yellow-faced whip snake lays up to 20 eggs, hiding the eggs away in forest litter or under rocks.

WESTERN BROWN SNAKE AND EASTERN BROWN SNAKE
Pseudonaja nuchalis and *Pseudonaja textilis*

LOCATION
The two species together are found throughout mainland Australia, the western brown not being present along the east coast, and the eastern brown not being recorded from the central and western mainland.

HABITAT
Both snakes can be found from wet forest

Size They are similar in size, with the average being about 1.5 m long, although larger specimens are not uncommon.

Distinguishing features They are both snakes of the daytime, and are incredibly quick-moving, covering the ground in a startling flash. They can be identified by their glossy brownish colouring, and their slim, speedy bodies. You should not tamper with them in any way, because they are protected animals and, also, they are extremely venomous.

ENVIRONMENTAL NOTES

Status Brown snakes play an important role in the control of species that have the potential to be pests, such as the house mouse.

Feeding habits Small mammals, other reptiles, birds and amphibians are taken as food.

areas to the arid zones. The western brown is even found in the central desert region. The eastern brown ranges from savannah and saltbush country, to the rocky ridges.

Predators All snakes, except the extremely large ones, are likely to be taken by birds of prey, such as kookaburras and hawks. They will also be eaten by goannas, other snake species and even members of their own species.

IDENTIFICATION

Colour Both snakes show a wide variety of colours from light copper-brown to almost black.

Reproduction Brown snakes lay up to 35 eggs, often hidden amongst grass, twigs and leaf litter on the ground.

Respect for Snakes

Snakes such as these should not be feared, but respected. When you are in the outback watch where you are putting your feet. Avoid walking through thick grass or broken, rocky country. Most importantly, be aware. Although brown snakes will avoid you whenever possible, they do not always retreat if you come across them. Several times I have been 'faced-off' by a very large brown snake that decided I was in the path it wanted to take. I did not bother to argue with it, but gave it right of way.

Do not make any attempt to kill *any* snakes that you see. Apart from the fact that in all states you are breaking the law, an angry brown snake is a dangerous animal.

Insects

BUSH FLY
Musca vetustissima

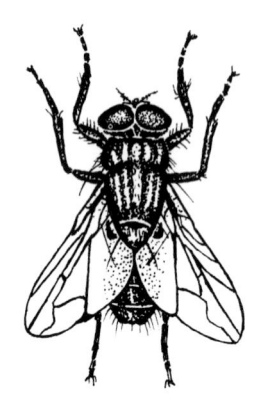

LOCATION
Throughout Australia.

HABITAT
Wherever quantities of the dung of large, herbivorous animals are available.

IDENTIFICATION
Colour Silvery-grey to blackish-brown, with two parallel dark lines along the back.
Size About 6 mm long, slightly smaller in size than the common housefly.
Distinguishing features The bush fly is one insect that you do not have to spend time looking for — it will find you. It is a small persistent fly, and many gather on your face to feed off your sweat, or collect on the back of your clothing as you walk. The bush fly is intrusive, and a daytime summer meal eaten outside can turn into a battle to keep it out of the food. It is often said that it is the prime cause of the 'great Aussie salute', as people wave their hands around in front of their faces to keep the flies away.

ENVIRONMENTAL NOTES
Status The better the season, the more vegetation grows, the more cow pats litter the ground, the more the bush fly breeds. Good winter rains in cattle-raising areas lead directly to an increase in the summer bush fly population.

For some years work has been going on to introduce dung beetles from other countries to assist in the reduction of the amount of cattle dung left lying in paddocks. Dung beetles quickly reduce fresh cow pats to a level where they are unsuitable for the bush fly to breed. It was necessary to introduce dung beetles from other parts of the world because the native Australian dung beetles have not evolved in such a way as to be able to deal with the massive quantities of cattle dung.

Research organisations are reporting pleasing results in the reduction of bush fly numbers in some areas of Australia.
Feeding habits The young maggot feeds in animal dung and the adult feeds *on* animal dung, sweat and blood to obtain protein, and sugary foods such as blossoms and, of course, picnic foods.
Predators Unfortunately, the natural predators such as spiders, other insects, birds and small lizards, can do little to control the incredible numbers of bush fly that appear in the warmer months.
Reproduction The bush fly breeds in dung, particularly the large pats left by cattle.

INSECTS

MARCH-FLY
Family Tabanidae

Although there are about 240 species of March-fly in Australia, the ones you are most likely to come across have some common characteristics. They are about the size of a small honey bee *(Apis mellifera)*, have flattened bodies, and large, colourful, pink iridescent eyes. They also tend to fly slower than the bush fly, and you are more likely to be able to swat them with a swipe of the hand.

ENVIRONMENTAL NOTES
Status In some countries the March-fly and its close relative, the horse-fly, are carriers of a range of debilitating and fatal diseases. This is not the case in Australia, but they nearly drive horses crazy.
Feeding habits It will bite all animals, but particularly large mammals. It will land on any exposed part of the skin, but prefers places like human ankles, where the blood flow is closer to the surface. The female is equipped with biting and sucking mouthparts and she lands on you to take a meal of blood.
Predators Birds, spiders and other insects.
Reproduction The eggs are laid in damp conditions, such as in rotting vegetation, or on the edge of tidal areas. The maggots then burrow into drier soil to pupate.

LOCATION
Throughout Australia.

HABITAT
Very varied, from seashore to arid inland areas, provided there is some dampness in which the larvae can develop.

IDENTIFICATION
Colour Varies according to the species, but usually greyish to grey-brown with some stripes or markings on the back.
Size About 1 cm in length.
Distinguishing features The first thing you will notice about the March-fly is its bite. The name 'March-fly' is not completely appropriate as it is likely to bite you in any warm month of the year.

Plants

WHITE CEDAR
Melia azedarach

LOCATION
NSW, Queensland, South Australia and Western Australia.

HABITAT
A range of soil and climatic types, from temperate high-rainfall areas to arid zones.

FARMLAND

IDENTIFICATION
Colour The leaves are a bright, shiny green, and the flowers are a pretty lilac. Fruit is bright yellow.
Size The white cedar is a handsome tree, that can grow as tall as 15 m. Each round fruit is about 1 cm across.
Distinguishing features It is deciduous, so that it spends part of the year with bare branches, an advantage if you want to get summer shade and winter sun. One of the best ways to identify the tree is when the fruit is present, as it hangs in large bunches.

ENVIRONMENTAL NOTES
Status The white cedar is really indigenous to rainforests, but is common in the outback because it is used as a shade and street tree. An unpleasant feature is that the white cedar attracts the hairy caterpillars of the white cedar moth *(Leptocneira reducta)*, and contact with the spines of the caterpillar can cause a sensation like a burn, and leave a nasty itchy welt.
Natural control agents The white cedar moth caterpillars will often completely strip a tree of all leaves.
Reproduction The fruit is often produced in such quantities as to be a nuisance, clogging gutters and covering the ground with its hard round centre. The fruit is also poisonous.

WESTERN BOOBIALLA
Myoporum montanum

LOCATION
All mainland states.

HABITAT
A wide range of soil types, but the trees do best if growing near a reliable source of water. Often seen around wet areas on farms, like dams and water run-offs.

IDENTIFICATION
Colour The shrub has dark-green leaves, and often looks out of place in its arid surroundings.
Size It is not a large tree, rarely growing more than 3 m high. However it happens

PLANTS

to be a very bushy and sturdy shrub.
Distinguishing features Boobiallas grow close together along a ready supply of water, like an irrigation channel or bore drain run-off. Superficially, in size and colour, the shrub looks a little like a garden camellia. Up close, you will notice that the leaves are much longer and thinner than those of a camellia, and the white flowers are tiny, only 1 cm to 1.5 cm wide.

ENVIRONMENTAL NOTES
Status It is commonly used as a windbreak. If the trees have been deliberately planted close together they can form an almost impenetrable barrier. The boobialla serves as valuable sanctuaries for nesting birds. The thick growth of branches and the dense outside covering of leaves keep nests well hidden and protected from most predators. Unfortunately, it is rarely enough to keep feral cats out of the nests.
Natural control agents Very few insects seem to attack the leaves, possibly as they contain toxins.
Reproduction The tree spreads by 'suckering', that is, sending up new trees from the spreading roots, or by seed.

NETTLE
Urtica spp.

Size Often up to 1 m tall, with leaves up to 8 cm long.
Distinguishing features The leaves have serrated edges and a fine covering of hairs. The nettle is 'weed-like' in its appearance, as it grows so thickly and stands out from the surrounding vegetation. The nettle is very noticeable and should be avoided, if possible. It is those fine hairs that you must watch out for. The merest brush against a nettle will cause a stinging, itching sensation, varying in intensity according to how much of the plant you touched, and your individual sensitivity.

LOCATION
Throughout all Australian states.

HABITAT
Areas that have been modified by flooding, rabbit warrens, or where rabbits have left the area eaten bare. Often in old sheep 'camps' under trees, and areas of heavy usage by animals or machinery.

IDENTIFICATION
Colour It is bright shiny green, ranging from dark to light green.

ENVIRONMENTAL NOTES
Status Widespread, particularly in farm areas around sheep yards, machinery sheds or rubbish tips.
Natural control agents Its natural defences seem to protect it from being attacked, although insects eat the tender new shoots.
Reproduction By wide dispersal of plentiful light seeds on the wind.

PEPPER TREE
Schinus areira

Size The tree can grow up to 15 m tall.
Distinguishing features The leaves have a pleasant distinctive odour if you crush them. The branches droop down to the ground, providing shady havens for sheep in stockyards, and for school children in the playgrounds of outback schools.

ENVIRONMENTAL NOTES
Status The pepper tree is one of the most common shade trees grown around farms in the outback. Pioneer families crushed the peppercorn to provide a type of pepper. The pepper tree is able to survive in very low rainfall areas, but it is a soil robber, and nothing else can successfully grow under it or near it.

Natural control agents Dozens of species of leaf-eating insects that are adapted to dealing with the strong taste of the leaves.

Reproduction This tree reproduces easily, producing an enormous quantity of seeds. The ground under an old pepper tree can be covered with the dry and hard fruit, so much so that they crunch as you walk.

LOCATION
NSW, Victoria, and South Australia.

HABITAT
Able to grow in a wide variety of soils, and with a wide variety of plants, but usually in areas of low rainfall.

IDENTIFICATION
Colour Thick, drooping foliage made of many fine, light green-grey leaves. The fruit is pinkish-red and small, only about 3 mm across, and inside is the hard 'peppercorn'.

CHAPTER THREE

Rivers, Swamps, Billabongs and Lakes

Some rivers, creeks and streams in the Australian outback often only have water in them after rain. Others may be permanent, deep waterways, with their own particular plants and animals. In dry times they become a series of unconnected pools, or dry up altogether.

Wet areas of all kinds provide the key to existence for many bird species. Some do not breed until floods occur, and others flock to feed along the shallow edges of swamps and billabongs. Mammals such as kangaroos do not breed unless water is available, and the water-rat can only survive where there is permanent water.

Swamps (known as marshes, fens or bogs in other countries) are shallow areas of water, usually full of reeds and other water-loving plants, and are very difficult to walk through. Swamps may be permanent, as is the case with the Macquarie Marshes in western NSW, or they may only be left after flood times. Early explorers of the east of Australia thought they had reached an inland sea when they came to the vast, impassable Macquarie Marshes. Some 'temporary' swamps become permanent if dams are placed on rivers, or if there is a major change in the flow of the river.

Billabongs (also called lagoons) are pools, sometimes quite deep, left when a river changes course. A portion of the riverbed is cut off, sometimes after very big floods have changed its course, leaving behind a closed off loop of water. Billabongs tend to be more permanent than swamps, although their level is often tied to the height of the river, and they can become very shallow between floods.

Outback lakes are large bodies of water, sometimes very deep, and sometimes so big you cannot easily see the other side. Their size does not necessarily make them a permanent body of water, as Lake Eyre in southern central Australia is more often a dry salt lake than a wet salt-water lake. However, when it is full, it provides an extraordinary habitat for billions of salt shrimp and thousands of waterbirds, along with hundreds of species of other animals.

Water is the key to the outback for humans as well. Aborigines fished the waterways for thousands of years. European settlers looking for land to farm followed the rivers and 'squatted' where they thought

RIVERS SWAMPS BILLABONGS AND LAKES

Willandra National Park, NSW

their sheep and cattle would find permanent food and water. The inland rivers served as water highways for paddleboats, travelling incredible distances into the outback, sometimes to be stranded for years while they waited for the next flood to pick them up.

The temporary nature of many outback 'wetlands' has meant that animals and plants have had to adapt to either escape as the water dries up, or stay behind and survive during the long, dry times. Added to this have been the changes caused by the damming of some inland rivers, and the introduction of species from other countries. Only the hardy species survive the combination of unreliable and infrequent rainfall, and the loss of habitat caused by changes in water depth and intrusion by introduced species.

Mammals

WATER-RAT
Hydromys chrysogaster

LOCATION
Scattered throughout all states of Australia, but absent from the arid areas of NSW and the central desert areas.

HABITAT
Rivers, creeks, streams, lakes and billabongs where suitable food exists (see 'Feeding habits' below), and shelter can be found.

IDENTIFICATION
Colour It has a wide range of colour on the back, from almost black, to slate-grey, but usually with a soft creamy-yellow underneath. Its long tail has a distinctive white tip starting at about the last quarter of its length.
Size Head and body length — male: up to 35 cm; female: up to 37 cm. Tail length — male and female: 32 cm. Weight — male: up to 1.3 kg; female: up to 1 kg.
Distinguishing features A water-rat in the wild is a joy to behold. While it is not often seen in full daylight, it occasionally can be observed feeding on a crayfish it has taken from the water, or swimming across a river to a favourite feeding place.

As would be expected it is an excellent swimmer, looking a little like a very small beaver, as it moves through the water with just the head showing. The water-rat will look rat-like to you at first glance, but you will see that it is larger, with movements that are more otter-like, being smooth and careful, rather than sly and scuttling. Its face is very unrat-like, being rounder and flatter on top, and in my opinion more appealing.

ENVIRONMENTAL NOTES
Status The fur of the water-rat is so thick and lustrous that it was vigorously hunted for commercial gain, also for sport, and sometimes by farmers on the pretext that it caused damage to the banks of irrigation channels. The damage the water-rat may have done was far outweighed by the benefits of its predation upon crayfish, whose burrows waste large amounts of valuable irrigation water every year. Natural controls such as predation and the availability of food maintain a population size suitable to the habitat.
Feeding habits It feeds on a wide range of crustaceans and molluscs, including crayfish and mussels, as well as fish and insects.
Predators The young are taken by snakes, fish and large waterbirds, while the adult is preyed upon by feral cats and birds of prey, such as the larger falcons.

Reproduction The young are reared in a nest in a burrow dug close to water, with 3 or 4 young in a litter. The water-rat is capable of reproducing as rapidly as introduced rats, but numbers are controlled (see 'Status' above).

Birds

AUSTRALIAN PELICAN
Pelecanus conspicillatus

Size A very large bird, up to 1.9 m long, with a wingspan of up to 2.6 m.

Distinguishing features The pelican has a huge, distinctive beak that is half as long as its body, and that has a sack on the lower portion capable of holding 6 litres of water. It is a fascinating bird to watch, whether just swimming around catching food, preparing for take-off for long sweeping flights over the water, soaring high up on thermal air currents, or coming in to land on water with its feet down to make a long, skidding landing. It is incredibly graceful in the air, and performs swimming ballets on the water, but it is a clumsy waddler on land.

LOCATION
Throughout Australia.

HABITAT
Any large area of fresh or salt water.

IDENTIFICATION
Colour Snowy white with black on the wings.

ENVIRONMENTAL NOTES
Status The pelican is a very common bird on waterways all over Australia. In some areas the pelican is attracted by regular handouts of food. This practice is very damaging to the natural behaviour of the

---

Fluctuating Pelican Populations

Following the flooding of Lake Eyre in southern central Australia in the late 1980s, thousands of pelicans flew to the lake to feed and breed. As the lake dried up young birds unable to fly were trapped, and the evaporating lake left a ring of bird carcasses as the water receded. The carcasses became food for a wide range of scavengers, from lizards to eagles.

bird. In a study I carried out on pelicans over a 12-month period, I found that they normally flew from their feeding sites back each afternoon to roosting or nesting sites, but when the pelicans were presented with handouts they did not leave the area at all, and stayed close to the unnatural food source. Any major breakdown in behaviour such as that has disastrous effects on the breeding and survival of the group.

Feeding habits You will sometimes see pelicans in large groups, swimming in formation as they drive schools of fish into a living 'net' of pelican beaks. Each bird then dips and sways into the schools of fish, coming up with its huge beak full of a mixture of water and fish. The water goes out and the fish goes down the gullet.

Predators The adult bird is too large to be preyed on, but the chicks are taken by large birds of prey.

Reproduction In some nesting sites the pelican gathers by the hundreds (even thousands). It lays its eggs on the top of bushes that sit out in the water, particularly after prolonged flooding. The eggs are hatched in this precarious position, and in big colonies it is not unusual to see floating eggs that have tumbled from the nests. The chicks display the most extraordinary behaviour following feeding, going into a form of convulsive fit.

HOARY-HEADED GREBE
Poliocephalus poliocephalus

LOCATION
Throughout Australia, with the exception of the tip of Cape York.

HABITAT
Almost any medium to large body of water, from fresh to brackish. Because of its shyness, it is unusual to see the hoary-headed grebe on small farm dams, as the body of water is not sufficient to allow it to get far enough away from the edge. Its most likely habitats are lakes or lagoons that provide a larger quantity of water, and shelter amongst clumps of water plants.

IDENTIFICATION
Colour Greyish, most commonly seen on the water in the distance where identification can be difficult.

Size A small bird, both male and female are up to 31 cm long.

Distinguishing features Trying to identify the grebe can be very frustrating, even with binoculars, as it takes off in splashing flight if danger threatens. Any small swimming bird, usually in pairs or small groups, that flies rapidly away, or dives suddenly, is likely to be a grebe. It is the Australasian grebe (*Tachybaptus novaehollandiae*) that dives to escape danger, giving rise to the nickname of 'diver'. During the nesting season the hoary-headed grebe may congregate in groups of several hundred.

ENVIRONMENTAL NOTES
Status Common to very common, although it is more often seen in pairs or small groups than huge flocks.

Feeding habits It feeds on the plants and small animals of its water habitat.
Predators The young are taken by fish and eels, and by birds of prey, but the adult is too wary to be easily caught.
Reproduction It builds its nest on the water, using plants that float, and attaching the nest to strong reeds to prevent it floating away.

LITTLE PIED CORMORANT
Phalacrocorax melanoleucos

IDENTIFICATION
Colour The white front and black back make it quite a distinctive bird out of the water and, when swimming, the white face and throat show clearly.
Size Up to 61 cm long.
Distinguishing features The cormorant is usually seen perched along the water's edge, often with wings outstretched to dry. It is a diving bird, and the low level of waterproofing in its feathers lowers the buoyancy of its body, thus requiring less energy to stay submerged. You can distinguish a slightly larger cormorant, the pied cormorant *(Phalacrocorax varius)*, by yellow-orange markings at the back of the bill.

LOCATION
Throughout most of Australia, with the exception of eastern Western Australia.

HABITAT
Large or small areas of water, both salt and fresh.

ENVIRONMENTAL NOTES
Status The little pied cormorant is a common bird along both salt, fresh and brackish water throughout Australia. It is a necessary and beneficial part of the water ecosystems, as it plays a large part

---

Cormorants Catch Fish For Humans

In Asian countries, larger species of cormorants are used to catch fish, like a living fishing line.

in the control of species that tend to take over in suitable habitats.
Feeding habits The little pied cormorant can swim considerable distances underwater, pursuing its prey as it twists and turns. If it catches a fish it brings it to the surface, flipping it around before swallowing it head-first down its throat. It feeds on a variety of aquatic animals, from fish to insect larvae.
Predators Its nest may be raided by an occasional adventurous goanna, but the adult bird is not prone to predation.
Reproduction A small platform of sticks is built in a tree over water, and in this nest 2 to 5 bluish-white eggs are laid.

DARTER
Anhinga melanogaster

LOCATION
Most of the Australian mainland, with the exception of eastern Western Australia and southwestern South Australia.

HABITAT
Most inland waterways, from large streams to lakes and swamps.

IDENTIFICATION
Colour It appears black in colour in the distance, but close up it shows a wonderful pattern of fawn and dark brown colours.
Size Up to 94 cm long.
Distinguishing features The darter can be recognised by its habit of perching above the water with its wings outspread to dry out its feathers. Unlike many waterbirds, the darter does not have waterproof feathers and must come out of the water to dry.

The darter may be mistaken for a similar-looking group of birds, the cormorants. They can easily be told apart in the water, as the darter swims with only the head and long neck showing above the water, and the cormorant swims with much more of its body out of water. On land, it is the very long neck (it is often called a snake-bird), and sharp, dagger-like beak that quickly identify the darter.

ENVIRONMENTAL NOTES

Status Fairly common on most suitable habitats, but rarely seen as more than a solitary bird or a pair.
Feeding habits The darter uses its long, sharp bill to stab food, like fish and other small water animals. The neck contains a special bone that 'locks' like a spring mechanism, releasing it suddenly forward when the darter wants to stab its prey.
Predators The adult bird is rarely preyed on, but the young are taken by large fish, eels and large waterbirds.
Reproduction Four or 5 greenish-white eggs are laid in a nest of a platform of sticks built in a tree that overhangs the water.

GREAT EGRET
Egretta alba

is pulled up into a tight 'S' shape. The great egret is a tall, stately bird that is almost regal in appearance. A hunting egret is a study in stillness as it waits for its prey to move, or slowly stalks along the water's edge. Often seen standing in shallow water, the great egret waits for the telltale ripple that indicates a fish is moving just below the surface. It then darts down with its stiletto bill.

LOCATION
Most of Australia, with the exception of the central desert area.

HABITAT
Any wetland that provides food.

IDENTIFICATION
Colour Snowy white, with yellow legs.
Size Up to 92 cm long. Legs are 45 cm long.
Distinguishing features It is easily identified when flying as the very long legs trail behind it in the air, and the neck

ENVIRONMENTAL NOTES

Status The great egret is a moderately common bird throughout the wetlands of Australia. In times past it was ruthlessly hunted for its beautiful feathers, as the long white breeding plumes were used as one of fashion's ornaments.
Feeding habits It feeds on all kinds of aquatic animal life, from small fish to frogs.
Predators Its large size and the positioning of its nest (see 'Reproduction' below) protect it from predation.
Reproduction The great egret builds nests of platforms of sticks in trees over the water, usually in the company of its own species or other waterbirds, and lays 3 to 5 blue-green eggs.

WHITE-FACED HERON
Ardea novaehollandiae

LOCATION
Throughout Australia.

HABITAT
Any area that has a small or large body of water that will provide food, including backyard fishponds. You may see the white-faced heron as a solitary bird stalking slowly along the water's edge, watching for prey, or flying overhead in large flocks. It will also be seen feeding in paddocks, particularly where irrigation is being used.

IDENTIFICATION
Colour Soft, grey-blue body with a white face and yellow legs.
Size Up to 69 cm long. Legs are 40 cm long.
Distinguishing features The white-faced heron is a slim, tall, long-legged grey bird, with a long, thin neck and dagger-like bill. It has a distinctive stance, often standing still on its long yellow legs, as it leans slightly forward to peer into the water. When resting, the neck takes a definite 'S' shape.

It is not very shy, and will often walk quite close to you if you are sitting still. It is territorial and aggressive, and will drive off intruders of its own species by flying at them and giving a harsh 'cracking' call. It will also mob predatory birds, such as white-bellied sea-eagles.

ENVIRONMENTAL NOTES
Status The white-faced heron is one of the most common waterbirds in Australia.
Feeding habits Its stately walk usually follows the fringe of the water, as this is the most likely area for the small aquatic insects that form its food. When it spots its prey, the head goes slightly back to lock the 'trigger' mechanism in the neck, and then the head is 'fired' forward to spear the animal.
Predators Although I have never seen a heron taken by a sea-eagle, the heron's reaction to one which perches in its territory seems to indicate that either adults or young are preyed upon by the larger birds of prey.
Reproduction A small, untidy nest of sticks is built in a tree over the water and 3 to 5 pale-blue eggs are laid in it.

ROYAL SPOONBILL
Platalea regia

LOCATION
Throughout Australia, with the exception of the central and southern desert regions.

HABITAT
Both fresh-water and salt-water wetlands are habitats for the royal spoonbill.

IDENTIFICATION
Colour White body with black legs and bill.
Size Up to 51 cm long.
Distinguishing features The royal spoonbill has long black legs and a very upright posture when standing or perching. It has a remarkable black bill, shaped like a long flat spoon. It would not be unusual for you to see sacred ibis and the spoonbill feeding together in the shallows. They can do this because their feeding techniques are very different. The spoonbill feeds with a sweeping motion, while the ibis probes as it goes.

The yellow-billed spoonbill *(Platalea flavipes)* is a similar bird but, as the name explains, the bill colour identifies the species.

ENVIRONMENTAL NOTES
Status The royal spoonbill is reasonably common throughout suitable habitats. Like many of the large waterbirds found in Australia, the spoonbill plays a vital role in the control of pest species.
Feeding habits The spoonbill feeds by swishing the flat end of its bill through shallow water and slush at the edge of any body of water. The mud and other junk is sorted out and the fish or crustaceans are swallowed.
Predators Its size, and the positioning of its nest (see 'Reproduction' below) make it unlikely to be taken by predators.
Reproduction When nesting, it may join colonies of several thousand birds of many species. Its nest is built over water and, in the huge temporary swamps that are formed after floods, it will tramp down the top of a lignum bush to lay 2 to 4 dull-white eggs.

BLACK SWAN
Cygnus atratus

LOCATION
Most of Australia, with the exception of the central and western deserts.

HABITAT
Usually on large areas of wetlands but occasionally found on small areas like farm dams.

IDENTIFICATION
Colour The black swan is a black bird, with a red bill.
Size Very large, up to 1.4 m long, with a wingspan of up to 2 m.
Distinguishing features When swimming it sits high in the water, with its long neck extended, and when flying a large white flash shows on the back edges of the wings. It is a superb flier, although it takes a fairly long run-off along the water to get its large body in the air. Once airborne its huge wings allow it to plane across the

BIRDS

sky. Often as it flies it will give a mournful honking cry that is particularly impressive at night.

ENVIRONMENTAL NOTES

Status The black swan can be in numbers from several hundred (into thousands) to a pair. Like all waterbirds, its distribution is dependent upon food supplies.

Feeding habits When feeding, the swan often up-ends, reaching the bottom of the river by stretching its long neck to the full, and with its tail and feet out of the water. It feeds on a wide variety of aquatic plants and also grazes on green pickings along the water's edge.

Predators The adult birds are too large to be taken by most predators, but I have found the bodies of swans that have been killed by marauding domestic dogs.

Reproduction It builds its nest in the shallows, usually far enough from shore to discourage predators such as foxes. The nest is made from a large heap of aquatic plants, pulled into a reasonably tidy mound. The 4 to 7 greenish-white eggs are 105 mm long, and are laid in a hollow at the top of the mound.

SACRED IBIS
Threskiornis aethiopica

HABITAT
All wetlands throughout its range.

IDENTIFICATION
Colour The sacred ibis has a white body and black, bare-skinned head, and a tuft of black feathers at its tail.

Size Up to 76 cm long. Legs are 35 cm long.

Distinguishing features Even at a distance, the most obvious feature of the sacred ibis is the sickle-shaped bill. A beautiful sight in the outback is the pattern formed by skeins of ibis as they fly across the sky. During times when the land is covered with floodwater, several hundred of these birds may be seen in flight, rippling across the sky in a beauti-

LOCATION
Throughout Australia, with the exception of southern Western Australia and western South Australia.

83

fully choreographed formation, that flaps and glides as if it were one bird.

ENVIRONMENTAL NOTES

Status The sacred ibis readily adapts to human habitation. At the Taronga Park Zoo in Sydney it became a menace, as it was so bold that it would steal food from a child's hand. In the wild this boldness has allowed it to survive and prosper in a wide range of habitats.

Feeding habits The ibis usually feeds along the muddy edges of swamps, lagoons, estuaries and rivers. It uses its long, curved bill to probe down into the mud and catch its prey. It feeds on many forms of aquatic animals, from salt-water snails to fresh-water crayfish.

It is an opportunist feeder, and will scavenge around the edge of garbage dumps, squabbling with ravens and silver gulls over scraps of edible material.

Predators No real predators because of its size and the remoteness of its nest.

Reproduction The ibis builds a large nest of sticks and reeds in trees, on the top of lignum bushes or in the midst of thickets or rushes.

Floating Eggs

I once was in the middle of a huge nesting area in Narran Lake in far northwestern NSW where thousands of waterbirds, including sacred ibis, along with many other species, had trampled the top of lignum bushes down to make their nests. There were so many birds and so many nests that hundreds of the eggs had rolled off the top of the bushes and were floating around in the water.

BLACK DUCK
Anas superciliosa

LOCATION
Throughout Australia, with the exception of eastern Western Australia.

HABITAT
Swamps, rivers, dams ... any water deep enough to supply food.

IDENTIFICATION
Colour Your first impression of a black duck seen on the water, or at a distance, will be of a very dark duck of one colour. Under closer observation you will see it is dark brown, with distinctive light fawn stripes down the face. When in flight, a flash of brilliant, opalescent green can sometimes be seen in the upper wings.

Size Up to 60 cm long.

Distinguishing features You will often see it in ponds in public parks and, in some places, it has become an expert beggar of bread and other food scraps. In the wild, the black duck is more likely to be seen in flocks than singly or in pairs. It rises quickly from the water when alarmed, and will often fly directly overhead as it circles. Its wings make the 'whiffling' noise common to all ducks, and an expert can differentiate between duck species by the speed of the wing beat.

ENVIRONMENTAL NOTES

Status The black duck is one of the most common of the wild ducks. As a result it is also the duck most likely to be taken by hunters. The controversy concerning the 'management' of wild species by hunting grows stronger every year, and it is an issue that governments are loath to face. Government controls have made significant inroads into the wanton destruction of waterbirds, but the basic issue of the value of hunting as a management tool is still not properly addressed.

Feeding habits It feeds on a wide range of water plants, both by grazing along the edge and 'duck-diving' to reach them. In rice-farming areas it occasionally makes a picnic of a small part of farmers' crops, but the damage is usually minimal.

Predators As well as hunting by humans, both adult and young birds are taken by foxes and dogs, and the adult bird is knocked out of the sky by large birds of prey. In some coastal lakes and lagoons, eels take ducklings.

Reproduction Like many ducks, the black duck is stimulated to breed by increases in water-level. It builds a nest in a scrape or hollow in the ground around the water's edge, and sometimes in the hollow stumps of old trees. It lays up to 10 dull-white eggs.

GREY TEAL
Anas gibberifrons

HABITAT
Any water deep enough to offer a food supply (see 'Feeding habits' below).

IDENTIFICATION
Colour Generally greyish, with no outstanding colours.

Size A relatively small duck, up to 46 cm long.

Distinguishing features You will often see grey teal in very large flocks, and sometimes perching on dead logs over and around water.

LOCATION
Throughout Australia, where food and water are available.

ENVIRONMENTAL NOTES
Status The grey teal follows the flood cycle in Australia. Its nomadic wanderings

are partly governed by the water made available after flood rains. It also requires permanent water refuges for times of drought.

Like the black duck, many grey teal are shot each year. The justification seems to become more cloudy as time goes on, as duck population control relies more on flooding and the availability of suitable habitat than on random shooting.

As it feeds on a wide variety of insects whose life cycles are tied to the water, the grey teal plays a vital role in controlling insect numbers.

Feeding habits It feeds upon a wide variety of aquatic plants and animals, grazing and foraging along the water's edge, as well as duck-diving in deeper water.

Predators Apart from human predation, which consists of just random shooting, the same comments apply as for the black duck (see page 84).

Reproduction The flooding of inland areas prompts the grey teal to breed. It builds a nest in any convenient spot where there is some structure to stop its eggs from rolling away. This includes tree hollows and scrapes in the ground at the water's edge.

BLACK-FRONTED PLOVER
Charadrius melanops

its underside white. It has a black mask around the red-rimmed eyes, with the mask going down the back of the neck. Its beak is red with a black tip.

Size Up to 18 cm long.

Distinguishing features The black-fronted plover is a charming bird not only because of its colouring, but also because of its action. It is a small bird, and quite difficult to see, despite its clear markings. It blends in well with its background, and it is often not until it moves that you realise it is there. When it moves, it moves rapidly, its little legs flickering over the ground. When it stops, it bobs its head up and down very rapidly several times. Like many birds it has a 'flight zone', and if you come within that zone it will take off, to fly quickly away, wings beating in a stop-start motion. As it flies it gives a high, peeping cry, over and over.

LOCATION
Throughout Australia.

HABITAT
Along the edges of fresh-water swamps, the stony edges of rivers and creeks, and farm dams in the middle of pasture.

IDENTIFICATION
Colour It is neatly 'dressed' with a black bib under a white throat, and the rest of

ENVIRONMENTAL NOTES
Status Common in suitable habitats

throughout mainland Australia. Apart from being an attractive bird to have around farm dams, the black-fronted plover is also important for its role in insect control.

Feeding habits Insects and other small animals that live around the edge of aquatic environments.

Predators Like other small waders its quick movements and alert carriage keep the adult bird out of danger, but the nest on the ground must rely on the camouflage of the eggs and the young birds to keep them out of danger.

Reproduction Up to 3 brown, mottled, camouflaged eggs are laid in a scrape in the ground, sometimes lined with any material that happens to be lying around, like twigs.

PURPLE SWAMPHEN
Porphyrio porphyrio

LOCATION
All of the eastern states, and the Northern Territory, eastern South Australia, and northern and southwestern Western Australia.

HABITAT
It is found in swamps throughout its range, and it also lives in parks and gardens that have large areas of water. It is not unusual to see groups of swamphens moving up from the water at dusk to feed on pastures or lawns.

IDENTIFICATION
Colour The colours of the purple swamphen are startling up close. The large bill and forehead are fire-engine red, and the throat and chest are iridescent purple. The rest of the body is black, and the long thin legs are reddish-purple. You can see the colours from quite a distance, making identification easy.

Size Up to 46 cm long.

Distinguishing features When alarmed, the purple swamphen flicks its tail up, displaying a patch of white feathers. This visual alarm signal warns other swamp-hens in the area that danger threatens. It is a very noisy bird and is often heard before it is seen. In some outback wetland areas I have seen it crossing the road during the day from one part of a swamp to another. Surprisingly, not many are hit by cars, probably because the swamphen is very fleet of foot.

ENVIRONMENTAL NOTES
Status Common in its range.
Feeding habits It feeds on a wide variety of aquatic plants, supplemented by the occasional small aquatic animal, like frogs and snails. It feeds on the reeds and rushes along the water's edge but also grazes out some distance from the water.

Predators The adult bird seems to have little to fear because of its size, but I was amazed to see one taken from the water's edge, right in front of me, by a white-bellied sea-eagle. Its nest is raided by foxes, cats and dogs.

Reproduction It builds a platform of trampled-down reeds, often cumbungi, in which it lays up to 5 very light-tan mottled eggs. The nest is often in clear view of the shore, although there may be a channel of water between land and reedbed.

WHISTLING KITE
Haliastur sphenurus

IDENTIFICATION
Colour The whistling kite has the appearance of being a soft, all-over brown when seen in the air. Closer inspection shows a dark tan colour with lighter mottling.
Size Up to 53 cm long. It is often mistaken for an eagle, as it is itself a very large bird. It can be easily distinguished from the wedge-tailed eagle, as the wedge-tail is much larger, and looks almost black in the air.
Distinguishing features You can identify the whistling kite in the air as one or two feathers are usually missing from its widespread, gliding wings. You are more likely to see it as a single bird or a pair, although a group may be seen feeding on the body of an animal killed by traffic on country roads.

This is one bird that is best known for its call, rather than its description. The beautiful whistling call that carries over great distance is heard in almost every Australian outback movie or documentary

LOCATION
Throughout Australia.

HABITAT
Over any open area, from rocky, arid, inland outcrop, to mangrove-lined estuary. The whistling kite is often seen over hills or paddocks, gliding easily as it searches out food.

ever made. Once the sound of its call is recognised, it becomes a haunting reminder of past experiences each time it is heard. It even calls in zoos and wildlife parks, where it lives in small enclosures, and when I hear the sound of its whistle, it brings back memories of wide open spaces and dusty haze-covered hills.

ENVIRONMENTAL NOTES
Status This large kite is a fairly common to very common bird throughout Australia, depending where you happen to be. It plays a valuable role in cleaning away carrion, and is an essential part of a balanced outback ecosystem.

Feeding habits Its food ranges from any dead animal found lying on the ground or floating in the water, to mammals and birds it catches itself.

Predators Like most animals at the top of the food chain, the kite has no natural predators.

Reproduction A bulky nest of sticks is built high up in a tall tree, and 2 or 3 blue-white mottled eggs are laid.

RED-KNEED DOTTEREL
Erythrogonys cinctus

bold white throat and black head and chest.

Size Up to 19 cm long.

Distinguishing features This is a small, active bird, that moves in fits and starts, running rapidly for a short distance to stop suddenly and probe in the mud for food. You can identify it by its bobbing head as it stands still, and the bold black and white of its head and throat.

When it feels threatened it prefers to run than to fly, skittering over the mud with legs moving quickly like a clockwork toy. It flies reluctantly, but when it takes to the air it will fly some distance before landing on another part of the swamp's edge.

LOCATION
In scattered populations throughout all of mainland Australia, with the exception of some coastal, desert and tropical areas.

HABITAT
The edges of wetland areas. Although it prefers fresh-water habitats, you will sometimes see it bobbing its way around the edge of brackish coastal swamps.

IDENTIFICATION
Colour It has a red bill and red knees,

ENVIRONMENTAL NOTES
Status Anything from single birds to quite large numbers, often mixed in with other small, wading birds can be seen. Studies suggest that it goes to the coast when drought conditions remove outback wetland habitats. If you see it in coastal areas it probably means that the outback is very dry at that time.

Feeding habits It eats insects and other small animals that live in and on the muddy edges of swamps and lagoons.
Predators Any small, wading bird has to be very alert to escape being caught by land predators like foxes. The adult dotterel would escape most predation by its keen eyesight and its quick escape flight.
Reproduction A scrape in the ground can become a nest, sometimes lined with twigs, or in the middle of pebbles. Four sandy-brown, dark mottled eggs are laid, only about 31 mm long.

BLACK-TAILED NATIVE HEN
Gallinula ventralis

LOCATION
Throughout inland mainland Australia, with the exception of the far tropical north.

HABITAT
The fringes of swamps, lagoons, and lakes, particularly where shelter can be found in bushes along the water's edge.

IDENTIFICATION
Colour The overall colour is brown-black and its orange-pink legs are easily noticeable.
Size Up to 36 cm long.
Distinguishing features You will usually see this bird along the edge of lagoons or swamps, where it moves quickly from cover to cover. It holds its tail erect as it moves.

It is a busy bird, constantly feeding around the edges of shallow water. It is usually timid in the wild, although there are records of it coming into farmyards to feed with domestic fowls. If you sit still at the edge of a lagoon you will often have the bird come quite close before it is aware of you. Its sharp, clacking alarm call will often be your first indication of its presence.

ENVIRONMENTAL NOTES
Status The black-tailed native hen is dependent upon the availability of water. When its swamp or lagoon dries up, it will fly great distances to find a replacement. In many of the inland areas the water only lasts for a few months after floods and then it is necessary for the black-tailed native hen to move on. It will often move down to coastal areas and remain there until inland wetlands have been replenished.

A phenomenon associated with this movement is the sudden appearance of a large number of birds in an area where none may have been present a short time before. Just as quickly, the population may disappear.
Feeding habits The black-tailed native

hen feeds upon water plants.
Predators Feral cats and foxes find that the shore-hugging habits of the native hen makes it easy prey, although its group watchfulness may protect it. Birds of prey, like marsh harriers *(Circus aeruginosus)*, take adults and chicks.
Reproduction A nest of grass or reeds is built along the edge of the water amongst thickets of lignum or other dense bush. Up to 7 pale-green mottled eggs are laid in the nest.

EURASIAN COOT
Fulica atra

LOCATION
Throughout Australia.

HABITAT
Swamps, lagoons and other large, open bodies of water; found in a huge variety of wetlands throughout Australia. You will see the Eurasian coot in city parks and gardens where it leaves the water to graze around the edge.

IDENTIFICATION
Colour Dark grey to black, with a white forehead and bill.
Size Up to 38 cm long.
Distinguishing features You will often see the Eurasian coot swimming with other similar-looking birds, either in groups of 2 or 3, or hundreds all together. At short range it is possible to see the toothpaste-white bill and forehead that distinguishes it from another waterbird, the dusky moorhen *(Gallinula tenebrosa)*.

If startled, the coot will burst from the water and stride across the top, wings flapping, until it has reached flying speed. The distance it travels depends on the seriousness of the danger. It is a noisy, busy bird. It is sometimes seen in 'rafts' where large numbers of birds congregate together on the water. These rafts will perform synchronised running, where the whole flock suddenly rush across the water, splashing and making a noise.

ENVIRONMENTAL NOTES
Status Very common, although more often seen in pairs or small groups than in huge flocks of just this species.
Feeding habits It feeds on a wide variety of waterweeds, and you will see it diving

down to then return to the surface with a bill full of choice greenery. Disputes occur over ownership of weeds brought to the surface, and this results in rapid chases across the water. This behaviour is particularly evident at breeding time.
Predators The adult bird is taken by marsh harriers *(Circus aeruginosus)* and other birds of prey, and the nest is raided by foxes, dogs and cats.
Reproduction A platform nest is trodden down on the top of waterweeds, or a grass nest is built in a log or a stump. Up to 7 light-tan, black-dotted eggs are laid.

RED-NECKED AVOCET
Recurvirostra novaehollandiae

LOCATION
Scattered populations are found throughout mainland Australia, apart from the eastern and southern coast and southern Western Australia.

HABITAT
Along the edges of swamps.

IDENTIFICATION
Colour The avocet has a red-tan head and neck, and white body with bold black markings along the edges of the wings.
Size Up to 46 cm long.
Distinguishing features It is the bill of this bird that will give you the clue to its identity. Instead of curving down at the end, like most other bird bills, it curves up. That fact is recorded in its scientific name, *Recurvirostra*, the 'recurve' part referring to the bill. The long thin legs, and long slim shape of the avocet also help with identification, being very similar in shape to the black-winged stilt (see below), but with quite different markings.

ENVIRONMENTAL NOTES
Status The avocet is not a bird that you are likely to see on every area of outback water. Occasionally you will find some areas where it is reasonably common, particularly in the southern part of the mainland. The shape of its bill allows it to feed in a fashion and in a 'niche' that is not being used by any other waterbird.
Feeding habits It feeds on aquatic animals such as insects and their larvae, other small animals and some plant material. Its long thin legs and long upward-curved bill, allow it to feed in shallow water some distance from the edge. As it feeds, it sweeps its bill backwards and forwards like a tiny, underwater scythe, catching small animals as it makes the sweeps.
Predators Similar to the black-winged stilt (see below).
Reproduction The nest is just a scrape in the ground, sometimes given partial shelter by a bush. Four dark-green eggs with camouflage colours are laid in the nest.

BIRDS

BLACK-WINGED STILT
Himantopus himantopus

is all legs. It is easily seen, as the black-and-white markings make it stand out against its watery home. You are likely to see a pair of birds, standing in shallow water, slowly and carefully stepping through the shallows, feeding as they go.

ENVIRONMENTAL NOTES
Status A fairly common bird in most shallow-water environments, although it is rarely seen in any numbers. Like all waders and aquatic feeders, the stilt has an important role to play in balancing populations.
Feeding habits It eats small shellfish, insects, and other small aquatic animals.
Predators Some adult birds would be taken by birds of prey like hawks and harriers, but the stilt's feeding position out in the water gives it some protection. The eggs and chicks are much more vulnerable to predation by any predator wandering along the water's edge.
Reproduction The long legs cause some problems for the stilt when it is on the nest. It has to spend some time folding its legs underneath it before it can sit down. The nest is made in vegetation along the muddy edges of swamps and lagoons, and 4 olive-green splotched brown eggs are laid.

LOCATION
Throughout Australia, with the exception of eastern Western Australia.

HABITAT
It forages around the edge of shallow wetlands.

IDENTIFICATION
Colour Its long, thin reddish-pink legs support a slim body boldly patterned in black and white.
Size Up to 38 cm long.
Distinguishing features Your first impression of a stilt is that it is a bird that

Reptiles and Amphibians

DESERT TREE FROG
Litoria rubella

LOCATION
Throughout the Australian mainland, except for a strip right along the southern coast.

HABITAT
It is found in environments as varied as wet coastal forests to the dry central desert. This frog is most commonly found sheltering under bark or under stones, somewhere near a temporary or permanent wetland.

IDENTIFICATION
Colour Mainly a grey, fawn or brown to blend in with its environment.
Size It is quite a small frog, only 3.5 cm long.
Distinguishing features It is not always an easy animal to see, as its colouring is designed to help it blend in with the background. It has a fat little body and a comparatively small head. It often has a black stripe down the side of the head, from the front of its nose, around the eyes and down to the shoulder. You are more likely to hear this frog than see it, as it croaks away from its hiding place in a tree or shrub.

ENVIRONMENTAL NOTES
Status This is quite a common frog in all areas of its range in the northern two-thirds of the mainland. It is one of a group of frogs that has adapted to living away from a constant source of water, and during the heat of the day it hides under rocks or loose tree bark to avoiding losing body moisture.
Feeding habits Frogs in general feed on a wide variety of insects and their larvae, as well as taking other small animals when the opportunity arises.
Predators Frogs are preyed upon by almost every carnivorous animal quick enough to catch them. This is why some frogs and toads have evolved into little packages of poison. The desert tree frog is not so lucky, so it is food for reptiles, birds and mammals.
Reproduction The desert tree frog is more likely to be active after summer rains, as this is its breeding time. The temporary ponds of water are used for the short time that they are available as egg-laying sites.

LONG-NECKED TORTOISE
Chelodina longicollis

LOCATION
Eastern mainland Australia, from south-eastern South Australian to northeastern Queensland.

HABITAT
Swamps, billabongs, and slow-moving rivers. It is not unlikely that you will find this tortoise wandering along a road during the middle of the day. At certain times it makes quite long journeys away from the swamp or lagoon in which it lives.

IDENTIFICATION
Colour The colouring of the back of its

REPTILES AND AMPHIBIANS

a clue as to its main feature. It has an extraordinarily long neck that appears to be almost as long as its shell. When the tortoise is at rest, basking in the sun along the bank of a swamp, it stretches its neck right out.

ENVIRONMENTAL NOTES
Status Very common in all suitable habitats; under no threat except for the possible loss of its habitat.
Feeding habits It feeds on a wide range of aquatic plants and animals.
shell is often a dull blackish-brown, and the undershell is a creamy-yellow.
Size Apart from its neck which is 20 cm long, it is not a large tortoise, as the length of its shell is rarely more 25 cm.
Distinguishing features Another name for this tortoise is the 'snake-necked tortoise', and this description will give you
Predators Tortoises are a favourite food of white-bellied sea-eagles and along rivers in NSW, it is not unusual to find the shells of long-necked tortoises under the eagle's favourite feeding tree.
Reproduction At least 10 eggs are laid in a hole in the bank of its wetland home. The hatchlings are orange and black.

MURRAY TURTLE
Emydura macquarii

of the more remote areas, you may see the Murray turtle along the banks of large billabongs, particularly if the water is beginning to recede in a dry time.

IDENTIFICATION
Colour Dark to dark brown above, creamy yellowish-white below.
Size This is a moderately sized turtle, as big as 30 cm along the longest part of the shell.
Distinguishing features It has a small head, short neck and short legs, with sharp claws. The small, white circle around the centre of the eyes might help you identify it. Sometimes the only evidence that you have that a river or waterhole contains a turtle is a line of bubbles that slowly move across the water.

LOCATION
In the rivers, large swamps and billabongs of the Murray/Darling river system of southeastern Australia.

HABITAT
Larger rivers and wetland areas. In some

RIVERS SWAMPS BILLABONGS AND LAKES

ENVIRONMENTAL NOTES
Status The Murray turtle is confined to the permanent waterways and waterholes of the Murray-Darling River system. It is fairly common throughout the huge length of watercourses that are part of this system.
Feeding habits It feeds on small aquatic animals like yabbies, mussels and fish.
Predators The smaller turtles are food for big fish like the Murray cod and the adults are prey for the white-bellied sea-eagle.
Reproduction About 10 brittle-shelled eggs are laid in a hole high up on the riverbank.

Fish and Crustaceans

GOLDEN PERCH
Macquaria ambigua

Size Golden perch can grow to be 80 cm long and weigh 23 kg.
Distinguishing features It has a small head with a distinctive bump behind the head in larger fish. Its scales are small, the tail is rounded, and it has a plumpish body.

ENVIRONMENTAL NOTES
Status Combine its size with the fact that it is a very tasty fish to eat and you find a good reason why it is sought after by anglers.

Like all native fish the population has been drastically reduced by changes to the habitat. The golden perch only spawns in streams above 23°C, and placing dams on rivers has caused water colder than this to be constantly in the rivers. This, combined with the intrusion of introduced fish such as the common carp, has resulted in a major asset in the river system being under threat.

Fish such as the golden perch have a role to play in the natural environment every bit as important as more visible animals such as the kangaroo. They also are potential economic assets, not just for

LOCATION
The river system of the eastern half of Australia.

HABITAT
The slow-moving, muddy rivers and large billabongs of the inland.

IDENTIFICATION
Colour The golden perch is probably more often called 'yellow-belly', particularly by the fishers who catch it. This gives you a good clue to identifying it, as there is a strong yellowish tinge all along its lower half.

FISH AND CRUSTACEANS

recreational fishing but also for commercial fish-farming, such as in farm dams.
Feeding habits Small, aquatic animals like yabbies, shellfish and fish.
Predators Small fish are taken by other fish, a range of waterbirds and turtles.
Reproduction Breeding is connected to a rise in the water-level and temperature. The eggs are laid at night and hatching occurs in 36 hours.

SILVER PERCH
Bidyanus bidyanus

LOCATION
The river systems of western NSW, western Victoria and southern Queensland.

HABITAT
This fish can survive in a variety of habitats, from warm and muddy rivers to fast-flowing water.

IDENTIFICATION
Colour As its name signifies, it is generally silver in colour, with a slightly darker colouring at the top.
Size It can grow up to 60 cm in length and weigh 8 kg.
Distinguishing features The silver perch is a very tidy looking fish, with a 'typical' fish shape. It has small scales, a small head and a broad tail with a very wide 'V' shape.

ENVIRONMENTAL NOTES
Status Because of its ability to live in a huge range of temperature variations and water conditions, the silver perch is a popular fish to introduce to farm dams. In many states a program of breeding and release has been happening for some time. In the wild, habitat conditions can be altered by damming rivers so that the silver perch is unable to breed.
Feeding habits It eats a wide variety of aquatic plant and animal life.
Predators As for the golden perch (see above).
Reproduction The cycle of breeding of this species is dependent upon the raising of the water-level in its part of the river system by at least 15 cm, and the water being above 23°C. The silver perch spawns in October, November and December, moving upstream to do so. You might be lucky enough to see large schools of silver perch congregating in the fast-flowing water under small dams and weirs.

CATFISH
Tandanus tandanus

LOCATION
The river systems of eastern Australia, particularly the Murray/Darling system, into South Australia.

97

RIVERS SWAMPS BILLABONGS AND LAKES

HABITAT
The larger rivers, streams and billabongs of the inland river system.

IDENTIFICATION
Colour Dark grey-brown to dark grey above, lighter grey underneath.
Size It grows up to 90 cm and can weigh 7 kg.
Distinguishing features The catfish is an extremely unpleasant-looking fish, in my opinion, with fleshy 'whiskers' around its mouth, dark slimy-looking bodies, and a shape that is more eel-like than fish-like. You will be told many stories about the catfish, including that it is poisonous to eat, and that it has a deadly spine in its backfin. These comments apply to some species of marine catfish, and not the *Tandanus tandanus*.

ENVIRONMENTAL NOTES
Status The catfish is fairly widespread through the river system and, as it feeds by stirring up the bottoms of rivers, it tends to muddy up the water. It is caught by recreational fishers and provides some 'sport' and good meat. Possibly because of its ugly appearance not many people eat it, even though the flesh is quite tasty.
Feeding habits The catfish feeds along the bottom on shellfish and shrimps.
Predators As for golden perch (see page 96).
Reproduction A saucer-shaped nest up to 2 m wide is made in sand or gravel in the bed of the river, and the eggs are laid in this nest. Hatching takes about 7 days. Breeding does not occur unless the water is above 24°C.

MURRAY COD
Maccullochella peeli

LOCATION
The river systems of eastern Australia, particularly western NSW, Victoria and Queensland.

HABITAT
Usually this fish is found in the deep-water areas of large rivers, and large deep billabongs.

FISH AND CRUSTACEANS

IDENTIFICATION
Colour The large fish is silvery grey and dotted with darker spots. The smaller fish tends to be patterned in large 'leopard spots' of colour along the back, growing lighter down the sides to almost fade away in the lower half.
Size The Murray cod is the largest of Australia's fresh-water fish, growing to a size of 1.8 m and a weight of 90 kg.
Distinguishing features You can recognise it partly by its size but also by its large head, big mouth and rounded tail.

ENVIRONMENTAL NOTES
Status It is a very good fish for eating and is sought after by both recreational and commercial fishers.

The Murray cod is stimulated to breed by river flooding, and any restriction to the natural flow of rivers restricts its rate of breeding. River red gums overhang rivers, and as the trees die and fall, the 'snags' they form in rivers become the homes for many species of fish. There have been many moves to 'de-snag' the bigger rivers, either to increase the flow, or provide better recreation areas for boating enthusiasts. Removal of the snags means removal of a vital part of the habitat for native fish.
Feeding habits It feeds on other smaller fish, crayfish and shellfish.
Predators As for golden perch (see page 96).
Reproduction It lays its eggs on the insides of submerged hollow logs, these logs often coming from the large, fallen branches of the river red gum.

COMMON CARP
Cyprinus carprio

LOCATION
The Murray/Darling river system of eastern Australia.

HABITAT
Rivers, lakes, streams, ponds, farm dams, swamps, billabongs . . . any area of water large enough to swim and feed in.

IDENTIFICATION
Colour It is greyish-gold in colour, the reflection of the scales causing changes in colour from grey to gold as they move.
Size Many carp grow to a tremendous size and can reach a weight of 50 kg. Fish of 45 cm in length are not uncommon.
Distinguishing features Your first clue to identifying this fish is the size of its scales.

99

They are comparatively huge, and on a big fish can be larger than 3 cm wide. The common carp has a large mouth and the tail is in the shape of a broad 'V'.

ENVIRONMENTAL NOTES
Status The common carp was introduced to Australia many years ago, probably deliberately to provide a species for commercial fish-farming. It has increased dramatically in number in the last decade, so much so that portions of the Darling River contain hundreds in a small area when the level of the river is low. It stirs mud into the water as it feeds along the bottom, destroying the oxygen-carrying capacity of the water, and thus threatening the life of native fish.

Control of carp in the river systems is essential if native fish are to re-establish themselves in any numbers. A properly controlled carp fishery would limit the spread of the species and provide a valuable resource for export. Carp is a valued food fish in many parts of the world.

Feeding habits It causes a direct threat to native fish by feeding on their eggs and young. The common carp will eat almost anything, from waterweeds to ducklings, ruining the habitat of other wildlife.

Predators As for golden perch (see page 96).

Reproduction Breeding occurs in the warmer months of the year, and spawning fish can be seen charging through water so shallow that the top third of their bodies is exposed. The eggs are scattered from the spawning fish and attach to any underwater surface.

MURRAY RIVER CRAYFISH
Euastacus armatus

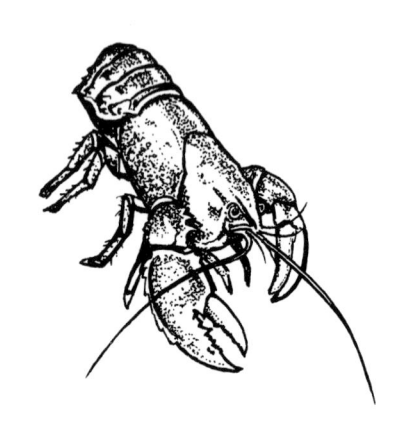

IDENTIFICATION
Colour You will instantly be able to identify the Murray 'cray' by its distinctive white claws and the white spikes along its tail, and dull china-blue body.
Size It is a large crayfish and can weigh up to 3 kg.
Distinguishing features The Murray crayfish is a large, fresh-water crayfish that looks a lot like the salt-water lobster (*Jasus* spp.) that is a seafood delicacy at restaurants.

LOCATION
The Murray, Darling and Murrumbidgee river systems of eastern Australia.

HABITAT
Rivers and larger billabongs.

ENVIRONMENTAL NOTES
Status The Murray crayfish is caught commercially in parts of southern Australia. It is an excellent food resource, but one which requires very skilled management of its habitat, and strict controls of the fishing.

FISH AND CRUSTACEANS

Feeding habits It feeds on small aquatic animals and carrion.
Predators The small crayfish is food for any carnivorous fish, bird or mammal. Even the larger crayfish would be a delicacy for the bigger predators, such as Murray cod.
Reproduction The female crayfish holds the eggs in a mass under her tail, and is said to be in 'berry'. A female caught in this condition must be returned to the water to ensure survival of the species.

YABBIE, MARRON AND GILGIE
Cherax spp.

LOCATION
Australia wide, in suitable habitats.

HABITAT
Rivers, irrigation channels, farm dams — any area of water that provides food and shelter.

IDENTIFICATION
Colour The fresh-water crayfish of the *Cherax* species varies in colour and size depending on its location. The small to medium sized *Cherax destructor* is the common crayfish of farm dams and irrigation channels in southeastern Australia. It is a muddy reddish brown in colour, with strong claws that are often of a lighter colour.
Size *C. destructor* grows to about 12 cm in body length, with the claws extending the body half as much again.
Distinguishing features It is very similar in shape to a small salt-water lobster (*Jasus* spp.)

ENVIRONMENTAL NOTES
Status *C. destructor*, as its name suggests, can be very destructive by burrowing in the walls of farm dams and along the banks of irrigation channels. The ideal feeding and breeding conditions in dams and channels allow the crayfish to be present in large numbers.

Fresh-water crayfish is a delicacy, and farm children have been catching the crayfish on a piece of string with meat on the end ever since the first farm dams were built.

The Western Australian crayfish, called a 'marron', with its combination of quick breeding and growth, is now being farmed commercially. It is hoped this industry will provide a worthwhile addition to other farming enterprises.
Feeding habits As for the Murray crayfish (see above).
Predators The water-rat is an important controller of fresh-water crayfish. Unfortunately, water-rat numbers were drastically reduced (see page 75). Hopefully, the numbers can build up again, saving farmers hundreds of thousands of dollars lost because of the damage caused by *Cherax destructor*.
Reproduction As for the Murray crayfish (see above).

Insects

DAMSELFLY AND DRAGONFLY
Order *Odonata*

LOCATION
Throughout Australia, in any suitable wet area.

HABITAT
The adult flies around and above the water, while the nymph is totally aquatic.

IDENTIFICATION
Colour Widely varied, from turquoise blue to daffodil yellow.
Size The damselfly grows up to 3 cm, with a wingspan up to 5 cm; the dragonfly grows up to 4 cm, with a wingspan of about 6 cm.
Distinguishing features The damselfly and the dragonfly are the miniature helicopters that fly around any reasonable body of fresh water during the warmer months of the year. They are superb fliers, being able to hover for long periods of time, and then zoom off at astonishing speed.

You can recognise the difference between the dragonfly and the damselfly usually by body size and the way they hold their wings. The damselfly holds its wings vertically above its body when it is resting, while the dragonfly holds its wings out flat. Both groups have very large eyes and long bodies. The damselfly is generally slimmer in the body.

ENVIRONMENTAL NOTES
Status They are very important control agents and are part of nature's cycle that occurs following floods. Floods mean wide expanses of shallow water for mosquitoes to breed and they soon reach pest proportions. If nature is allowed to restore the balance and no pesticides are used, then huge swarms of dragonflies and damselflies arrive to feed on the mosquitoes.

They are both completely harmless to humans.
Feeding habits The damselfly and the dragonfly are insect eaters, particularly small insects like mosquitoes that they catch on the wing. The nymph feeds on any tiny animals it can catch in the water. It is a fierce feeder, and its face and jaws form a savage-looking 'mask'.
Predators Many birds take the adults on the wing, and the young are eaten by a wide range of carnivorous fish and fowl.
Reproduction Eggs are laid by the female either directly onto the water, or along the stems of aquatic plants. The young, or nymph stage, lives in the water. When the nymph is ready to change to an adult, it climbs out of the water up the stem of a water plant, its back splits open and the adult dragonfly or damselfly flies away.

Plants

RIVER RED GUM
Eucalyptus camaldulensis

LOCATION
Mainland Australia.

HABITAT
Riverbanks and flood plains.

IDENTIFICATION
Colour Its trunk is predominantly white to whitish-grey with rough grey bark up about the first third of the trunk, and the leaves are grey.
Size This tree is a large eucalypt, up to 30 m tall. The trees in some areas can be huge, being more than 2 m through the trunk.
Distinguishing features The river red gum is always closely associated with water. You will often see a whole forest spreading back from the banks of rivers and billabongs to cover many hectares of flood plain. Whenever you come to a river or large open body of water in the outback, look along the banks. It is highly probable that the large white-trunked eucalypt that you are seeing is the river red gum.

ENVIRONMENTAL NOTES
Status Apart from its tremendous importance in stabilising the banks of waterways, the river red gum provides habitats for many creatures, from spiders under the bark, to pink cockatoos in the hollows in the limbs, to water-rats under the roots. Even when the branches are dead and have fallen into the river, the hollow logs provide homes and places for fresh-water fish to lay eggs.
People also profit from the rich nectar given off by the cream, spring and summer flowers. As you travel along riverbanks look out for the hives left by apiarists so that their bees can collect a honey bounty from the river red gum.
Natural control agents Leaf-eating and trunk-eating insects, and the availability of water.
Reproduction As with all eucalypts, the seeds are protected in a woody fruit that is covered with a little 'gumnut baby' cap until they start to ripen.

RIVERS SWAMPS BILLABONGS AND LAKES

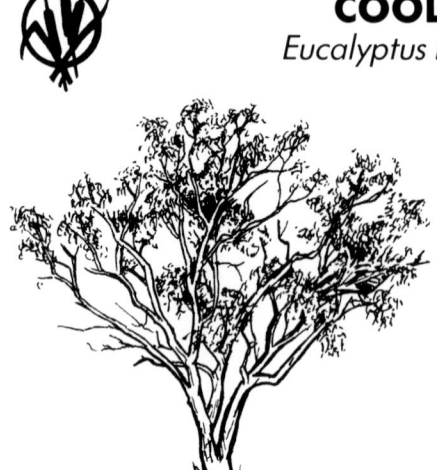

COOLIBAH
Eucalyptus microtheca

IDENTIFICATION
Colour The coolibah has bluish-grey to grey-green leaves, and a dark-grey trunk.
Size It is a medium-sized eucalypt, rarely more than 15 m tall.
Distinguishing features This tree, made famous in song and verse, really does not have a lot of remarkable features. You will find it near water, although not necessarily right on the riverbank. It has bushy, spreading branches, and the bark on the trunk is rough and continues up to the main branches. The smaller branches are bare.

LOCATION
All mainland states, with the exception of Victoria.

HABITAT
Heavy clay or sandy soils near watercourses and rivers, particularly if these are covered in flood times.

ENVIRONMENTAL NOTES
Status Common, not as huge monospecific forests, but as individuals or small clumps of trees.
Natural control agents As for the river red gum (see above).
Reproduction As for the river red gum.

Under the Shade of a Coolibah Tree
If the swagman wanted to camp under the shade of a tree he should have chosen the river red gum as it would have provided more shade. However, because the river red gum has a habit of dropping big branches in hot weather, he was safer under the smaller coolibah.

RIVER COOBA
Acacia stenophylla

LOCATION
Mainland inland Australia, in areas of permanent water or occasional flooding.

HABITAT
On heavy clay soils not far from water, often grouped with black box and river red gum.

IDENTIFICATION
Colour The long leaves are grey-green and the slim trunks dark brown. If you

PLANTS

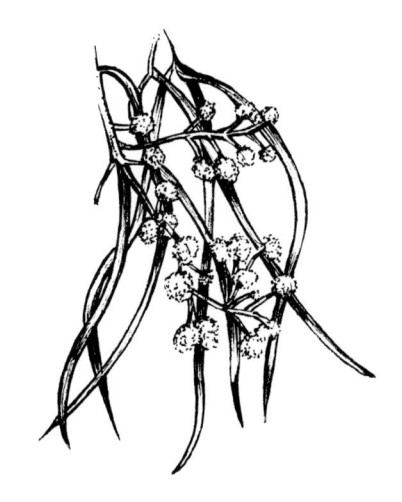

see it when it is in flower in the summer and early autumn it has the round and yellow flowers that are typical of the 'wattle' or acacias, although it does not put on the extravagant show of many wattles.

Size It can grow up to 10 m tall, although most are shorter than that.

Distinguishing features River cooba is a very common tree that you can recognise by its closeness to water and the drooping nature of the branches. It looks enough like the introduced willows to be given the name of 'native willow', as it has long thin leaves that hang down from the branches.

Status Very common around inland flood-prone areas in the semi-arid zone.

Natural control agents Acacias are prone to many insect predators, and you will often find round shapes on them that look like strange fruits. These are the galls made by the tree to encase the eggs of several species of gall wasps that are parasites to acacias. They are also attacked by trunk-boring insects.

Reproduction Acacias produce pea-like pods in which are contained the very viable (easily grown) round seeds.

BLACK BOX
Eucalyptus largiflorens

LOCATION
NSW, Queensland, Victoria and South Australia.

HABITAT
Along the edges of dry lakes, or the dried-up areas left by swamps or periodic floods. Black box is often found in association with lignum and nitre goosefoot.

IDENTIFICATION
Colour The bark is very dark brown and the foliage mid-grey.

Size It can be up to 20 m tall, and its large spreading top provides very welcome shade in the heat of summer.

Distinguishing features You can recognise it by its very rough, dark bark that has deep furrows running up the trunk. The bark runs up the branches, covering all but the smallest twigs right at the tips.

ENVIRONMENTAL NOTES
Status Black box is a very common tree on the dry plains, particularly in areas that go under flood on a regular basis. If you are camping in a flood plain, you will probably be camped in the shade of a black box. Its branches often come right down to the ground, providing excellent places for the attachment of lamps and other camping equipment.
Natural control agents As for the river red gum (see page 103).
Reproduction As for the river red gum.

LIGNUM
Muehlenbeckia cunninghamii

leafless shrub, but has tiny cream flowers carried in little bunches along the stem.
Size It forms a matted bush which can be up to 4 m high, but is usually between 2 and 3 m high.
Distinguishing features Depending where you are, lignum could either be clumpy isolated bushes, or a dense impenetrable barrier.

LOCATION
The inland areas of mainland states.

HABITAT
In and around swamps and river flats, sometimes on flood plains some distance from permanent water.

IDENTIFICATION
Colour It is a grey, thick, twiggy and

ENVIRONMENTAL NOTES
Status It is very widespread in Australia, and covers huge areas of swamps, providing shelter and nesting places for a wide range of animals. Feral pigs love lignum. It provides cover and protection, as well as shade in the hot parts of the year. One of the problems of eradicating pigs from swamp areas is the total cover provided

Lignum Survives Drought and Floods

In places like Narran Lake in northwestern NSW, the lignum thickets can be high and dry for years. Then there will be torrential rain somewhere in the catchment, perhaps hundreds of kilometres away. The lake expands, covering up to 20 000 hectares, and creating a huge, swampy lake all around the lignum. Waterbirds in their thousands flock in from everywhere and build their nests on top of the lignum, the weight of the birds sometimes flattening the lignum down into the water.

PLANTS

by lignum thickets. Foxes also like to 'camp' in the thickets, and vixens will make a nest in the thickest parts for their young cubs.

Natural control agents Very few insects seem to attack this dry and spindly plant.
Reproduction It can flower throughout the year.

NITRE GOOSEFOOT
Chenopodium nitrariaceum

green, and produces many small orange-coloured flowers at the end of stems.
Size It is only about 2.5 m high, often sprawling over the same width, and it has a generally untidy look.
Distinguishing features At first glance you could mistake it for one of the saltbushes, but it is much more spiny in appearance. It grows in the same area as lignum and black box, growing as a shrub right up against them.

LOCATION
In the semi-arid areas of all mainland states.

HABITAT
The depressions and river flats of flood plain areas, particularly in clayey soils. Often sheltered by other shrubs and tall trees.

IDENTIFICATION
Colour It is a dull, battleship-grey colour, sometimes broken with small patches of

ENVIRONMENTAL NOTES
Status Nitre goosefoot is very widespread in inland flood plain areas. Its many slim and spiny branches provide ideal cover for small nesting birds.
Natural control agents Like many arid shrubland plants, nitre goosefoot presents a tough meal for most insects. However, it is eaten by hungry sheep and cattle. It is usually controlled by the harsh climatic conditions under which it grows.
Reproduction It can flower throughout the year.

COMMON NARDOO
Marsilea drummondii

LOCATION
The Australian mainland.

HABITAT
Floating on top of temporary or permanent wetlands.

IDENTIFICATION
Colour Various shades of green to greenish-yellow.
Size The individual leaves are 2 to 7 cm across, but the mass of plants may cover a huge area.

RIVERS SWAMPS BILLABONGS AND LAKES

Distinguishing features Nardoo looks like a floating four-leaf clover, but it is not related in any way to the clover.

ENVIRONMENTAL NOTES
Status In some parts of the outback it will multiply to cover huge areas of water left after floods, dying back as the water dries out. Where nardoo is growing as a permanent waterweed on shallow lakes and billabongs it can serve as an indicator of the depth of the water. Once the water increases beyond half a metre, the nardoo stops growing, although patches of it may be torn up by wind and floods and drift into deeper areas, where it dies and sinks. It is also susceptible to water quality, and if there is a major environmental change in the water, the nardoo will disappear.

Natural control agents Many aquatic animals feed on nardoo.

Reproduction If the water on which it floats dries up, it produces reproductive bodies called 'sporocarps', carrying the spores for the next generation.

Nardoo Flour
The Aborigines collect the sporocarps and grind them into a form of flour. We are told that Burke and Wills starved to death on a diet of nardoo flour.

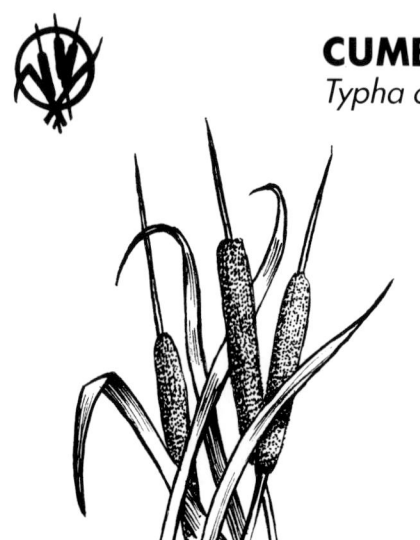

CUMBUNGI
Typha orientalis

LOCATION
In suitable wetland areas throughout Australia.

HABITAT
Along the edges of swamps, billabongs, irrigation and drainage channels, or any swampy area where water is held for some time.

IDENTIFICATION
Colour Light-green tall stalks, with dead brown leaves at the base. When it is flowering it carries a 'bulrush' head of

PLANTS

flowers that are tan in colour.
Size Up to 2.5 m tall. The 'bulrush' flowers are one above the other on the same spike, and each is about 20 cm long.
Distinguishing features Cumbungi is very common in all sorts of watercourses, from lakes in golf courses to inland billabongs. You can recognise it by its tall, spear-like shape, and its thick growth around the edges of many wet areas.

ENVIRONMENTAL NOTES
Status Cumbungi has both its good and bad sides. Its good side is that it is an ideal habitat for waterbirds, providing nesting material and protection from predators. The bad side is the amount of water it requires to exist, and this makes it an economic problem for farmers if it grows in their irrigation channels. As well as using valuable water, it also quickly clogs the channels, causing more water loss.
Natural control agents Apart from the tramping down by bird species, cumbungi seems to have few natural control agents.
Reproduction The plant dies back in winter, leaving an enormous mass of organic matter that serves to fertilise a fresh, vigorous growth in the spring. The top part of the 'bulrush' contains the male flowers and the lower part the female. The seed, that comes from the female part, is carried by the wind.

RED AZOLLA
Azolla filiculoides

LOCATION
Throughout Australia, with the exception of the Northern Territory.

HABITAT
Swamps, billabongs and lakes.

IDENTIFICATION
Colour Individual azolla plants form a floating carpet of greenish-red over the surface of huge areas of shallow water.

Size Individual plants are only about 2 cm across the floating top, but a mass of plants may cover hectares.
Distinguishing features You will notice it during the warmer months on any large body of water that has little or no current. From a distance it looks a little like the green scum that algae forms on the water, but up close you can see the small fern plants that make up the carpet.

ENVIRONMENTAL NOTES
Status Azolla moves freely from place to place with the wind and quickly colonises suitable habitats. In areas where the water is affected by fertiliser run-off from farms, the azolla spreads even more rapidly to the point were it can block waterways.
Natural control agents As for common nardoo (see page 107).
Reproduction The plant usually spreads by pieces breaking off and growing elsewhere, and rarely by spores.

CHAPTER FOUR

Forests and Woodlands

As you travel the outback it is worthwhile to do some mental arithmetic and work out how many trees it takes to build a fence with timber posts. Then mentally multiply by the hundreds of kilometres of fencing just one large property may have, and then multiply that figure by the number of large farms. The figure becomes astronomical, and you have to ask how it is that any trees remain in the outback. The answer is that they are a renewable resource, one which can be managed in a way that provides the greatest environmental and economic benefit.

Prior to white settlement 200 years ago, the Aboriginal people periodically set fire to many forest, grassland and woodland areas, to provide green pick for the native grazing and foraging animals like

Riverbanks, Darling River

FORESTS AND WOODLANDS

kangaroos and emus. Some explorers record that they could tell whether the area they were approaching was inhabited or not by the presence or absence of bushfire smoke.

The outback forests and woodlands have been vastly changed since the arrival of European settlers. Timber has been used for fencing and for houses, and trees cleared away when the land was needed for farming. Some of the land has reverted to open woodland or even closed forest when it has been allowed to regrow, so some areas have been through up to 4 or 5 lots of clearing and regeneration in the last 200 years.

The plants and animals of the forest and woodland have had to adapt to these constant changes to their environment. But this was not the most important adaptation. They had to be able to survive in a hot and dry climate, where rainfall was uncertain, and often only fell in small amounts when it fell at all. Some of the smaller animals went several generations without experiencing a fall of rain, and all the water they needed had to come from the food they ate.

Some of the modifications to the forest and woodland benefited native species. The open woodland areas, with pasture under the trees, allowed kangaroos to increase. The clearing of vast stands of grey box to make way for wheat farms prepared a banquet for the huge mobs of galahs, now common in the outback. However, it was not all good news, as the clearing of mature trees, with their collection of hollow branches, knotholes and hollow trunks, took away the sheltering and nesting places of animals like the pink cockatoo.

Mammals

SHORT-BEAKED ECHIDNA
Tachyglossus aculeatus

LOCATION
Throughout Australia.

HABITAT
From sandy, seaside dunes, to tablelands and eucalypt forest, to the central arid zones. Its ramblings are dependent upon the heat of the day. In cooler zones and seasons, it can be seen snuffling along at any time, but in very hot areas it will shelter in logs or caves until the cool of night.

IDENTIFICATION
Colour It is covered with sharp yellow spines with black tips.
Size Head and body length: up to 45 cm; weight: up to 7 kg.
Distinguishing features It waddles as it walks, and it rolls up into an impenetrable ball of spikes if disturbed. The echidna is not a porcupine or a hedgehog, and it shares little with these animals apart from having sharp spikes on its body. The echidna is like no other animal. If you see it before it rolls up, it has a beak-like snout and claws on the back legs that seem to point the wrong way. As it eats ants, it also eats dirt, and it is often possible to find the rock shelters where echidnas camp during the heat of the day by the cube-shaped droppings made up of dirt and ant remains.

ENVIRONMENTAL NOTES
Status The echidna is fairly common throughout its range, particularly where there are extensive areas of woodland and open forest. It is unable to survive the type of disturbance that accompanies any sort of urban development, both because of the loss of food and habitat, and because of its incapacity to adapt to interference by people and their pets. Its population is gradually shrinking back into the better protected areas of national parks and nature reserves.
Feeding habits The echidna eats ants, so the name 'spiny ant-eater' may be appropriate, but not correct. It uses its powerful front claws to dig its way into ant nests, including the concrete-hard termite nests, where it uses its sticky tongue to feast on the scurrying insects.
Predators Its strong spines and the habit of curling into a ball protect it from most predators, although persistent dogs and dingos do manage to get at its softer underside.
Reproduction It is a monotreme, an egg-laying mammal, a characteristic it shares with only one other creature, the platypus

(Ornithorhynchus anatinus). The soft-shelled egg is laid straight into the pouch of the female, and the young remains there when it 'hatches', lapping milk from special mammary glands, for about 3 months.

FEATHERTAIL GLIDER
Acrobates pygmaeus

sum-like than mouse-like in its movements, and its tail is fur-fringed, giving a feather-like appearance. Not only is the feathertail glider a beautiful, delicate creature to behold, it also has the amazing capacity of being able to glide from tree to tree. It can glide up to 20 m, and this is a prodigious distance for such a small creature. Nor does it have to glide in a straight line, it can also use its tail to steer itself around obstacles and change direction as it glides.

LOCATION
Eastern Australia, and just across the southeastern border of South Australia.

HABITAT
You are more likely to see the feathertail glider in the wetter forest areas of the eastern coastline than in the drier areas of outback, but it does live in the scattered, dry woodlands. As for many nocturnal animals, the way for you to find it is to know its likely locations and its preferred habitats within those locations. Then it is only a matter of patience and luck!

IDENTIFICATION
Colour It is soft grey on top and creamy white underneath.
Size It has a tail as long as its body, and each is only up to 8 cm. It weighs only 14 g.
Distinguishing features It is more pos-

ENVIRONMENTAL NOTES
Status The survival of the feathertail glider is threatened by the destruction of its forest and woodland habitat.
Feeding habits It has a wide range of food preferences, from tree sap to insects. After larger possum species have made cuts in the bark of trees to make the sap run, groups of the tiny feathertail glider will often gather around to feed on the flowing sap.
Predators This tiny creature is no match for prowling feral cats. In a catless environment its number would be controlled by night-time predators like owls and spotted-tailed quolls *(Dasyurus maculatus)*.
Reproduction A female can be pregnant while still carrying up to 3 young in her pouch, so there is a capacity for rapid reproduction. In the northern part of their range feathertails can breed the whole year round, but not in the cooler southern areas.

COMMON BRUSHTAIL POSSUM
Trichosurus vulpecula

LOCATION
Very widespread in eastern Australia and parts of southwestern Western Australia.

HABITAT
Its outback habitat is open forests providing nest holes and a wide range of food plants, but you can find it in a wide range of forest and woodland habitats.

IDENTIFICATION
Colour Dark silvery-grey to dark grey-brown, with some deep-brown ones in Tasmania. The underside is dark cream, with the males having a stain from the scent gland down the centre.
Size The brushtail can grow to the size of a Persian cat (50 cm long) and have the same fluffy fur in the colder months. The male can weigh up to 4 kg and the female up to 3.5 kg.
Distinguishing features It has large ears that present a quickly recognisable profile when seen head on. Above the pink, hairless nose are two large, bright eyes.

ENVIRONMENTAL NOTES
Status Unlike many native Australian animals it has adapted to most of the changes made by humans, and it profits from our food supplies.
Feeding habits Very varied, from the leaves of native trees, to kitchen refuse. The brushtail is a great raider of rubbish bins and food stores.
Predators Dogs, dingos, foxes, carpet

Brushtails Raid Campsites

It is the unwise camper who leaves containers of food on a camp table overnight. Brushtails are bold and curious, and will quite happily rattle around in the pots and pans of a campfire, looking for food scraps. Be warned, they also have sharp claws, specially designed to climb the smooth trunks of trees. Sharp claws and a short temper has resulted in many a scratched camper.

MAMMALS

pythons, goannas and very brave cats eat the adult and young. The young are taken by owls as well.
Reproduction The baby possum is carried in a deep pouch for about 5 months.

The young, mature, mother brushtail carries her young ones on her back, and on moonlit nights a lucky watcher may see a baby being 'piggy-backed' amongst the branches.

KOALA
Phascolarctos cinereus

Size Head and body length — male: up to 82 cm; female: up to 73 cm. Weight — male: up to 13.5 kg; female: up to 9.8 kg. Koalas in Queensland tend to be smaller than those in the south of Australia.
Distinguishing features Probably the best known of all Australian animals, you soon recognise it as the cute and cuddly 'teddy bear'. The big ears, black 'rubber' nose, tail-less body and squat shape, have been seen all round the world, in pictures or in reality.

ENVIRONMENTAL NOTES
Status The koala survived the savage hunting of the early part of the 20th century when millions were slaughtered for their skins. Books written about pioneering days of farming in Australia often contain references to 'bear' hunts. The koala is not related to bears but its shape is vaguely similar.

Today the koala has to survive an accelerating destruction of its natural eucalypt habitat, and a fatal disease that is decimating populations in some areas.
Feeding habits It feeds exclusively on the leaves of eucalypts, such as river red gum, and a small number of other species, including some paperbark species. The species it prefers is totally dependent upon locality.
Predators Apart from people, the adult koala has had little to fear in the way of predation. The young are closely protect-

LOCATION
Limited to mainly coastal eastern Australia, with scattered populations on the fringe of the eastern outback.

HABITAT
Restricted to the areas where it can find its eucalypt food trees. Although very difficult to see in the outback, as it blends in so well with its treetop homes, it is always worth checking trees in remote and heavily timbered areas. This is particularly so in western Victoria and parts of western Queensland.

IDENTIFICATION
Colour Generally a soft mid-grey, and clean white underneath, although large males often have fronts stained with secretions from scent glands.

ed by the adults. Some are taken on the ground by dingos and wild dogs.
Reproduction During the summer breeding season the night-time forests can echo to the pig-like snorts and grunts of males establishing territories. The young makes its way as soon as it is born into a rear-facing pouch. The baby weighs less than 0.5 g at birth and remains in the pouch for about 7 months.

LITTLE MASTIFF-BAT
Mormopterus planiceps

Size It is less than 11 cm long from tip of nose to tip of tail, and weighs less than 15 g.
Distinguishing features Your best method of distinguishing this bat from others is by its tiny size. Up close, it does not have the fearsome crushed bulldog face of other mastiff bats. For bat observers, the best time to spot it is at dusk. Different species utilise different 'flight lanes' at different heights above the ground, although occasionally there is disagreement when the flight lanes cross.

ENVIRONMENTAL NOTES
Status Like many animals of the outback, this bat depends upon hollow trees to provide shelter. Extensive clearing of 'over-mature' forests has had a marked effect on the bat population.
Feeding habits This tiny bat is able to catch its insect prey on the wing over treetops or along creeks, and also to climb around tree trunks and along the ground to scurry after it.
Predators Probably its ability to squeeze into tiny places enables it to escape predation by cats, at least while it is roosting. Any bat scurrying along the ground or on a tree trunk would be easy prey for a cat. When roosting, a few bats are taken by owls.
Reproduction Little is known of its breeding habits.

LOCATION
Western NSW, Victoria and Queensland, South Australia, and southern Northern Territory and Western Australia.

HABITAT
In the drier outback areas, only limited by suitable roosting places and food. Often seen along creek beds that provide an open avenue for flying. This bat makes its home in any suitable small hole or cavity, several bats often sharing the same hollow in a tree.

IDENTIFICATION
Colour Dark grey on top and lighter coloured below.

MAMMALS

LESSER LONG-EARED BAT
Nyctophilus geoffroyi

LOCATION
Throughout Australia, with the exception of northern Queensland.

HABITAT
Extremely varied, from the arid outback to the humid coast. It will roost in any enclosed space that gives it shelter, warmth and humidity. This may be a cave, a tree hollow or under the eaves of a shed.

IDENTIFICATION
Colour Soft grey-tinged brown on top and lighter underneath.
Size This is a very small bat, with a head and body length of 5 cm, and a weight of up to 8 g.
Distinguishing features It has extremely large ears in relation to the size of its body. You may also distinguish it by its slow, fluttering flight, as it hunts just above the ground.

ENVIRONMENTAL NOTES
Status This bat is one of the most common over its range. Its habit of foraging on the ground makes the lesser long-eared bat a potential victim for cats. It is also vulnerable because of the chemical sprays used by agriculture to control the insects that are its food. Despite this it seems to be holding its own, even to be increasing. This comes about through its ability to adapt to the changes that European settlement has made to its environment. Houses and sheds provide potential roosting places for the tiny bat, and crops attract the insects it feeds upon. The value of bats in the control of insect pests has probably yet to be realised.
Feeding habits As for the little mastiff-bat (see above).
Predators As for the little mastiff-bat.
Reproduction Breeding colonies are formed, containing from 10 to 100 bats. The young bat is born naked and feeds from the mother's nipples, or clings to her fur. When she leaves to feed, the babies hang suspended from the top of the roost.

GOULD'S WATTLED BAT
Chalinolobus gouldii

LOCATION
Throughout Australia, with the exception of northern Queensland and northeastern Northern Territory.

117

FORESTS AND WOODLANDS

and dark brown below.
Size Head and body length: up to 7 cm; tail: up to 5 cm. Weight: up to 18 g.
Distinguishing features This bat has adapted to the different seasonal variations throughout Australia. In the hot, dry zones it is active the whole year round, while in cooler areas it will fall into a form of hibernation during the winter months.

ENVIRONMENTAL NOTES
Status It is abundant throughout its range.
Feeding habits It feeds on a wide variety of insects, from beetles to moths.
Predators Less likely to be taken than bats that forage on the ground, it could still be attacked in its roost by feral cats and goannas. It is also taken on the wing by owls and other predatory birds that wait outside the roosts for the bats to emerge.
Reproduction Similar to the lesser long-eared bat (see page 117), although the colonies vary in size.

HABITAT
In most wooded areas in Australia. Its preferred feeding place is just below the tree canopy.

IDENTIFICATION
Colour This bat is darker in colour than many other species, being black on top

---

Bats Are Extraordinary Flying Mammals

Bats' flying ability is due to the adaptation that has turned the forelimbs into extended supports for membranous wings. It is easy to forget that bats are mammals, in the same broad group as whales. Not only have they evolved the extraordinary capacity of flight, they also have the amazing echo-location method of navigating the night sky.

Birds

PINK COCKATOO
Cacatua leadbeateri

LOCATION
The outback areas of mainland Australia.

HABITAT
Open savannah and grasslands, provided

BIRDS

yellow band.
Size Up to 36 cm long.
Distinguishing features Unlike the noisy and gregarious galah, the pink cockatoo seems to be a wary and shy bird. It is often difficult to find in the wild and you will need patience and luck to see it. It does not gather in huge flocks like other cockatoos, and is more likely to be seen in pairs or small groups.

ENVIRONMENTAL NOTES
Status Unfortunately, the pink cockatoo is not a common bird. It is tied to the native plants that form its diet and, with the clearing of these areas, its population appears to be on the decline. It is not only the clearing of food trees that creates problems, it is also the removal of the old trees that provide hollows for nesting.
Feeding habits It feeds on fruit and seeds, including the seeds of the bitter wild melons.
Predators The nest hollows of the pink cockatoo are raided by goannas and the adult bird is taken in the air by hawks.
Reproduction A hollow in a tree is roughly carpeted with tree scraps or pebbles and 2 to 4 white eggs are laid.

there are sufficient trees for food and shelter. It also must have ready access to water. A clue for discovering its whereabouts is to find the thickets of the trees that provide its food. Stands of native cypress pine and she-oaks are good places to start.

IDENTIFICATION
Colour Once seen, the pink cockatoo (often called the Major Mitchell cockatoo) is not forgotten. It is the softest pink underneath, fading to white, with white upperparts. It has a truly startling crest of white and orange, interspersed by a thin,

RED-TAILED BLACK COCKATOO
Calyptorhynchus magnificus

LOCATION
Queensland, western NSW and Victoria, the Northern Territory, and northern and southwestern Western Australia.

HABITAT
Forests and woodlands.

IDENTIFICATION
Colour The male is rich black, with a red flash under the tail, and the female is black

FORESTS AND WOODLANDS

spotted with yellow flecks, with a much paler yellow-orange marking on the tail.
Size Up to 66 cm long.
Distinguishing features If you see the red-tailed black cockatoo flying you will have no trouble identifying it from the brilliant orange flash under its tail. You will also notice it because of the noise it makes as it flies, a very harsh grating sound like the opening of a very large, rusty gate.
  Although easy to spot and find with its noise, this cockatoo is not easy to approach in the wild. Flocks will settle high up in a tree and give their harsh alarm cry if approached, flying away as a group, the males flashing their brilliant tails.

ENVIRONMENTAL NOTES
Status The red-tailed black cockatoo is moderately common over its range, but the clearing of its food trees has caused major shifts in population.
Feeding habits It feeds on the fruits of eucalypts and casuarinas, cracking the hard fruit open with very powerful beaks.
Predators As for the pink cockatoo (see above).
Reproduction One white egg is laid in a tree hollow, usually high up.

Red-tailed Black Cockatoo Predicts Rain
In my childhood the harsh, grating calls of the red-tailed black cockatoo were said to be a sign of approaching rain, and in some localities they were called 'storm-birds'. These cockatoos share this legendary capacity with several other totally unrelated species.

BLACK FALCON
Falco subniger

HABITAT
Timbered watercourses and eucalypt woodlands.

IDENTIFICATION
Colour As its name suggests this bird is uniformly charcoal grey-black.
Size Up to 56 cm long, with a wingspan of 93 cm.
Distinguishing features The solid dark colouring may help you with identification, as most other falcons, kestrels and hawks have some colour patterning. You

LOCATION
All of the eastern and northern mainland.

may also be helped by its habit of pursuing birds through the timber, giving its attacking scream as it does so. It is a very rapid flier, and a fierce hunter, and will follow its prey with great tenacity.

ENVIRONMENTAL NOTES
Status The black falcon is a fairly uncommon bird throughout its range, living as it does amongst the sparsely timbered areas of arid zones. It is thought to move with the migration and movement of prey species, like quail.

Feeding habits It feeds on many birds and mammals, particularly quail and rabbits. It will pick up its prey from the ground without hesitating in its flight and then roost in a tree to eat it. It also feeds on plague locusts.

Predators Like all large birds of prey, the black falcon is safe from predation, being at the top of its food chain.

Reproduction Two to 4 freckled reddish-white eggs are laid in the old nest of a hawk or crow.

HORSFIELD'S BRONZE-CUCKOO
Chrysococcyx basalis

Distinguishing features It takes an expert to quickly tell the bronze-cuckoos apart, but it will often be the call that will lead you to the Horsfield's bronze-cuckoo. It is a persistent, repeated, descending scale of notes. You will need to follow the sound to the caller, as the bird's colouring does not make casual observation easy.

ENVIRONMENTAL NOTES
Status Fairly common throughout its range.

Feeding habits Ecologically, the bronze-cuckoo has a valuable role to play. It is one of the few species of birds that can feed on hairy caterpillars. The 'hairs' or spines on hairy caterpillars deter most birds. Hairy caterpillars cause damage to some species of plants and occasionally appear in 'plague' proportions, and if their spines come in contact with human skin a nasty rash can occur.

LOCATION
Throughout Australia.

HABITAT
Open woodland, scrubland, marshland, orchards and margins of densely forested areas.

IDENTIFICATION
Colour A generally dull brown-green back. On the underside it has bold brown stripes on a dull-white background.
Size It is a smallish bird, up to 17 cm long.

Predators Birds of prey would take a few bronze-cuckoos, although the cuckoos liking for dense undergrowth gives them protection.

Reproduction Like cuckoos world wide,

FORESTS AND WOODLANDS

the Horsfield's bronze-cuckoo is parasitic, laying its eggs in another bird's nest. The female lays her egg in the nest of another species, and then leaves the 'foster parents' to hatch and bring up her baby. The young cuckoo is almost always bigger than the other babies in the nest and it uses its strength to tip the others out. The foster parents then rear the cuckoo chick as their own, taking turns to feed its large appetite until it flies away a fully fledged bird. Records show that this species of cuckoo parasitises over 60 other species of birds.

SULPHUR-CRESTED COCKATOO
Cacatua galerita

instantly recognise its incredibly loud and harsh call that sounds a little like dragging a large metal garbage can along a rough metal surface. The brilliant white of its feathers would make it ideal for a clothes whitener commercial. To cap it all, it has a bright lemon-yellow crest that it lifts above its head.

ENVIRONMENTAL NOTES

Status The sulphur-crested cockatoo is a very common cage bird, although a dismal bird in a cage is nothing like the white splendour of a bird in the wild. This cockatoo is not just a bird of the outback. It has moved into many cities in eastern Australia, and is very common in national parks based on city boundaries. It does not make the best neighbour for suburban dwellers, as it is noisy at all the wrong times of the day, and takes particular delight in tearing many outside wooden structures to pieces. This is something that it does in the wild, as it searches for grubs in tree branches, or rips up strips of bark for nest lining.

Feeding habits A wide range of foods from grubs to fruit, and occasionally farmer's crops.

Predators As for the little corella (see below).

Reproduction Two to 3 white eggs are laid in a tree hollow.

LOCATION
Throughout eastern and northern Australia.

HABITAT
Widely varied, from coastal mangroves to inland scattered woodland, but usually associated with the availability of fresh water.

IDENTIFICATION
Colour Brilliant white, with a sulphur-yellow crest.
Size Up to 51 cm long.
Distinguishing features Large, very obvious and extremely noisy, the sulphur-crested cockatoo is one of the most extroverted of all Australian birds. You will

BIRDS

LITTLE CORELLA
Cacatua sanguinea

LOCATION
The Australian mainland, with the exception of the central and western desert.

HABITAT
Timbered and open country, particularly around watercourses.

IDENTIFICATION
Colour It is mostly white, has a small crest on its head, and up close you will see the red mark behind its bill and the bluish circle around the eyes.
Size It is smallish for a cockatoo, hence its name. Up to 40 cm long.
Distinguishing features Probably the first thing you will notice about the little corella is the sheer numbers in a flock. In the evening when they come to land in their favourite roosting tree near a watercourse, the tree will appear to be covered in huge noisy, white blossoms. When flocking, corellas fill the air with their calls. Even if they cannot be seen they can soon be tracked to their roosting places by their noise.

ENVIRONMENTAL NOTES
Status The corella was the cause of a local 'war' in the northwest of Australia. When a new dam was built to open land up for irrigated crops the corella reaped the harvest. It flocked to feed on every type of grain planted, and particularly enjoyed the grain sorghum. Every scheme was tried to remove the birds from the crops, from poisoning to mechanical scarecrows. The battle continues with various levels of intensity all over the corella's range.
Feeding habits The little corella eats seeds, fruit and some insects.
Predators Although its flocking behaviour does protect it, some birds are taken by hawks and falcons. The nests are raided by goannas.
Reproduction Three to 4 white eggs are laid in a nest in the hollow of tree.

SOUTHERN BOOBOOK
Ninox novaeseelandiae

LOCATION
Throughout Australia.

HABITAT
From dense forest to desert fringe. The boobook nests in hollows in trees but does not rest in these during the daylight hours, choosing instead to seek the thick cover of trees. It is not solely an outback animal, as it is found everywhere from rainforests to suburban yards.

IDENTIFICATION
Colour An owl of softest fawn, broken up

123

FORESTS AND WOODLANDS

by vertical and horizontal bands of dark brown, with dark brown markings underneath.
Size Up to 36 cm long.
Distinguishing features As the boobook is a nocturnal animal, your chance of seeing one is fairly small, but you will soon learn to recognise its call. It is a highly distinctive 'boobook', or some would say, 'more-pork', with the first sound higher than second. When seen at night in car headlights it is just a ghostly grey shape gliding across the dark. When full darkness occurs it begins to hunt and on lucky occasions can be seen sitting in trees in suburban backyards, silhouetted against house lights, waiting for a small animal to show itself.

ENVIRONMENTAL NOTES
Status The boobook is common throughout its range and it survives well in all but the most urbanised areas.
Feeding habits Like all owls, it has a very valuable role in controlling the outbreaks of small animals that may become pests. This includes insects such as moths and mammals such as the house mouse.
Predators As a big bird of prey, it is rarely preyed upon.
Reproduction Two to 3 eggs white eggs are laid in a tree hollow.

Boobooks Get Mobbed

On rare occasions you may be drawn to an incredible racket as several species of birds 'mob' a boobook that has taken up a daytime roost in their territory. As many as 10 different species of birds may mob the owl at one time, and the noise is amazing.

TAWNY FROGMOUTH
Podargus strigoides

LOCATION
Throughout Australia, with the exception of some areas in western Queensland and eastern Western Australia.

HABITAT
Closely associated with a wide range of woodland types. Widespread through many suburban areas. Unfortunately, you are more likely to see one dead than alive, killed as it was feeding along the road. This is made worse by its habit of swooping down to feed on its prey while it is illuminated by car headlights. Occasionally, after severe storms, it will be driven from its normal night-time roosts

Size Up to 47 cm long.
Distinguishing features Although the tawny frogmouth is a nocturnal hunter you are more likely to see it in the daytime than other nocturnal birds, such as owls. It often roosts in dead trees that match its slate-grey and mottled brown colouring to perfection. In daylight, or when disturbed at night, it sits still with its head up, mimicking a broken, dead branch.

ENVIRONMENTAL NOTES
Status Common, but not as common as previously, due to the widespread use of pesticides to control the insects on which it feeds. It is attracted to the insects and other small animals that gather along roads and around street lamps, and often falls victim to passing traffic.
Feeding habits It eats insects.
Predators Apart from being killed by cars, some frogmouths are taken from their daytime roosts by cats.
Reproduction One or 2 eggs are laid on a shaky nest of sticks built in the fork of a tree.

to less sheltered areas where it is more visible. It is not unusual for it then to spend the hours of daylight pretending it cannot be seen before flying off at night to a more secure roosting site.

IDENTIFICATION
Colour Predominantly shades of dark and light grey, occasionally with splashes of light brown.

LAUGHING KOOKABURRA
Dacelo novaeguineae

LOCATION
Eastern Australia and southwestern Western Australia.

HABITAT
Open woodland, to the edges of dense, closed forests. The kookaburra is not just a bird of the bush, it is also a bird of the suburban garden.

IDENTIFICATION
Colour Fawn with darker brown on the wings, tail and back.

Size 46 cm long.
Distinguishing features It has many names that indicate one of its most identifiable features: its laugh. It is called 'laughing jackass', or 'bushman's clock', the last name coming from its habit of announcing the false dawn (when light appears in the sky before sunrise) by giving its laughing call.

You will have no trouble recognising this large bird, with its oversized, cruel looking bill. It watches you as you watch it, and decides very quickly whether you are any threat to it at all.

FORESTS AND WOODLANDS

ENVIRONMENTAL NOTES
Status Very common throughout its range.
Feeding habits It takes anything as food, from tiny lizards in the garden, to cooking sausages off a barbecue. The kookaburra does kill and eat snakes, but it is only one of a wide range of foods, from large insects to small birds. As I sat writing this book a kookaburra visited our fishpond and took a goldfish through a wire mesh.

Predators In the wild very little will bother it, as that powerful bill is a fearsome weapon, although large goannas will occasionally take eggs and young from the nest in a hollow tree. The kookaburra has its revenge, as it mercilessly takes any small lizard that it spots with its sharp eyes.
Reproduction The laughing kookaburra lays white eggs 45 mm long, making its nest in a hole in a tree.

COMMON BRONZEWING
Phaps chalcoptera

LOCATION
All of Australia, with the exception of Cape York Peninsula.

HABITAT
Any area with tree cover, from banksia thickets to the scattered scrubs of inland Australia. Like all members of the dove group, the common bronzewing needs to be near water. It may range widely during the day in search of food, but it returns to drink after sunset and again just before dawn.

IDENTIFICATION
Colour It is generally brown in colour and

BIRDS

plump in shape, and it has the distinguishing flash of bronze-green that shows on the upper wings as it moves.
Size The common bronzewing is a comparatively large bird of the dove group, being up to 36 cm long.
Distinguishing features You are most likely to see bronzewings in pairs or small groups as they move among the scrub or scattered trees. It seems to me to be a shy, almost secretive bird, as it tends to avoid observation where possible. If it is disturbed enough to fly it takes off in clattering flight, to land in a nearby tree and watch to see what you will do next.

ENVIRONMENTAL NOTES
Status Common in its range, but not a pest species, as it tends to stay away from habitation.
Feeding habits It wanders in search of seeds, both from farmers' crops and wild grasses.

Predators It is worth considering how vulnerable the behaviour of the bronzewing makes it to the predation of feral cats. Its characteristic of moving from place to place by walking would seem to make it easy prey. Although it is a reasonably large bird it has no defence against a hunter that is easily able to kill a fully grown rabbit.
Reproduction Like most of the doves and pigeons, the common bronzewing builds a flimsy and shaky nest of sticks and twigs. In this it lays 2 white eggs.

BUSH THICK-KNEE
Burhinus magnirostris

LOCATION
In very scattered populations throughout mainland Australia, but not saltbush or spinifex country.

HABITAT
Open woodlands and plains, areas of short grass, particularly near watercourses or other wetlands.

IDENTIFICATION
Colour Strongly streaked with dark brown over a lighter brown, creating a mottled effect like broken shadow.
Size Up to 58 cm long.
Distinguishing features Your best way to identify the bush thick-knee is by its ability to stand absolutely still, determined to fool humans and predators that it is really a grass tussock. It is a large bird, but very slim when standing upright, with

FORESTS AND WOODLANDS

an oversize head and long, lumpy legs. Its general colour is that of dry grass in the shade, and it is extraordinarily well camouflaged in its natural open woodland habitat. The bush thick-knee is also called a 'curlew' because of its cry.

ENVIRONMENTAL NOTES

Status Despite the scattered nature of the population, and its habit of nesting and feeding on the ground, the bush thick-knee does not seem to be in any danger of extinction in the near future. For some reason it has become a popular bird for zoos and wildlife parks, since it is reasonably large and easily seen by visitors because of its habit of standing or sitting in the open. Thankfully, it is still present in farming areas where extensive clearing and cultivation has occurred.

Feeding habits Mainly insects and other small invertebrates, like spiders, that it takes as it stalks over the ground.

Predators Its greatest danger to survival would seem to be predation by foxes and feral cats.

Reproduction Two eggs, 59 mm long, incredibly camouflaged in light and dark browns and grey, are laid directly on the ground.

Bush Thick-knees and Bunyips

It is very likely that the call of the bush thick-knee is the origin of the bunyip legends of the outback. Bunyips are said to live in and around large bodies of water in the inland, a favourite habitat for the thick-knee. Bunyips are supposed to make night-time blood curdling cries, as does the bush thick-knee. It is quite an experience the first time you hear the eerie 'curlew' call of the thick-knee carrying across the stillness of a moonless outback night.

RUFOUS WHISTLER
Pachycephala rufiventris

LOCATION
Most of mainland Australia with the exception of the tree-less, desert areas.

HABITAT
Typically open woodland and scrubland, but also some of the thicker forested areas. You will hear it in areas ranging from low mallee scrubland in the dry outback to scattered timberland along inland waterways.

IDENTIFICATION
Colour The male bird is very dapper, having a white throat with a black collar

and a rich, rufous red underbelly. The female is much plainer and hard to see amongst the camouflage colours of undergrowth and treetops.
Size Up to 18 cm long.
Distinguishing features You will most probably hear the rufous whistler before you see it. One of its calls is best described as 'ee-chong', with the 'chong' slightly lower than the 'ee'. In the scrubland of the outback, this call carries over long distances, and goes on for long enough to become slightly irritating. This is made up for by occasional bursts of more melodic whistling. When you hear the call it is worth testing your powers of observation and bush skills by attempting to track down its source. Its mixture of colours stands out quite startlingly once the bird is located.

ENVIRONMENTAL NOTES
Status The rufous whistler is a fairly common bird.
Feeding habits It is an insect-eating bird often seen hunting for insects in the lower canopy of trees.
Predators As for the red-capped robin (see page 130).
Reproduction The nest is a loosely made cup of grass and twigs in which 2 to 4 browny-green mottled eggs are laid.

CRESTED BELLBIRD
Oreoica gutturalis

LOCATION
Scattered through the inland areas of Australia.

HABITAT
The dry scrub and woodland areas inland, plus the dry coastal zones of Western Australia and South Australia.

IDENTIFICATION
Colour It has a distinctive white throat and face and a wide black collar that reaches down to the breast.
Size Up to 23 cm long.
Distinguishing features Its voice has been described as one of the most beautiful of all inland birds. One of its common names is 'pan-pan-panella', the name given to it by the Aborigines to describe its call. The range and volume of notes in the call, and the method of delivery, tend to make it ventriloquial, that is, it seems to be coming from where the bird is not. This can make it hard for you to track it down.

ENVIRONMENTAL NOTES
Status This small, slim bird is common throughout much of the saltbush zone of the Nullarbor Plain and many other parts of the dry interior. It may be seen as a single bird or part of a small group.
Feeding habits It is a ground feeder, hopping about amongst the scrubs and bushes on the lookout for insects. During nesting time the bird catches hairy cater-

pillars and immobilises them by crushing their mid-section. The caterpillars are then placed around the rim of the nest. Some observers believe that the partly paralysed caterpillars serve as a store of food.
Predators As for other small bush birds.

Reproduction An untidy cup of bark, twigs and bits of grass is built in the fork of a bush or tree, usually no more than 3 m from the ground. It lays 3 or 4 blotchy white eggs.

RED-CAPPED ROBIN
Petroica goodenovii

LOCATION
Throughout Australia, with the exception of the tropical north, southern Victoria, and Tasmania.

HABITAT
The woodlands and scrubland in the drier areas of Australia, and timbered fringes of wetlands.

IDENTIFICATION
Colour The male bird is like a living flame, with a bold red breast and red cap to his head. The red is highlighted by a white outline on the sides of the chest and the black back and face. The female bird is drab compared to the male, having only a slight pink colouring on the forehead. The rest of her body is a general grey-brown colour.
Size Up to 12 cm long.
Distinguishing features Your first sighting will probably be of a sudden flash of red amongst the trees. It is a restless bird, seeming unable to sit still. It flicks and flits along branches or fencing wire, filled with nervous energy. It can usually be approached to within a few metres, then it will fly a short distance away with a quick flick of wings and tail.

ENVIRONMENTAL NOTES
Status The red-capped robin is usually seen only as a single bird or in pairs, but it is reasonably common in its range. It performs a very valuable function in the control of insects and their larvae.
Feeding habits It is a great hunter of insects. It will sit on fenceposts or low branches, peering down at the ground, watching for any insect to move. When one is spotted it dives down to pounce on it, and then returns to the perch to eat it.
Predators Like all small birds, the robin is taken by many birds of prey, as well as feral cats and large reptiles.
Reproduction The nest is a superbly built cup made from bark and grass and bound together with spiderweb. In it 2 to 4 tiny freckled bluey-green eggs are laid.

BLACK-FACED CUCKOO-SHRIKE
Coracina novaehollandiae

LOCATION
Throughout Australia.

HABITAT
From house gardens to arid lands. In the outback the cuckoo-shrike is often seen in open woodland, either waiting for the movement of insects in the air or on the ground, or flying in its looping flight from perch to perch.

IDENTIFICATION
Colour Mainly a beautiful soft dove-grey, with a black head and face.
Size Up to 36 cm long.
Distinguishing features An easy feature for identification is its dipping flight, as it flaps and swoops in a short glide, then flaps and swoops again. When it lands it carefully folds one wing over the other, in an exaggerated show of neatness. It is not a shy bird and the species is sufficiently common for even the casual observer to quickly recognise it.

ENVIRONMENTAL NOTES
Status The black-faced cuckoo-shrike is a common bird in most parts of Australia, although not necessarily the whole year round.
Feeding habits This bird is a busy insect-eater and will be seen 'hawking' after insects in flight. It is particularly busy in the years when cicadas are plentiful, and it takes cicadas in flight, to return to a perch to eat them. Sometimes the first indication you will have of the black-faced cuckoo-shrike is the plaintive cry of a cicada being dismembered.
Predators Birds such as butcherbirds and currawongs take young chicks.
Reproduction A neat, shallow nest of twigs and cobwebs is built in the horizontal fork of a tree, at least 6 m above the ground. Two to 3 dark green or greeny-blue freckled eggs are laid.

BROWN TREECREEPER
Climacteris picumnus

LOCATION
Eastern mainland Australia, with the exception of the far north coast and the far south coast.

HABITAT
Dry forests and woodlands, and timbered country around wetland areas in the outback.

IDENTIFICATION
Colour The brown treecreeper does not stand out by its colouration as it is generally grey to greyish-brown.

FORESTS AND WOODLANDS

from tree to tree as it finishes its inspection.

The brown treecreeper spends a large part of its time on the ground, turning over sticks and leaves. This species lives and hunts in small groups, rather than as a pair or a solitary bird. You can tell if treecreepers are in a patch of trees by the single ringing note that pings out at regular intervals.

ENVIRONMENTAL NOTES
Status Common where suitable food trees remain.
Feeding habits Its principal food is ants, although it eats a wide range of insects and their larvae.
Predators As for other small bushland birds (see page 130).
Reproduction It nests in the hollows of trees and it has been recorded that an introduced bird, the common starling *(Sturnus vulgaris)*, competes with the treecreeper for nesting space. It lays 2 or 3 pink eggs with red or purple freckles.

Size Up to 18 cm long.
Distinguishing features You will be able to identify it by the way it moves in the trees that are its source of food. The treecreeper moves in a spiral fashion around the trunks of living and dead trees, searching in cracks in the wood and ripping off bark to find insects. It is a very active bird, moving rapidly over the bark of a tree or over the ground, and it swoops

YELLOW-THROATED MINER
Manorina flavigula

LOCATION
Throughout the Australian mainland with the exclusion of the whole of the east coast, from Cape York to the Victoria–South Australia border.

HABITAT
Dry woodlands and scrub country, particularly around watercourses and wetlands; also grasslands where there is a plentiful supply of flowering shrubs.

IDENTIFICATION
Colour Generally greyish, with some yellow marking on the wings, and the underside a pale fawn-grey. There is a thin black mask around the eyes, and a washed-yellow colouring on the throat.
Size Up to 28 cm long.
Distinguishing features The yellow-throated miner is very similar in appearance to the noisy miner *(Manorina melanocephala)* of the east coast of Australia that many people are familiar with. The main difference is that the noisy miner has a bolder black 'mask' over the eyes and the yellow-throated miner has a small patch of yellow at the back of the

ENVIRONMENTAL NOTES

Status The natural limitations of food in the drier areas would provide a limiting factor to the expansion of population of the yellow-throated miner. Studies indicate that the yellow-throated miner is less able to tolerate the spread of suburbia than its noisy relative (see 'Distinguishing features' above).

Feeding habits Although it is classed as a honeyeater, it spends a great deal of its time walking over the ground picking up anything edible, from ants to fallen fruit.

Predators The miner tends to be a very aggressive bird when in a flock, and I have often seen them drive off potential predators by sheer weight of numbers and volume of noise. Even the most cunning of hunters, the cat, is soon spied by miners, and they scream out to let everyone know of its presence.

Reproduction Three or 4 blotched orange-pink eggs are laid in an untidy cup-shaped nest made of grass, twigs, wool, spiderwebs, and a variety of other materials.

bill. Another major difference between the two species seems to be behavioural. It is not unusual to see large numbers of noisy miners acting aggressively towards others species of birds, particularly around suburban feeding trays and favourite food trees. As their range overlaps there are records of the two species interbreeding, creating a hybrid species.

SPINY-CHEEKED HONEYEATER
Acanthagenys rufogularis

LOCATION
Inland mainland Australia from the Great Dividing Range in NSW to the coast of Western Australia, but excluding the tropical north.

HABITAT
The dry inland forests and scrublands, through to orchards and gardens.

IDENTIFICATION
Colour It is boldly marked on the front with long stripes, and has a creamy-yellow throat and white cheeks. It has the long

FORESTS AND WOODLANDS

bill and slim head of a typical honeyeater. The front half of the bill is black and the back half pink.
Size Up to 26 cm long.
Distinguishing features A very active and alert bird, watching the world through bright eyes. The spiny-cheeked honeyeater is also a noisy bird, particularly when in a mob feeding on a thicket of favourite flowering shrubs. It will occasionally take off in the air, giving a gurgling cry, then returning to the business of feeding.

ENVIRONMENTAL NOTES
Status The benefit that the honeyeater provides by helping to control insect pests has still to be realised, particularly when the birds feed on the insects that attack orchard fruit. Unfortunately, the practice of heavily spraying orchards with pesticide puts these natural controllers at risk.

Feeding habits It eats nectar and insects.
Predators As for other small bushland birds (see page 130).
Reproduction A flimsy deep cup of grass and spiderwebs is hung in the outer foliage of a tree or shrub, and 2 or 3 whitish-cream mottled eggs are laid inside.

GREY SHRIKE-THRUSH
Colluricincla harmonica

LOCATION
All of Australia, with the exception of some of the drier desert areas.

HABITAT
From coastal and mountain forests to inland woodland and scrub. The grey shrike-thrush is not just a bird of the outback, as it is found in timbered areas throughout Australia. It is a curious, cheeky bird, often sitting on logs or the sides of trees to peer back at the observer, or scratching and feeding on the ground or on the lower parts of the trunks of trees.

IDENTIFICATION
Colour Generally grey, but with a slight shading of fawny-brown on the back.
Size Up to 27 cm long.
Distinguishing features The eyes are large, bright and black, and wonderfully observant. When resting in a bushland area it is not unusual to feel you are being watched and look up to see the bright eye of the grey shrike-thrush observing you. This is one bird you need to know, as it is very likely you will see (or hear it) in any bushland setting. Its colouration is not outstanding, as it is a uniform grey, but it is its beautiful song and perky behaviour that make it quickly identifiable. The Latin species name *harmonica* gives the clue to this bird's song. The melody is beautiful, as the bird runs through a variety of melodic scales. Even when the unfortu-

nate bird is kept in the captivity of a zoo aviary it will give its song, running through the musical passages as it investigates its confined home.

ENVIRONMENTAL NOTES
Status Common in suitable woodlands.
Feeding habits The shrike-thrush is a vigorous feeder. It eats insects and a range of other invertebrates.
Predators As for other small bush birds (see page 130).
Reproduction It builds a large bowl-shaped nest of twigs, grass, bark and other pieces of vegetation in which are laid 2 to 4 lightly freckled white eggs.

BLACK-FACED WOODSWALLOW
Artamus cinereus

LOCATION
Throughout mainland Australia, with the exception of the southeast coast and the tip of Cape York.

HABITAT
Open country, from scattered woodlands to the rocky deserts.

IDENTIFICATION
Colour The black-faced woodswallow is a dapper, two-tone grey, with darker grey on the back, and the black face that gives it its name.
Size Up to 20 cm long.
Distinguishing features The woodswallow always looks beautifully dressed. It is also a noisy, 'talkative' bird, and will often tell you where it is before you see it. You will find communities of the birds nesting and feeding together and it is their chattering that will lead you to them.

ENVIRONMENTAL NOTES
Status Its life is tied to the availability of trees, particularly dead trees, in which to perch. If such perches are available, then it can exist in dry, sparsely vegetated areas where saltbush and spinifex predominate.

Groups of birds are often found in clusters, where dozens to hundreds of birds may be found in the same tree, although this is only a short-term phenomenon.
Feeding habits It feeds on insects mostly taken in flight.
Predators Like the yellow-throated miner, the woodswallow mobs predators, giving them little chance to pick off a solitary bird.
Reproduction It builds a neat, cup-shaped nest of grass and other plant material in a shrub or small tree, and lays 3 or 4 blueish-white eggs blotched with darker colours. When rains occur in the drier areas of its range, the black-faced woodswallow is prompted to breed immediately. Rainfall means a bounty of insects will soon follow, and the woodswallow is guaranteed food for its young.

FORESTS AND WOODLANDS

CHESTNUT-RUMPED THORNBILL
Acanthiza uropygialis

amongst the smallest group of birds in Australia, only the weebill *(Smicrornis brevirostris)* being smaller. The chestnut-rumped thornbill is well described by its name as its only real distinguishing feature, apart from its size, is the small patch of orange-red above its tail.

This species can be distinguished from other similar looking thornbills by its habit of feeding on or close to the ground. Thornbills tend to be in groups when you find them out of the breeding season, and you may spot several species feeding together in and around trees. While they feed they move among the leaves and branches giving off a constant twitter.

LOCATION
Inland mainland Australia, from west of the Great Dividing Range in NSW to the coast of Western Australia. Not the tropical north or southwestern Western Australia.

HABITAT
The drier woodlands of central Australia, particularly when associated with saltbush and other arid-land shrubs.

IDENTIFICATION
Colour Generally pale grey-brown with a chestnut patch just above the tail.
Size Up to 12 cm long.
Distinguishing features The thornbill is

ENVIRONMENTAL NOTES
Status Common to very common, dependent on suitable trees for food and nesting.
Feeding habits It feeds on a range of invertebrates, including insects and spiders.
Predators As for the shrike-thrush (see page 134).
Reproduction It is unusual in that it nests in the holes or hollows of trees, or any other suitable cavity, whereas other thornbills build bulky grass nests. It is often the presence of dead trees that determines whether a habitat is suitable or not. It lays 2 to 4 tiny white eggs with a scattering of red dots on one end.

PIED BUTCHERBIRD
Cracticus nigrogularis

LOCATION
Mainland Australia, with the exception of the southeastern coast, and some parts of the arid inland.

HABITAT
A wide variety, from parks and gardens to the drier inland, but more typically near watercourses in the drier interior.

BIRDS

A common sight in the outback is a pied butcherbird sitting on a television aerial in the early morning. It is also seen on the dead branch of a tall tree that overlooks an open paddock or an area around a farm dam. From this high perch it will plummet down to take its prey.

IDENTIFICATION
Colour Visually, the bird is outstanding, with a snowy-white underside, bold black head and throat, black on the outer wings, and a broad white saddle behind the neck.
Size Up to 38 cm long.

Distinguishing features Your introduction to the pied butcherbird may well be its beautiful song. It has a sweetly melodic whistle that sounds a little like the first few notes of Beethoven's Fifth Symphony. It has the heavy, dagger-like hooked bill of all butcherbirds.

ENVIRONMENTAL NOTES
Status Common throughout its range.
Feeding habits It eats small animals such as insects or mice. The butcherbird gets its name from its habit of hanging dead prey on thorns and spikes of bushes, presumably as a form of larder. Its beautiful cry can cause panic among smaller birds, particularly if the birds are confined in an aviary where there appears to be no escape. The reason for the panic is that the butcherbird often preys on young birds in nests.
Predators A superb predator like this has little to fear from any other animal.
Reproduction An untidy nest of twigs and sticks is built in the fork of a tree about 10 m from the ground, and in this nest the female lays 3 to 5 brownish-green mottled eggs.

Reptiles and Amphibians

COMMON DEATH ADDER
Acanthophis antarcticus

LOCATION
NSW, Queensland, northern Northern Territory, southern South Australia and southern Western Australia.

HABITAT
Half-buried in sandy or light soil or leaf litter, often close to the trunks of trees and bushes.

IDENTIFICATION
Colour Light grey to reddish brown, usually with bands of a darker colour.
Size The death adder is only a small snake, rarely more than 1 m and usually less than 0.5 m long.
Distinguishing features You are unlikely to see it during the day unless you happen to disturb it in its hideaway of leaves and

soil. As its greyish-brown colouring is designed to camouflage, you will need all your powers of observation just to see it.

Its body is fatter and flatter than most snakes, with the tail sharply tapering to a point. At the end of the tail is a 'lure' that it flicks in the air just above the ground to attract prey, like mice. The lure has nothing to do with its venom, as that is carried by the fangs in the mouth. This venom is a very good reason to be extremely careful where you place your hands when clearing around trees and shrubs in the bush. The death adder is very venomous. It does not move unless forced to, and then can strike with blinding speed.

ENVIRONMENTAL NOTES
Status The death adder is fairly common throughout its range.
Feeding habits It takes lizards, other snakes, mice and birds as prey.
Predators Although a deadly foe, small death adders would be eaten by other snakes, large lizards and birds of prey, particularly owls. Large death adders have little to fear.
Reproduction Fifteen to 20 live young, each about 15 cm long, are born during the summer and autumn months.

LACE MONITOR
Varanus varius

LOCATION
Eastern mainland Australia from just below Cape York in Queensland, through mid-western NSW, to southeastern South Australia.

HABITAT
Usually in the tall trees of forests and woodlands, but also on the ground, as it hunts for food. On hot summer days you will occasionally see it watching you from its home in the hollow branches of big trees.

IDENTIFICATION
Colour It is often boldly striped over a dark background, but these stripes are not so obvious in the really big lizards.

REPTILES AND AMPHIBIANS

Size The lace monitor grows to more than 2 m in length.

Distinguishing features You will have no problem recognising this lizard, as it is very large, and unmistakably like the dragon of legends. If you come across one in the bush, it is likely to crash off through the undergrowth at great speed, body raised off the ground. When it reaches a suitable tree it will climb rapidly, pausing when in safety to see what you are doing. The lace monitor is very well equipped to defend itself and should be left well and truly alone. It has strong jaws with sharp teeth, long claws used for climbing trees, and a whip-like tail that it lashes in angry defence. A large, angry monitor can be a fearsome looking animal.

ENVIRONMENTAL NOTES

Status The lace monitor is more commonly known as a goanna, and it is a common part of eastern Australian forest and woodland. In some national parks on the western slopes of NSW, it becomes so used to the rubbish left by visitors that it visits the bins at all hours of the day and night. It will even wander in amongst picnickers.

Feeding habits The monitor takes a huge range of foods from carrion to live chickens. I have seen one so full of hens' eggs that it was unable to get back into its burrow in a termites' nest. It is very adept at killing snakes, its tough skin giving great protection from bites.

Predators A fully grown monitor is more than a match for any other predator, but young lizards are taken by many birds of prey.

Reproduction Six to 20 eggs are laid in a suitable retreat, such as that made in the side of a termites' nest. The young are about 25 cm long when hatched.

TREE SKINK
Egernia striolata

LOCATION
NSW, southern and eastern Queensland and eastern South Australia.

HABITAT
Under bark, and in the hollow limbs and cracks of trees. Look out for old trees that have many cracks and hollows and, as you move quietly through the trees, you will be rewarded by seeing the quick, scuttling movements of this lizard. Its habit of stopping just inside its bolt-hole will give you a chance to have a good look at it.

IDENTIFICATION
Colour It is a very neat and smooth lizard, pale brown to fawn in colour, with an even pattern of lighter dots and darker stripes

FORESTS AND WOODLANDS

running in parallel lines down its back. Its colouring makes it very well camouflaged.

Size The average length is about 15 cm from head to tail.

Distinguishing features The tree skink is small when compared to lizards like the lace monitor. It is a lizard of the daytime, so you are likely to see it hunting over the bark of trees in warm weather. It will dart back to its hiding place with a noisy scamper when you disturb it, stopping once it is inside to see what you are going to do next.

ENVIRONMENTAL NOTES

Status This is a common lizard throughout its range.

Feeding habits It hunts out insects and other small invertebrates from under the bark of trees.

Predators Its camouflage colouring and quick movement saves it from most predation, but long-beaked birds like kookaburras and butcherbirds can prise the lizard out of its bolt-hole.

Reproduction Three to 4 live young are produced.

TREE DTELLA
Gehyra variegata

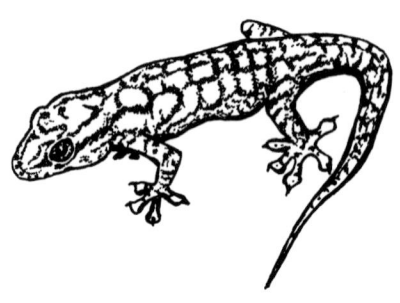

LOCATION
All of mainland Australia, except for the northwest and the southeast.

HABITAT
Trees and shrubs, and under bark in the daytime.

IDENTIFICATION
Colour It is a general grey colour, with darker grey splotches and patterns scattered over its body.

Size The tree dtella is a very small gecko lizard, usually not longer than 10 cm.

Distinguishing features It has a longer and slimmer tail than most geckos, but you will be able to recognise it as a gecko by its huge eyes, adapted to its nocturnal lifestyle, and its pad-like toes.

If you disturb one under bark or in a crack in a fencepost, it will give a sharp squeaking noise. Like all geckos, it will drop its tail if roughly handled, to grow another one in its place. The dropped tail twitches and flicks to distract a predator from the rest of the gecko.

ENVIRONMENTAL NOTES

Status This is the gecko that you are most likely to find, as it is the most common over its range.

Feeding habits It feeds on insects and other small invertebrates.

Predators The tail-dropping and the sharp squeak are meant to deter most predators, but the dtella would still often be food for birds, mammals and other reptiles such as snakes and lizards.

Reproduction One egg is laid in hollows in trees or in leaf litter.

Insects

SWIFT MOTH
Abantiades spp.

LOCATION
The southern and eastern portion of Australia.

HABITAT
Restricted to areas where it can find a suitable food tree, usually a species of eucalypt.

IDENTIFICATION
Colour Soft grey-brown, streaked with darker brown.
Size Body length: up to 6 cm; wingspan: up to 8 cm.
Distinguishing features You have two main guides to the identification of this moth. One is its size, as it is large winged and heavy bodied, the other is that the adult moth often emerges from its pupa in large numbers after heavy falls of rain.

ENVIRONMENTAL NOTES
Status Common to very common to plague proportions when the weather conditions are perfect. Swarms occur only when prolonged dry periods are followed by heavy rains in the evening and early night.

Feeding habits The adult moth does not eat at all. The caterpillar feeds on the roots of trees.

Predators Following a swarm of moths, birds such as kookaburras, magpies and butcherbirds appear from everywhere. For a short while all insect-eating animals in the area feast on the swarming moths. The moths begin to die in about a day after emerging, so the chance to gorge is short-lived.

Reproduction The female randomly scatters thousands of eggs from which hatch the larvae that then tunnel into the soil. A sudden downpour in warm weather can trigger the pupa to push away the plug at the entrance to its burrow in the ground or in a tree trunk, and emerge as an adult moth. The moth often begins to emerge while it is still raining, particularly if the rain begins in the evening. By the next morning, every light-coloured surface has a covering of these large, grey-brown moths. It is important that as many moths as possible be around for the short time the moth is alive so that breeding can take place. If you happen to be camping during an emergence your tent, lantern and fire will be swarming with moths.

FORESTS AND WOODLANDS

CICADA
Family Cicadicae

LOCATION
Throughout Australia, where suitable food trees are found.

HABITAT
In any habitat that has some tree or shrub cover.

IDENTIFICATION
Colour Very varied, from black and orange to bright lime-green.
Size Body length: up to 5 cm; wingspan: up to 7 cm.
Distinguishing features The cicada is the world's noisiest insect. Once you have heard its summertime song you will never mistake it for anything else. Depending on the species, it ranges from a gentle trilling to a piercing shriek. During 'cicada summers' you will find the cast-off nymph skins everywhere there are trees. You would know that cicadas were about, even if they made no noise.

ENVIRONMENTAL NOTES
Status Widespread and common, although the numbers vary from year to year. In 'cicada summers', the months of November and December can be deafening.
Feeding habits The adult feeds on the sap of the upper parts of trees, while the nymph feeds on the sap of tree roots.
Predators Many birds take the cicada as food, and the half-eaten bodies of the insects, the soft parts gone, are often found trying to crawl away to shelter.
Reproduction The cicada has an amazing life cycle. It is reported that some species pupate under the ground for as long as 17 years, but it is more likely that it ranges from 3 years to 7 years, depending on the species. The adult female cuts a slit in the bark of a branch or twig and lays her eggs along the slit. The tiny cicada nymphs that hatch out drop to the ground and burrow down to feed on the roots of trees. At the appointed time they burrow out, leaving the characteristic round hole in lawns and gardens.

Once out of the burrow the nymph climbs a fence or a wall, usually to about 1 m from the ground, and in the early-morning sun the back of its skin splits open and the adult cicada emerges.

BULLDOG ANT
Myrmecia spp.

LOCATION
Throughout Australia, where suitable bushland environments exist.

HABITAT
Ground level, often amongst undergrowth, and in clearings in the timber.

INSECTS

fiercest stinging ants in Australia. Any disturbance of the nest on a warm day brings a rush of its inhabitants out of one or two exits. The ants will fiercely attack anything that comes within a couple of metres of their nests. Occasionally scouts will be seen foraging some distance from the nest, so be cautious with these as well. Their sting is in their tail, and one ant can sting repeatedly, unlike honey bees that lose their sting and die.

IDENTIFICATION
Colour Varies according to the species, but the colours are usually bright gingery red or shiny black.
Size Also varies with species, but some species can be up to 1.5 cm long.
Distinguishing features The best guide to identify this ant is the conical mound that it builds, up to 45 cm high. It is often covered with small twigs and stones, and blends in very well with the soil and growth around it. If you see one, leave it alone, as it is the home of one of the

ENVIRONMENTAL NOTES
Status The bulldog ant is very common in some parts of its woodland and forest habitats.
Feeding habits It kills and eats many small ground-dwelling insects and invertebrates, including other ants.
Predators Its sting deters most predators, although bulldog ants away from the nest are taken by birds and other ant species.
Reproduction The nest is guarded by the savage workers equipped with stings. Inside, other workers tend the eggs laid by the queen.

Bulldog Ants Sting
The sting of a bulldog ant is painful but not dangerous unless a person has an immune reaction to such bites. The pain can be relieved by a wide range of pharmaceutical products designed for that purpose, or by very effective home remedies that contain an alkali to neutralise the acid of the sting. Time is the best cure, as the pain begins to diminish in a few minutes.

MEAT-ANT
Iridomyrmex purpureus

LOCATION
The meat-ant is to be found throughout Australia.

HABITAT
In clay soils, particularly in open woodland, or near citrus orchards.

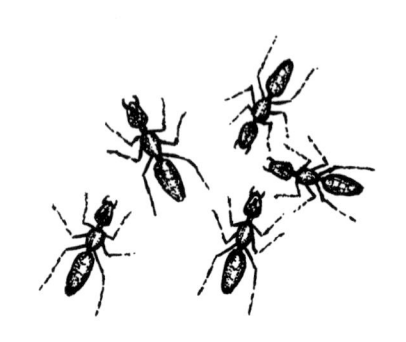

IDENTIFICATION
Colour The overall colour is a reddish-brown.
Size The meat-ant is about 6 mm long.
Distinguishing features You will come to recognise its nest mound which can vary from a few centimetres across to a few metres, and stand up to 20 cm above the level of the surrounding ground. It is always kept totally bare of all vegetation, and the top is 'decorated' with small pebbles, twigs or the dry fruit of eucalypts and other plants. It does not stand out in such an obvious way as the nest of the bulldog ant, but shows as a gently sloping bare clay mound, often of quite a considerable size.

The meat-ant is extremely active in warm to hot weather. If you disturb the nest on a summer's day, the worker ants swarm out from the many holes of the nest, looking for the cause of the disturbance. They will savagely attack anything that walks on their nest, or comes within range of the trails that lead from the nest. They do not sting with the tail (unlike the very painful sting of the bulldog ant) but bite with powerful jaws that hang on to you.

ENVIRONMENTAL NOTES
Status Common to very common in its preferred habitats.
Feeding habits If the animal that falls on the nest is small enough to be killed, it will be torn to pieces in a very short time. I kept a record of how long it took meat-ants to clean all the meat off the body of a large (dead) snake. In 5 days in mid-summer all that was left was the bare bones. However, the ants do not just wait for animals to walk on their nests: they go hunting for their food. You can track the ants to and from their food source by following the wide ant 'highways' that come out from the nest mound, like irregularly placed wheel spokes.
Predators Similar to the bulldog ant (see above). Some birds actually use meat-ants to 'anoint' their bodies, a process known as 'anting'. The reason for this behaviour is not known.
Reproduction As for the bulldog ant.

Plants

MUGGA IRONBARK
Eucalyptus sideroxylon

LOCATION
NSW, Queensland and Victoria.

HABITAT
Along the low ridges and slopes of the western districts of the eastern states. It

PLANTS

rough, deeply furrowed bark. This is visible even at some distance, and if you see a tree with a very dark bark, that carries through right up into the branches, you can be almost sure it is an ironbark. Some species, such as the widespread silver-leaved ironbark *(Eucalyptus melanophloia)*, can be recognised by the colour of its leaves.

ENVIRONMENTAL NOTES

Status It was a very popular tree for fenceposts and slab walls for huts, even though the timber is very hard to cut and work with. This hardness makes it extremely durable, and some fences that were constructed more than a hundred years ago are still standing today. As you drive through the outback, watch out for the 'post and rail fences' made of split and shaped ironbark. Calculate how many trees it took to build just one fence a kilometre long, and consider the time it took to make every rail and fence post.

Natural control agents As for other species of eucalypts, like the yellow box (see below).

Reproduction As for other species of eucalypts, like the yellow box.

can tolerate a wide range of habitats, although it is often an indicator of 'poor' country.

IDENTIFICATION
Colour A tree with very dark bark, and greyish foliage.
Size The ironbark can grow up to 20 m high, its height depending upon the soil and rainfall of the area.
Distinguishing features The outstanding feature of all ironbarks is their dark, very

YELLOW BOX
Eucalyptus melliodora

LOCATION
NSW, Queensland and Victoria.

HABITAT
The sandy or rich soils of flood plains. Heavy clay soils that are periodically covered by floods show the best growth of yellow box. This area can often be some distance from permanent water. You will see yellow box as ancient trees standing beside the road, or as a tall forest, with little or no understorey.

IDENTIFICATION
Colour Yellow box has grey-green leaves and light brown bark, sometimes with a yellowish tinge.
Size Up to 20 m tall.
Distinguishing features The yellow box is a tall, noble tree that you often see

FORESTS AND WOODLANDS

You will quickly come to recognise it by its browny-yellow bark on the lower part of the trunk, and the bare trunk and branches above. The bark on the older trees hangs in untidy tatters.

ENVIRONMENTAL NOTES
Status Yellow box is commercially very valuable as it supplies huge amounts of nectar for the honey industry. Next time you are in a supermarket look for the honey with the label 'Yellow Box'.
Natural control agents Leaf-eating insects such as the group known as scarab beetles can devastate eucalypt forests.
Reproduction Although the blossoms supply valuable nectar, they are barely noticeable from the ground. They produce a copious amount of seed, contained in the typical hard fruit of eucalypts.

growing in large groups in flood plain areas. It can be distinguished from river red gum by the colour of its straggly bark.

GREY BOX
Eucalyptus microcarpa

HABITAT
Grey box grows in a wide range of soil and climatic conditions, but it is usually found in the medium to low rainfall areas.

IDENTIFICATION
Colour The bark is a uniform light, slaty grey and the foliage is grey-green.
Size A tall tree, up to 20 m high.
Distinguishing features You will recognise it by its grey bark, made up of small scale-like pieces, that go right out to the main branches. From a distance the bark looks smooth, but up close you will discover its rougher nature. Its general appearance is very neat. The first branches begin to grow a third of the way up the trunk, and slant sharply upward. A mature tree looks a little like an upside-down pyramid with a round base.

LOCATION
NSW, Queensland, Victoria and South Australia.

PLANTS

ENVIRONMENTAL NOTES
Status Grey box is a very common tree in the inland of the eastern states. It has been a very important tree for farmers, as it has supplied them with excellent fenceposts and fuel from the very early days of white settlement. Careful farmers have left blocks of grey box in wheat paddocks and pastures because of the shade they provide for stock. The presence of grey box is an indicator of good grazing country.

Predators As for other species of eucalypts, like the yellow box (see above).

Reproduction As for other species of eucalypts, like the yellow box.

BELAH
Casuarina cristata

Distinguishing features The belah belongs to a group of trees called 'bull-oaks' or 'she-oaks'. Your key to identification comes from the 'leaves' that look something like the 'needles' of a pine tree, and form little circles along the tiny branchlets. The bark of the belah is shaped into small tile-like squares. It is darker in colour than most eucalypts, and the older trees develop the shape of an upright rectangular prism.

ENVIRONMENTAL NOTES
Status Belah is a common tree, seen as single trees left in paddocks, and as dense single species stands, or in assocation with other woodland trees such as wilga.

She-oak wood has a very straight grain and a rich colour. It has been used for making roofing shingles since the early days of white settlement.

Natural control agents All members of the casuarina group are prone to attack by hairy caterpillars. These animals are the larvae of a wide range of species of moths.

Reproduction Casuarinas have distinctive male and female flowers, the male flowers carrying pollen on small spikes, the female flowers being more bunched into groups. The fruit is cone-shaped, about 2 cm long, and very rough and woody.

LOCATION
All mainland states.

HABITAT
Very varied, often mixed in with a variety of other trees. Can tolerate a wide range of soil types throughout its climatic range.

IDENTIFICATION
Colour Very dark green 'foliage', with dark grey bark.

Size Some species of casuarina grow into forest giants, but the belah grows to a medium height for a woodland tree, about 15 m. The leaves are tiny, only 1 or 2 mm across.

WILGA
Geijera parviflora

IDENTIFICATION
Colour The leaves are dark green, long and drooping.
Size It grows up to 12 m high.
Distinguishing features Wilga grows in amongst other trees of the arid woodland, such as belah. It has a clumpy shape, with branches hanging right down to the ground. If you crush the leaves, a very aromatic peppermint scent is given off. Look for a medium-sized tree, with a very rounded shape and drooping leaves almost touching the ground.

ENVIRONMENTAL NOTES
Status Wilga is very common throughout its range, usually found mixed in with other species.
Natural control agents The strong aromatic smell of the wilga protects it from most leaf-eating insects.
Reproduction Although it produces a great deal of seeds, very few of them grow into new plants, in contrast to shrubs in the acacia group.

LOCATION
NSW, Queensland, Victoria and South Australia.

HABITAT
Widely variable, but in the low rainfall areas. On most soil types, but rarely on river flats.

QUANDONG
Santalum acuminatum

LOCATION
All mainland Australian states in low rainfall areas.

HABITAT
From sandy soils to rocky hillsides, usually with a variety of other woodland plants.

IDENTIFICATION
Colour The quandong is not an easy tree to identify immediately unless you see it in fruit, and then the bright-red colour stands out amongst the olive-green leaves.
Size The tree is not very tall, usually no more than 5 m. The fruit is about 3 cm across.
Distinguishing features The drooping, spindly branches and leaves hang down toward the ground. The fruit is fleshy, tart in taste, and contains a large stone.

ENVIRONMENTAL NOTES
Status The tree is moderately common to very common throughout its range. The

PLANTS

wood has several uses, including as a form of sandalwood to make fragrant ornamental containers. The Aborigines use it as a type of firestarter, as its oily nature makes it easily combustible. The fruit is very edible, and formed a part of the diet of Aboriginal peoples and white settlers alike. The fruit and seed are also a popular food for emus.

Natural control agents The quandong is parasitic on other woodland plants in the early part of its life, therefore the clearing of woodland by natural or unnatural causes, means that the quandong would not be able to establish itself.

Reproduction Through the fruit and seed detailed above.

SPIDER-FLOWER
Grevillea spp.

species. In the arid areas, look for spindly shrubs that have flowers that are bright red, orange or creamy-yellow. In some areas the flowers can even be grey.

Size Outback grevillea grows in many shapes and sizes, from trees like the beefwood *(Grevillea striata)* that grows up to 12 m tall, to shrubs like the honeysuckle spider-flower *(Grevillea juncifolia)* that is less than 3 m tall.

Distinguishing features This is one group of plants that you will be able to recognise immediately when it is in flower, as its spider shape is unmistakable. Use the references listed in the back of this book to discover which grevillea you have found.

Often you will be led to the spider-flower by the noise and movement caused by honeyeaters and other birds as they feed on the nectar contained in the flowers.

LOCATION
Throughout Australia.

HABITAT
Very varied.

IDENTIFICATION
Colour Very varied according to the

ENVIRONMENTAL NOTES
Status Grevillea has become so wide-

149

spread in its use as a garden flower that most people recognise the spider-shaped flowers that give them their common name. It is decorative, and wonderful for attracting birds to suburban gardens.
Natural control agents A control agent in the wild is the presence or absence of the honey-eating birds that use the plant as a food source. It is interesting to speculate if the decline in honeyeaters caused by predation by feral cats will show a decline in the health of outback grevilleas.
Reproduction By local scattering of the ripe seeds. As birds and insects collect nectar they also cross-pollinate the plants ensuring a healthy sharing of genetic material.

MISTLETOE
Lysiana spp. and *Amyema* spp.

Size Very varied, according to the species, although never larger than the host plant.
Distinguishing features You can recognise mistletoe because it seems out of place in its host tree. It usually hangs down from a branch or stem in a thick bunch, and is often of a much different colour from the tree it is growing on. To make it even more of a contrast, it often has brightly coloured flowers and fruits against a host tree that is uniform grey, and it can be in flower at any time of the year.

ENVIRONMENTAL NOTES
Status Mistletoe is parasitic, that is it taps into the host plant for nutrients.
Natural control agents The mistletoe is usually a relatively succulent plant in a harsh environment, and so it is attacked by insects that eat it. This form of natural control seems to falter in areas where major disturbances have occurred, such as on the edge of roads, and in clearings in woodland areas.
Reproduction The seeds of the mistletoe are sticky and when they pass through the intestines of birds that eat them, they stick to the branch the bird is perching on. The seed then grows into the branch and a new mistletoe begins.

LOCATION
Throughout Australia.

HABITAT
Widely varied, wherever 'host' trees are available. You will see mistletoe growing everywhere, from trees beside the road, to struggling shrubs in the arid outback.

IDENTIFICATION
Colour Very varied, according to the species, with leaves of light yellow-green through to dark olive-green, and flowers from white through yellow to bright red.

PLANTS

LEOPARDWOOD
Flindersia maculosa

LOCATION
NSW and Queensland.

HABITAT
Sandy soils and flood plains. It is most commonly found on sand plains and along sandy river flats, but it also grows in rocky soil conditions.

IDENTIFICATION
Colour The leaves are shiny dark green and the bark is mottled and patched with orange-and-yellow blotches on a light grey background.
Size It can grow up to 12 m high.
Distinguishing features The leopardwood is unlike many other trees in the low rainfall zone as it has a very neat and graceful shape, its branches spreading up from the trunk in an upside-down umbrella shape. Your best method of identification is by looking at the bark, as the tree gets its name from the blotches. Even from a distance you will see the patterned bark.

ENVIRONMENTAL NOTES
Status Leopardwood is a common tree once you get to the edge of the low rainfall zone.
Natural control agents Yellow mistletoe parasitises and damages this tree.
Reproduction The young tree grows in spiky clumps, looking nothing like the adult tree. One of the spikes becomes the main trunk of the new tree and the rest die out.

CURRAWONG
Acacia doratoxylon

LOCATION
NSW, Queensland, Victoria and Western Australia.

HABITAT
Rocky slopes and hillsides. It grows amongst other woodland trees such as

mugga ironbark, or in vast thickets by itself. You will also find the currawong growing along roadsides, where you will be able to examine it more closely.

IDENTIFICATION
Colour The foliage is greyish in colour, very long and thin, and the flowers are golden-yellow. It has many small reddish branches.
Size It can grow up to the size of a small tree, about 10 m tall. The flowers grow in thick spikes about 3.5 cm long.
Distinguishing features If you are driving through the outback in early spring and summer you may come across a whole hillside that is a band of bright yellow, the colour standing out for some distance. This will be a mass of currawong plants growing along the contour of a ridge, giving their show of golden 'wattle' flowers.

ENVIRONMENTAL NOTES
Status The currawong is a very common shrub.
Natural control agents Like other acacias, currawong is attacked by leaf-eating insects and wasps that parasitise the stems.
Reproduction Acacias produce seeds in pea-like pods, allowing the ready dispersal of very strong seed, and the rapid colonisation of an area.

BUTTERBUSH (BERRIGAN)
Pittosporum phillyreoides

LOCATION
All mainland states.

HABITAT
In areas of very low to moderate rainfall, often forming part of a woodland with a wide variety of other trees and shrubs. A wide range of soil and climatic areas when cultivated.

IDENTIFICATION
Colour This tree stands out from others because of its bright-green leaves and the startling colour of its fruit, which is bright apricot-orange when it splits open. Flowers are creamy-yellow.
Size Up to 6 m high. Round fruit, about 2 cm across.
Distinguishing features In autumn and winter, it is covered with a fruit that has orange seeds inside, surrounded with sticky sap. Even when it is not in fruit you will notice it immediately, as its green colour is such a contrast to the mostly grey-green shrubs that grow around it.

ENVIRONMENTAL NOTES
Status The appearance, flowers and fruit of this tree make it a popular ornamental

for suburban gardens.

Some species of pittosporum have become a pest plant in disturbed areas, such as along coastal sandstone creekbeds. You will recognise these by their similar bright foliage but the fruit is a dull yellow-green.

Natural control agents Pittosporum is attacked by several species of insects that lay their eggs between the layers in the leaves. The plant reacts by growing galls about 1 mm across, giving the leaves a characteristic pimply look.

Reproduction The flowers of the pittosporum grow in profusion if the plant is in wetter conditions.

CHAPTER FIVE

Scrubland and Shrubland

Much of outback Australia is wide, open, flat plain country, but it is not all an empty expanse. A lot of it is covered with scrubby trees and shrubs, and these provide an ideal habitat for animals.

One of the most common of these scrubby trees is the eucalypt known as the mallee. 'Mallee' actually describes the form of the plant rather than the species, because many eucalypts that grow in dry or windy areas take the mallee shape. Instead of having one trunk, the tree sends out many smaller trunks, all from the same root base. The root becomes thick and strong, and searches out any available water or nutrients.

Farmers discovered that mallee areas were suitable for dry land crops like wheat, and thousands of acres of mallee were cleared. The technique often involved pulling a huge heavy ball and chain behind steam-driven tractors. This cleared away the tops but left the strong

Saltbush plains, NSW

SCRUBLAND AND SHRUBLAND

thick roots behind, making any sort of cultivation a nightmare. To combat this a 'stump-jump' plough was invented with a strong spring that took up tension when it hit a root, and then moved over the obstacle without snapping the plough, or its attachment to the horses or tractor.

A common shrub of the outback is the species known as saltbush. It is a very hardy plant, and can live in areas where rainfall is very low and unreliable. It helps to bind the soil together, provides cover for a wide range of animals and helps maintain the balance in a very fragile environment. Unfortunately, like the mallee, it has suffered since much of the shrubland was taken up for farming and grazing. In this case it has not been so much that the farmer has deliberately cleared the land for cropping, often the rainfall in the area is too low for that, but that the plants have been eaten out of existence. Saltbush is very palatable to grazing animals and there is often not much grass in the areas where it grows. Sheep can do very well on a diet of saltbush and other dryland plants, and thousands of hectares were denuded within three human generations.

The clearing of the mallee did create many new wheat farms, but it also created the potential for a 'dust bowl'. Frightening dust storms blotted out the sun as the wind carried the farmers' paddocks many kilometres away. The city of Melbourne was blotted out with such a dust storm in the 1980s, but fortunately they are not as frequent as they were earlier in the 20th century.

Rabbits had as big a role to play as sheep in the destruction of the saltbush plains. What they did not eat they dug under and around, ruining the fragile soil structure and driving native animals out of their habitats. A beautiful native marsupial, the bilby *(Macrotis lagotis)*, has been forced to the edge of extinction because the rabbit has destroyed its habitat.

If you would like to see the effect that domestic grazing animals and rabbits had on the saltbush ecosystem, travel to a state national park, like Kinchega in NSW, and see how the areas that are now protected are regenerating. Compare these with areas still being grazed, or used for grazing until recently.

Farmers are often good managers of the land — they have to be, otherwise they do not survive. In recent years more and more farmers have taken to planting saltbush, so that they can continue to graze marginal land and not destroy it in the process.

Management of the scrubland and shrubland does not mean locking it up so that it can never be used. It means understanding the complex and delicate balance that lets it survive, and then using the land for the greatest long-term benefit for all Australians.

SCRUBLAND AND SHRUBLAND

Mammals

FAT-TAILED DUNNART
Sminthopsis crassicaudata

Distinguishing features As its name describes, you can recognise the fat-tailed dunnart by the swollen base of its tail. It also has larger eyes and ears than seen on the common house mouse. It will move rapidly away when disturbed and probably only be glimpsed as a flash of grey.

ENVIRONMENTAL NOTES
Status There are several species of dunnarts (marsupial mice), that you might find in outback Australia. They range from the very rare to the more common, like the fat-tailed dunnart.
Feeding habits It eats insects and other small animals, and does not need to drink as it obtains its moisture from its food. This is very important for the survival of animals in the dry outback. The fat tail serves as a store of food to get the animal through hard times.
Predators Any prowling carnivore, from cats to dingos, preys on the dunnart. It is also taken by owls.
Reproduction Breeding can take place from the middle of winter until the end of summer. The female can give birth to up to 10 tiny young, and they each attach to a nipple in her deep pouch. Usually only 5 survive until weaned.

LOCATION
Throughout most of outback Australia.

HABITAT
From dry saltbush areas, to open woodland, to farmland. Although it is unlikely you will see it during the day, as it is mostly nocturnal, there is a chance you may disturb it and it will come out of its nest from under a log, or from a deep crack in dry soil.

IDENTIFICATION
Colour The fat-tailed dunnart is greyish-brown in colour.
Size It is a tiny, mouse-like animal, about 16 cm in length, the head and body up to 9 cm, and the tail about 7 cm long. It weighs only 20 g.

NARROW-NOSED PLANIGALE
Planigale tenuirostris

LOCATION
Outback NSW, Queensland and northern South Australia, but they are not found in Western Australia.

HABITAT
This animal is often found in grassy areas and where dry soils have been opened up with deep cracks caused by drought.

active on winter days, often looking for a nice warm place to bask in the sun.

ENVIRONMENTAL NOTES
Status It is not a common species, and does not occur in large numbers anywhere, but you may still be lucky enough to spot one on a warm winter's day as it soaks up the sun.
Feeding habits The planigale is a savage hunter and would be a very fearsome animal if it were any larger. It can eat its own weight in food in a day, and obtains all the moisture it needs while doing it. It attacks insects that are as large as it is (which is not very large) and then crunches them into submission with strong jaws. Often it will eat its food while sitting up, holding it in its front paws, like a child eating a giant icecream.
Predators As for the fat-tailed dunnart (see above).
Reproduction As for the fat-tailed dunnart.

IDENTIFICATION
Colour Rusty brown fur with a grey face.
Size It is mouse-like in size and shape, and is less than 13 cm from tip of nose to end of tail, weighing less than 9 g.
Distinguishing features You will be helped to identify it by the sharply pointed face. If you were to see a narrow-nosed planigale in the day, it would be most probably in wintertime, as it is more

HAIRY-NOSED WOMBAT
Lasiorhinus latifrons and *Lasiorhinus krefftii*

LOCATION
The two species of hairy-nosed wombat are separated by some distance, with *Lasiorhinus latifrons* occurring in a tiny area of Queensland, and the *Lasiorhinus krefftii* in southern South Australia and Western Australia.

HABITAT
For both species, arid grassland has now become their typical habitat. If you are travelling in the remote areas south of the Nullarbor plains you may see one of these large, lovable animals late in the evening or early in the morning. During the hot daylight hours they remain below ground in huge, cool and humid burrow systems, thus limiting the loss of water from their bodies.

SCRUBLAND AND SHRUBLAND

> **Wombat Tunnels Are Big**
> Wombats build huge complexes of interconnecting tunnels. They are so large that a school boy in Victoria studied wombats by crawling into the tunnel complex!

IDENTIFICATION
Colour Soft grey fur, shading to fawn.
Size The wombat is a large animal, being up to 1 m in length and weighing more than 30 kg.
Distinguishing features Its short-legged, waddling walk is unmistakable, as it proceeds like a small, furry, living army tank from one point to another. The hairy nosed wombat has a squatter, rounder face than the common wombat *(Vombatus ursinus)*, and softer grey fur.

ENVIRONMENTAL NOTES
Status Hairy-nosed wombats are rare and endangered. It is believed that the northern hairy-nosed wombat, *Lasiorhinus latifrons*, is threatened because it is unable to compete with grazing animals such as sheep and cattle. It is the rarer of the two species.
Feeding habits It grazes on a wide variety of plant material.
Predators Small wombats would be taken by dingos, wild dogs and birds of prey, but a fully grown wombat is too formidable.
Reproduction The female has a backward opening pouch, the current theory being that this is to stop it filling with dirt when she is tunnelling. The single baby is born in spring or summer, and remains in the pouch for about 9 months.

YELLOW-FOOTED ROCK-WALLABY
Petrogale xanthopus

LOCATION
A very small area of central Queensland, western NSW and eastern South Australia.

HABITAT
You will only find this shy, small wallaby amongst the ledges and caves of places like the Flinders Ranges in South Australia.

IDENTIFICATION
Colour Up close it is a beautiful animal, with soft brownish-grey fur on its back, creamy white underneath, a white flash under its forearm and on its hip, fawn front legs and back legs, and a fawn tail with bold black stripes.
Size Head and body length: up to 65 cm. Tail length: up to 70 cm.
Distinguishing features Visitors to the yellow-footed rock-wallaby habitat areas in the ranges of South Australia may well glimpse this beautiful and elusive animal,

particularly if they are with a guide with good local knowledge.

ENVIRONMENTAL NOTES
Status The yellow-footed rock-wallaby has been hunted almost to extinction because of the colour qualities of its skin. It also has to battle with drought, and the destruction of its habitat, along with predation by foxes. Feral goats now compete directly with the rock-wallaby for food and water. It is wonderfully adapted to its rough rocky home but its very specific adaptations may make it even more endangered. It is tied to the permanent waterholes that are filled after the very rare rainfalls that occur in its habitat areas.
Feeding habits Dryland grasses, herbs and shrubs are eaten.
Predators Foxes, dingos, wild dogs and large birds of prey, like the wedge-tailed eagle, all prey on the wallaby.
Reproduction The breeding cycle is similar to all members of the kangaroo and wallaby group, in that the young makes its way to the pouch in an undeveloped state and remains there for some time.

COMMON WALLAROO
Macropus robustus

LOCATION
Throughout the outback, with the exception of parts of the tropical north, and all of Victoria and southern Western Australia.

HABITAT
The rocky hills and slopes of the outback. Being largely a solitary animal living away from centres of population, the wallaby is less likely to be seen by the 'main road' traveller. The camper or bushwalker who moves up into the outback hills in the late evening or early morning will be rewarded by finding the wallaroo, as it is then moving back from its night-time feeding to its daytime shelters. Because the location in which it lives is the hottest part of the outback, it seeks shelter in caves and under overhanging rocks during the day.

IDENTIFICATION
Colour Dark grey to greyish-brown.
Size Head and body length — male: up to 1.1 m; female: up to 0.8 m. Tail length — male: up to 0.9 m; female: up to 0.8 m. Weight — male: up to 47 kg; female: up to 25 kg.
Distinguishing features At first glance, it is often difficult to tell the difference between the red kangaroo and the wallaroo. The location will help, as the wallaroo is more likely to be seen sheltering in or near rocky outcrops. A better guide is that you will see the wallaroo on its own, while other kangaroos tend to be in family groups or large mobs.

ENVIRONMENTAL NOTES
Status The wallaroo is quite numerous

SCRUBLAND AND SHRUBLAND

throughout the outback and, in certain locations, you can find large numbers sheltering in the rocky hills and valleys. However, its population varies greatly, depending upon local rainfall and competition for the very limited grazing.
Feeding habits Dryland grasses and shrubs are eaten. It shelters in the shade during the day to conserve essential moisture obtained from its food.
Predators Dingos and large birds of prey kill and eat even the adult.
Reproduction As for the western grey kangaroo (see page 16).

WESTERN PYGMY-POSSUM
Cercartetus concinnus

LOCATION
Western Victoria, southern South Australia and southern Western Australia.

HABITAT
Scrubby areas that have a good proportion of flowering plants, such as paperbarks (melaleucas), spider-flowers (grevilleas) and banksias. The most likely people to find the western pygmy-possum are the quiet night-time walkers moving among the low flowering shrubs, occasionally shining a bright light on likely flower heads. Unless it is deliberately taken out of its nest and awakened, it is unlikely you would see one in daylight hours.

IDENTIFICATION
Colour A soft fawn to a ginger colour on top, and lighter below.
Size As its name indicates, the pygmy-possum is tiny, its total length being less than 20 cm and its weight less than 20 g.
Distinguishing features It is mouse-like, but more appealing, with big ears and large bright eyes. It also has a prehensile tail that grips onto tiny branches. It is a favourite subject for wildlife films, as it performs acrobatics amongst the brilliant red and paintbox yellows of Western Australian wildflowers.

ENVIRONMENTAL NOTES
Status As the pygmy-possum is tiny and nocturnal, it is not often seen. However, it is quite numerous within its limited location, and as a species appears to be able to survive the predation of cats and foxes by its ability to breed rapidly.
Feeding habits It eats pollen and insects.
Predators The biggest danger comes from feral and domestic cats, as this tiny possum is easy prey.
Reproduction It builds a tiny leaf nest in which it curls up during the day, and the tiny young are left in this nest. The young leave the nest after about 25 days. The female is able to have several litters in quick succession, each one having up to 6 babies. She is able to mate soon after a litter is born, and as soon as she is free of the litter in the pouch, the next lot develops and is born.

PLAINS RAT
Pseudomys australis

Size It is a small rodent, only 25 cm from tip of nose to tip of tail, with the body a little longer than the tail, and ears more than 2 cm long.

Distinguishing features If you happen to be walking or driving in the rather limited range of the plains rat, you would recognise it by two main features: the huge expanse of its burrow system and its beautiful fur. The burrow system can be enormous, a scientific study showing one lot of inter-connected burrows extending more than 40 kilometres.

LOCATION
Southeastern Queensland, northern South Australia, eastern Western Australia.

HABITAT
The arid interior of southern and central Australia. The plains rat digs its burrows directly into the hard-packed soil or amongst the piles of windblown soil under shrubs.

IDENTIFICATION
Colour Its general colour is a soft, shiny grey-brown.

ENVIRONMENTAL NOTES
Status The numbers appear to be dwindling, but it can appear in some years in plague proportions, when a combination of mild seasons and good rains coincide.
Feeding habits Some insects are eaten, but it mainly exists on seeds.
Predators Foxes, cats, owls and other birds of prey take many plains rats.
Reproduction The plains rat is a rodent, so it does not have a pouch. It is thought that in the wild the young are only born after rain. Up to 7 can be in a litter.

MITCHELL'S HOPPING-MOUSE
Notomys mitchelli

LOCATION
Restricted to a small area of western Victoria, southwestern NSW, southern South Australia and eastern Western Australia.

HABITAT
A fringe desert dweller, dependent upon some water to survive, and thus restricted from the true desert. The most likely sighting of a hopping-mouse you would have in the daytime would come about by disturbance of its deep burrows, although it is reported to sometimes be found in surface nests.

IDENTIFICATION
Colour It is light greyish-brown above

SCRUBLAND AND SHRUBLAND

and lighter below.
Size Body length: up to 13 cm; tail: up to 16 cm; weight: up to 60 g.
Distinguishing features The hopping-mouse is superficially like a house mouse, but with larger eyes and ears, and the long tail is tufted at the end. The tail is longer than its body, and the legs are very well adapted for a hopping gait. Its large dark eyes are the true indicators of its nocturnal habits, and the savage temperatures of its limited range would restrict life on the surface.

ENVIRONMENTAL NOTES
Status Uncommon to rare, but not yet threatened as a species.
Feeding habits Its night-time forays are in search of seeds, green plants and insects.
Predator Feral cats, foxes and birds of prey all take the hopping-mouse.
Reproduction The hopping-mouse is not a marsupial, it is a placental mammal, belonging to the group collectively called rodents. Up to 5 young are born and live in a nest in a burrow.

Hopping-mice in Other Countries

In other countries of the world where similar harsh climatic conditions occur, animals that look remarkably similar to the Mitchell's hopping-mouse are to be found. The animals are not related, but have evolved many of the same bodily structures and behaviour patterns that allow the Australian hopping-mouse to cope with its environment.

DINGO
Canis familiaris

LOCATION
Scattered populations throughout all of non-urban Australia.

HABITAT
Widely varied, from rugged and wet forest country to the dry central desert.

IDENTIFICATION
Colour The colour varies, but a 'characteristic' colour is yellow-orange.
Size Head and body length — male: up to 98 cm; female: up to 89 cm. Tail length — male and female: up to 38 cm. Weight — male: up to 19 kg; female: up to 16 kg.
Distinguishing features The dingo is very similar in all aspects to the domestic dog, with which it can breed. You will notice that the dingo has a heavier head than most domestic breeds, looking

something like a cross between a golden labrador and a german shepherd.

ENVIRONMENTAL NOTES
Status Scientists believe that the dingo was introduced to Australia by the Aborigines at some time in the last 5000 years. It has established itself well, and it is the largest land-based predator on the Australian mainland.

The concept of the conservation of the dingo causes arguments on a regular basis. Dispute continues concerning whether it is a 'natural' part of the Australian environment, or a recent introduction that threatens native species, and controversy will continue for years about the stock losses it may or may not cause.

Availability of water plays a part in its ability to populate an area.

Feeding habits It feeds upon a wide variety of animals, from wombats to kangaroos, lizards to young emus, and will also kill domestic stock, such as sheep and young cattle. It also preys on rabbits, but the dingo population would have to increase many-fold to have a long-term effect on the rabbit population.

Predators It is at the top of its food chain and is not preyed upon.

Reproduction The dingo finds a hidden and sheltered spot to give birth to its pups, up to 8 being in a litter, although only a small number of those would survive to breed.

CAMEL
Camelus dromedarius

LOCATION
The shrubby, arid heart of mainland Australia.

HABITAT
The dry centre of the continent, in areas where there is a wide range of plants suitable for food.

IDENTIFICATION
Colour Dirty brown to sandy brown,
Size Head and body length: up to 3.5 m. Weight: up to 700 kg.
Distinguishing features You will have no trouble identifying the camel of central Australia as it is the same camel of the zoo and circus.

ENVIRONMENTAL NOTES
Status Australia is the only country in the world to have feral camels, and estimations of their numbers vary from 30 000 to 100 000.

The camel was brought to Australia in the last half of the 19th century as a beast of burden. It carried supplies to remote stations (farms) and provided the vital link between towns in the arid centre. Then, early in the 20th century it was replaced by the railroad and a road system that allowed motor vehicles to move more easily through the outback. No longer wanted, many were left to run wild, and the modern herds have come from those released animals. There has been concern that the camel is damaging the fragile environment that it lives in, particularly by its grazing. It is obvious that it directly competes with native animals for the very scarce supplies of water. However, studies by two German scientists show that the camel eats such a wide range of plants that it may have little impact on particular species. Only time will tell the true scale of damage that can be directly blamed on the camel.

Feeding habits It is a very large animal and requires a high intake of plant material, eating a wide range of species.
Predators None.
Reproduction The male rounds up a harem of females and then spends much time and energy driving off other males. Gestation takes over a year and the baby is about 40 kg at birth.

DONKEY
Equus asinus

LOCATION
Western Queensland, central and northern South Australia, the Northern Territory and scattered locations in Western Australia.

HABITAT
The desert fringes and arid areas of central Australia. Because both water and grazing are in short supply in dry times, large mobs tend to congregate around waterholes and food supplies.

IDENTIFICATION
Colour Dark grey, with a white belly and white nose.
Size Up to 140 cm at the shoulder, weighing up to 350 kg.
Distinguishing features The wild or feral donkey is basically no different in appearance from the domestic donkey.

ENVIRONMENTAL NOTES
Status Like the wild horse, the donkey was an escapee from domesticity. The donkey is well adapted to the arid centre of Australia, as it was domesticated many centuries ago from species that were native to the North African arid lands.

With a population estimated to be well over one million, the hard-hoofed grazing donkey is damaging the fragile ecosystem of the arid areas. Plants that are adapted to contending with droughts and searing temperatures are not able to cope with being cropped by the hungry donkey. The concentration of large numbers in a small area increases the damage. Control of the donkey population may be even more difficult than that of the horse, as there does not seem to be such a demand for redomestication. Someone, somewhere, may have to make the unpalatable decision that a drastic eradication program is the only solution.

Feeding habits It feeds on a wide range of dryland plants.
Predators It is possible that dingos and wild dogs take young donkeys, but I have never seen it recorded.
Reproduction As for the domestic donkey.

MAMMALS

FERAL GOAT
Capra hircus

LOCATION
Western NSW and Queensland, eastern South Australia, western Western Australia.

HABITAT
Rocky ridges, caves, rock overhangs and bush thickets.

IDENTIFICATION
Colour Generally brindled, a mixture of white, black and dark brown.
Size Head and body length — male: up to 162 cm; female: up to 147 cm. Tail length: about 17 cm for both male and female. Weight — male: up to 63 kg; female: up to 49 kg.
Distinguishing features The feral goat has the same appearance as the domestic goat, the stock that it came from. The only noticeable difference you will see is the wide variety of colours, shapes and wool covering. Some will be white and short-haired, others will be brindled tan, black and white with long hair, and there will be every mixture in between.

ENVIRONMENTAL NOTES
Status The goat was brought from England with the First Fleet in 1788, and it is certain that some escaped. Pioneer settlers used the goat for milk and meat, as it was easier to keep than a cow. At various times in Australia's history the goat was seen as a better way of making money than sheep, and when these schemes failed, goats were left to run wild. The results are the herds scattered throughout arid Australia, estimated to number in total over 500 000, but no-one knows the true numbers.

The goat is incredibly destructive, particularly in a fragile ecosystem like the Australian outback. It selectively grazes the plants it likes, tramples the ground with its sharp hooves, and drives native animals from its habitat by taking their caves and rock overhangs. It also takes the precious reserves of water that sustain animals like wallaroos and rock wallabies.

Another frightening aspect is the likelihood that an escaped goat may be the carrier of exotic diseases like foot-and-mouth disease. Any disease that got into the wild herds could not be controlled, and would get into domestic sheep and cattle. The result would be devastating.

Feeding habits Surprisingly, it does not like lush pasture grasses, but prefers the tough grasses and shrubs of the arid lands. This is one reason why it does so much damage to the fragile ecosystem.
Predators Dingos, dogs, foxes and eagles take young goats.
Reproduction As for the domestic goat.

Birds

DIAMOND DOVE
Geopelia cuneata

LOCATION
The majority of mainland Australia, with the exception of the east coast, the tropical north and southwestern Western Australia.

SCRUBLAND AND SHRUBLAND

HABITAT
Always linked to the availability of water, but able to survive well in arid zones that have some tree cover. At any suitable watering place you can see a very large pre-dawn gathering of diamond doves. They sit in trees and shrubs around the water's edge until first light, and then move down to drink. During the heat of the day the doves will move into the shade of trees to roost and rest. In cooler weather they will often find patches of dust in a sunny spot and have a vigorous dust bath to remove parasites and generally clean their feathers.

IDENTIFICATION
Colour It has the softest grey colouring and bright eyes rimmed with red. The wings are speckled with white, giving the origin of its common name.
Size Up to 22 cm long.
Distinguishing features It is little wonder that the dove has been used as a symbol of peace when you see the diamond dove. It is a calm and gentle-looking bird. Its soft cooing call also exactly fits its peaceful image.

ENVIRONMENTAL NOTES
Status Common to very common, but it prefers areas away from people.
Feeding habits The diamond dove usually feeds on seeds on or near the ground, and flies with a rapid whirring flight if disturbed, which can be startling if you do not notice it before it flies. The dove does not need to lift its head to drink — it is able to consume large amounts of water, and then move out quickly.
Predators Foxes and cats take many doves, mainly while they have their heads down, feeding. Cats also rob the nests. Falcons and hawks take birds on the wing.
Reproduction If you ever see a dove nesting you will wonder how it ever survives to the next generation. The nest is a very shaky platform of sticks on which sit 2 white eggs. It appears as if the slightest breeze would cause disaster.

MALLEEFOWL
Leipoa ocellata

LOCATION
Southern Australia, from western NSW to the southern third of Western Australia.

HABITAT
Predominantly the dry inland scrub country, including the mallee scrub that gave it the name.

IDENTIFICATION
Colour Beautifully marked and mottled with dark brown over a lighter brown, with splashes of chestnut and fawn.
Size Up to 61 cm long.
Distinguishing features You will find that this is a much larger bird than it appears from photographs — it is more

BIRDS

the size of a small turkey than a large hen. Its legs are relatively short but powerful looking. Away from its normal shadowy habitat, the bold brown marks on its upper wings stand out clearly.

During the hottest part of the day the bird lies in the shade, camouflaged by the dappling of the leaves.

ENVIRONMENTAL NOTES
Status Malleefowl numbers have been in decline for many years, not only through the clearing of the mallee for farming but also by predation by foxes.
Feeding habits It feeds on plant food such as fruits and seeds, as well as insects.
Predators Foxes.
Reproduction The malleefowl is one of a group of mound-building birds that construct huge piles of twigs, leaves and soil as incubators for their eggs. It can sometimes be seen standing on the top of its mound, almost motionless except for the occasional scratching of a powerful foot. The construction of the mound requires many hours of work and then constant attention once the eggs are laid in it. The male has biological and behavioural mechanisms that allow him to determine and regulate the correct temperature of the mound, thus ensuring that the heat incubates the eggs.

AUSTRALIAN BUSTARD
Ardeotis australis

LOCATION
Western Australia, western South Australia, Northern Territory, western Queensland, with scattered populations in NSW and Victoria.

HABITAT
It is a true bird of the outback, being almost unknown near any centres of population. Open country, often with sparse, dry grass cover and scattered trees.

SCRUBLAND AND SHRUBLAND

Also crop areas where hunting or predation has not reduced the population. Usually seen standing amongst or near grass tussocks.

IDENTIFICATION
Colour Its overall colour is mid-brown with a white neck and chest.
Size Up to 1.5 m long, with a wingspan of up to 2.1 m.
Distinguishing features Once you have seen a bustard you will not forget it. It is a tall bird, and it may stand perfectly still for some time, its head held high, with the bill held pointing slightly upward.

ENVIRONMENTAL NOTES
Status The bustard has been the victim of indiscriminate hunting throughout European settlement in Australia. It is now gone from large areas of NSW and Victoria, where it was once reasonably plentiful. Bird counts carried out over the last decade indicate that numbers are increasing in some areas, particularly in Queensland. It is to be hoped that this is a trend Australia-wide.
Feeding habits Small animals, such as insects, particularly grasshoppers, and some plant material.
Predators Its first response to danger is to freeze. If pursued, it will run and then take flight. The young bird squats down when danger occurs, hoping its colouring will hide it. This is not a good defence against one of its main predators, the fox.
Reproduction One or 2 brownish-green eggs, 78 mm long, are laid on the bare ground, sometimes near a grass tussock.

BUDGERIGAR
Melopsittacus undulatus

LOCATION
The inland of Australia in all states.

HABITAT
A wide range, from arid grassland and saltbush to scattered woodlands along watercourses. Budgerigar existence is tied to water and huge flocks gather at waterholes during times of drought. There is a great deal of luck in seeing flocks of budgerigars. Often the population will be in small flocks, hiding away from the heat of the day in trees and shrubs, completely camouflaged from the casual observer. Then it can happen that you will be in an area where flocks of thousands of the birds are coming in at dusk to drink at an isolated waterhole.

IDENTIFICATION
Colour In the wild it is beautifully camouflaged with light yellow-green underneath, and thin black stripes over green on the back. Up close, you may be able to see patches of blue on the cheeks and tail.

Size Up to 20 cm long.
Distinguishing features The budgerigar of the wild is identical in shape and size to the caged 'lovebird', but its colouring is consistent with that noted above. Multicoloured budgerigars in cages are the result of selective breeding.

The budgerigar is truly a bird of the outback, which makes it even more remarkable that it has been able to adapt to the role of being the caged 'lovebird' familiar to everyone.

ENVIRONMENTAL NOTES
Status Although it is probably the most popular caged bird in Australia, and one of the most numerous of the parrot family in the wild, the budgerigar is not always easy to find in the outback. The flocks move and disperse as the arid land that is their home has times of plentiful seed and water, followed by hard times.
Feeding habits Seeds of a wide variety of growing plants are eaten.
Predators Flocking gives a measure of protection to the species, but many budgerigars are taken by birds of prey and cats.
Reproduction Four to 6 white eggs are laid in the hollow of a tree, the bottom of the hollow being lined with woodchips and wood dust.

SPOTTED NIGHTJAR
Caprimulgus guttatus

It spends its day sitting on the ground in the most unlikely places, and it is possible you may literally stumble on one as it is so well camouflaged that spotting it is difficult. Incredibly, it is able to tolerate the direct heat of the inland sun beating down on it as it sits in its roosting spot.

IDENTIFICATION
Colour When it is not flying its general colour is mottled dark greyish-brown, matching beautifully the red soil, pebbles, leaves and twigs amongst which it sits.
Size Up to 33 cm long.
Distinguishing features It is a nocturnal bird, beginning its hunting at dusk and taking flying insects on the wing. What you will see is a medium-sized, dark-looking bird whose eyes flash startling ruby-red in the headlights, and whose wings flash white as it flies. Often it will fly for some distance along in front of the car, as if using the headlights as a guide.

LOCATION
Scattered over mainland Australia, with the exception of the east and south coast.

HABITAT
Woodland, dry eucalypt forest, and scrubby rock and sand plains. The most likely place for you to see the spotted nightjar is as you drive along country roads at night.

SCRUBLAND AND SHRUBLAND

ENVIRONMENTAL NOTES
Status Uncommon but not rare.
Feeding habits It feeds on insects.
Predators Like all ground-dwelling birds, it is taken by foxes and cats.
Reproduction One creamy-green and camouflaged egg is laid on the ground in leaf-litter.

MALLEE RINGNECK
Barnardius barnardi

LOCATION
Western NSW, eastern South Australia and southwest Queensland.

HABITAT
As its name suggests, it lives amongst the stunted eucalypt trees called mallee, but also along watercourses and in lightly timbered areas.

IDENTIFICATION
Colour Its main colours are bright green and light blue on the front with darker blues and greens on the back. The name 'ringneck' comes from a band of yellow around the back of the neck, with a dark patch above it.
Size Up to 36 cm long.
Distinguishing features You will most likely first see the mallee ringneck in small groups as it crosses the road, or a path where you are walking, its colours flashing. It has a dipping, swooping flight that quickly takes it into cover.

ENVIRONMENTAL NOTES
Status The mallee ringneck is fairly common throughout its range.
Feeding habits It is a dawn feeder in the hot parts of the year, and you will find it feeding on the fruit of bushes like emu bush. It will sometimes be in groups of up to a dozen, quietly and busily feeding close to the ground. It also feeds on a wide variety of other plants, as well as insects. Sometimes it can be seen eating the seeds of wild melons after the melons have been smashed, or dried and split open.
Predators Birds of prey, such as falcons and hawks.
Reproduction It uses a hollow in a eucalypt as a nest and lays 4 to 6 white eggs in it.

RAINBOW BEE-EATER
Merops ornatus

LOCATION
Throughout Australia, with the exception of the southeast and southwest coasts.

HABITAT
Open country, from pasture lands to desert fringes.

BIRDS

IDENTIFICATION
Colour Its back is many-hued, the most noticeable colour being green-yellow. It has a bright-yellow upper throat, with a collar of dark brown.
Size Up to 28 cm long.
Distinguishing features The rainbow part of its name gives you some clue to the colouration of this small, bright bird. It is slim and upright, with a long thin bill similar to the family of honeyeaters.

ENVIRONMENTAL NOTES
Status Common to very common, as the bee-eater is a migratory bird and moves through some outback areas in large flocks during its migration. It moves from the south in autumn, to northern Australia for the winter, some continuing on as far north as the Solomon Islands.
Feeding habits Its name, 'bee-eater', gives you the clue to much of its behaviour and its feeding habits. It is not the friend of the apiarist, as each bird is capable of eating several bees a day. It also eats other flying insects, such as dragonflies and wasps, all of which it catches on the wing.
Predators Birds of prey, such as falcons and hawks.
Reproduction During the spring breeding season the birds burrow into sandy banks and construct a nest chamber. Four to 5 white eggs are laid in the nest. In some parts of NSW the birds may congregate in nesting colonies.

BOURKE'S PARROT
Neophema bourkii

LOCATION
Central Australia.

HABITAT
Scrubland in the arid area, particularly mulga and mallee.

IDENTIFICATION
Colour It has a pastel grey-pink underside and bright blue front to the sides of its wings. The rest of its body is brownish,

171

allowing it to 'disappear' when it keeps still.
Size Up to 23 cm long.
Distinguishing features The best time to see it seems to be just after dawn, before it hides away to escape the savage heat of the day.

Once you have found where it feeds it is an ideal subject for photography, as it will return to the same feeding area until the seeds are exhausted. It is relatively tame, and will let you approach to within about 10 m before flying away a short distance. It does not travel in big flocks or make a lot of noise, but the occasional flash of blue and pink as it flies lets you know it is there.

ENVIRONMENTAL NOTES
Status Bourke's parrot is not very common, although some areas in its range show high populations.
Feeding habits In parts of its range it can often be seen feeding on the seeds of *Cassia* species, moving in small groups close to the ground.
Predators As for other parrots (see page 119).
Reproduction Three to 6 white eggs are laid in a tree hollow near the ground.

BROWN SONGLARK
Cinclorhampus cruralis

LOCATION
All of mainland Australia, with the exception of the tropical north.

HABITAT
Pasture land, saltbush country and other low vegetation, and grasslands. The brown songlark is often seen sitting on the top of scrubby bushes only a metre or two from the ground. The habitat in which it lives provides large areas of open space under bushes and shrubs, and it is here where it hunts for its insect food. In pasture land, where growth is lush, it will often avoid the thickest grasses to feed among the coarser tussocks and roost on the scattered 'roly-poly' bushes.

IDENTIFICATION
Colour Generally drab-brown in colour, with dark and light-brown markings on the head.
Size The male is 26 cm long; the female 19 cm long.
Distinguishing features There are no major distinguishing marks that you can see, but the bird characteristically keeps its tail in a 'half-cocked' position, holding it out and up above the horizontal. Its breeding behaviour will help to identify it, as it flies slowly into the air, singing as it goes, to slowly descend, like a softly falling feathered parachute. Its song has been described variously as guttural, musical, metallic and mechanical. Outside of the breeding season you will be lucky to see the brown songlark, as it is very secretive in its behaviour.

ENVIRONMENTAL NOTES

Status Clearing of timber and scrubland to create open grassland for stock has benefited the brown songlark by providing more of its preferred habitat.
Feeding habits It feeds on insects and seeds.
Predators As noted before, all birds that feed on or near the ground are easy prey for cats.
Reproduction It builds a deep cup of grass in amongst tussocks in which are laid 3 or 4 orange-pink eggs, speckled with red.

WHITE-BROWED BABBLER
Pomatostomus superciliosus

LOCATION
Southern inland mainland Australia.

HABITAT
Scattered timber, scrublands and mallee of the dry interior. To find the white-browed babbler simply walk quietly through the dry scrubland and scattered timber that is its preferred habitat. If you come across a noisy group of small, grey birds feeding on the ground you have found your quarry.

IDENTIFICATION
Colour Generally dull grey-brown, with some lighter markings on the throat and around the face.
Size Up to 22 cm long.
Distinguishing features The babbler is an incredibly busy, noisy bird that spends a great deal of its time in argumentative groups, foraging over the ground, looking for insects. Its behaviour is the key to its identification, and you will see it moving busily along the ground or in the lower branches of scrubby bushes, chattering away all the time. It is obviously this last characteristic that gives it its common name.

If you come close enough to a group to alarm them they will give a sudden harsh cry and clumsily fly a short distance to sit motionless and wait until the danger has passed. They will then return to the business of turning over leaves, twigs and small rocks, looking for insects.

ENVIRONMENTAL NOTES
Status Very common in its preferred habitats.
Feeding habits It feeds on insects and seeds.
Predators Because of its noisy, flocking behaviour, the babbler is less prone to predation than many ground-feeding and nesting birds.
Reproduction During the nesting time a whole family group will build the nest and feed the young. The nests are built in scrubby bushes about 2 m from the ground. Two to 6 fawn-brown to dark-brown eggs with dark scribbly marks are laid.

SCRUBLAND AND SHRUBLAND

RED-BACKED KINGFISHER
Halcyon pyrrhopygia

Size Up to 24 cm long. The red-backed kingfisher is a small member of the kingfisher family, being approximately half the size of the biggest and best-known kingfisher, the laughing kookaburra.
Distinguishing features It can be distinguished by its slim shape, and a long sharp bill that is outsize for its body.

ENVIRONMENTAL NOTES
Status This species of kingfisher is most unusual in that its life is not tied to ready access to water. It is able to live on the water contained in the bodies of its prey.

While it is not common anywhere in its range you might see one sitting motionless on a bare branch or electric light pole, waiting for a small animal to move below.
Feeding habits It eats reptiles, insects and small mammals.
Predators The nest is also preyed upon by dingos and foxes.
Reproduction The red-backed kingfisher often excavates a nesting tunnel in the banks of a dry creekbed. Four or 5 white eggs are laid in the nest. On those rare occasions when it rains in the arid outback, its nest can be flooded or collapsed by the rising creek.

LOCATION
All of inland Australia with the exception of southwestern Western Australia.

HABITAT
The dry scrub and foothills of arid Australia, often far from water.

IDENTIFICATION
Colour As its name suggests, the red-backed kingfisher has orange-red colouring on the rump immediately above the tail. The other predominant colour is the soft, powdery blue of the outer wings.

ZEBRA FINCH
Poephila guttata

LOCATION
In scattered locations almost throughout Australia, with the exception of some of the southeastern and southwestern coastal areas, and the Cape York Peninsula.

HABITAT
Once a common bird in a huge range of grasslands and open woodland. Still common in many outback areas where it has ready access to water, food plants and

shrubs and small trees for nest-building. It is common around permanent waterholes, coming to drink several times a day when the weather is hot.

IDENTIFICATION
Colour The male has white-speckled fawn colouring in front of the wing, a striped throat with a narrow black bib, a fawn-orange face and a bright orange bill. The female is a drab fawn-grey but she has a bright-orange bill.
Size Up to 10 cm long.
Distinguishing features The zebra finch is a very popular cage bird because of its bright, chirpy behaviour and its beautifully patterned colouring. It is a small bird, and the male is the one with all the beauty.

In its wild state the zebra finch is a fascinatingly busy little bird. You will soon learn to recognise its thin, piping call and this will lead you to flocks of this bird feeding busily on the seedheads of a wide variety of plants.

ENVIRONMENTAL NOTES
Status The zebra finch was once very common around major centres of population. There was a huge decline in population in the 1950s due to the widespread use of DDT as a controller of insect pests. Another cause for decline was the trapping of finches for sale as cage birds.
Feeding habits It feeds mainly on a wide variety of seeds, although occasionally it will take insects.
Predators Finches of all sorts are easy prey for cats, and I have found half the nests in a large nesting colony torn apart by them. The cats were recognised as the villains as they left their paw prints in the dust at the base of the shrubs. Goannas also take eggs and young.
Reproduction If you are observant as you drive along country roads you may see clumps of large, bottle-shaped grass nests in thickets along the side of the road. These could be the nests of the zebra finch, built out of the long, light stems of the grasses on which it feeds. It lays 3 to 7 tiny blue-white eggs.

CRIMSON CHAT
Ephthianura tricolor

LOCATION
Inland mainland Australia, from western NSW and Victoria to the Western Australian coast.

HABITAT
The crimson chat can be found in the low shrubs of the arid inland, particularly in the open areas.

IDENTIFICATION
Colour The male is a glowing red gem. He has a red cap and white throat, with a brilliant red belly. These colours are set off by a narrow black mask over the eyes and a black back with a red dab over the rump. The female is a fairly drab grey, with just tinges of pink where the male has bright red.
Size Up to 12 cm long.
Distinguishing features This bird is a blessing to the outback visitor. It is easy to recognise, although at a first quick glance you could confuse it with one of the red-breasted robins. It is about canary size, with the habit of scuttling along tracks and open areas in front of the observer.

If you happen to be in an area where you think the crimson chat may be found, look at dusty roads or animal pathways to see if you can find the tiny imprints of its footprints. Particularly look around plants that flower close to the ground, or where plants lean down to the ground.

ENVIRONMENTAL NOTES
Status Its life cycle and movement through its range is closely tied to the amount of water available, and large numbers will suddenly appear in usually arid areas that have had a good rainfall. It also appears to have some preference for the areas around saltpans and salt lakes.
Feeding habits It feeds on insects found on the ground, in the foliage or in the flowers of low bushes.
Predators Cats and goannas eat the chat, as do birds of prey such as falcons, kestrels and hawks.
Reproduction The deep, cup-shaped grass-and-twig nest is built close to the ground in grass or bushes, and 3 or 4 white speckled eggs are laid.

VARIEGATED WREN
Malurus lamberti

LOCATION
From coastal NSW to coastal Western Australia, but not southern Victoria and southern Western Australia.

HABITAT
From the damp verges of coastal eucalypt forest streams to the saltbush and spinifex plains of inland Australia.

IDENTIFICATION
Colour You will know this blue jewel by the russet orange-red of a saddle of colour across its wing. Only the breeding male is coloured in this way, all other members of the group in which it congregates being soft fawn-grey to blue.
Size Up to 14 cm long.
Distinguishing features Wrens in general

are tiny, lively, noisy colourful birds. There are several 'races' of this species of wren, and the colours show some variation depending whether you see it on the eastern slopes or the western plains. However, all of them have the russet patch somewhere on the upper body.

They move as pairs or small groups, keeping close to the ground, chattering and chittering as they go. They are constantly busy, whether flying up to take a flying insect on the wing, or turning over a leaf to catch a small spider.

When alarmed, a harsher sound is made, that draws the group close and into the protection of the thickest part of the undergrowth. When the danger has passed, the song returns to a thin, descending and ascending trill.

ENVIRONMENTAL NOTES
Status The variegated wren is fairly common throughout its range. The race that lives amongst the saltbush and spinifex of the outback shows the typical foraging behaviour of blue wrens everywhere.
Feeding habits It feeds on insects.
Predators Cats take many wrens.
Reproduction A small, domed nest with a low side entrance is made of grass, bark and other plant material, usually near the ground. In it are laid 3 or 4 whitish, lightly speckled eggs, only 15 mm long.

WHITE-WINGED FAIRY-WREN
Malurus leucopterus

LOCATION
Central inland Australia, not the tropical north nor the southwest of Western Australia.

HABITAT
The low scrubland of the drier inland, usually where trees are absent. It is truly at home in the densest parts of dryland thickets. It does not fly easily, but it moves with continuous leaps and bounds through the thin twigs and spiky branches of saltbush and spindly forms of melaleuca.

IDENTIFICATION
Colour Seen in the sunlight the blue colour of this tiny bird glistens like shimmering water, and the contrast of the white stripe on the wing is startling. The female is a drab fawn-grey above, with a lighter colouring underneath.
Size Up to 13 cm long.
Distinguishing features Unlike the friendly and curious blue wren that lives in suburban gardens, this blue-and-white bush gem is very shy. It will move into the densest parts of saltbush and spinifex at the slightest sign of danger, hiding its

flashing colours by keeping still.

Like most wrens, the white-winged fairy-wren is busy and noisy. The best way for you to find this elusive species is to listen for the reedy and soft trilling of its song, locate the thicket it is hiding in, and then sit quietly and wait.

ENVIRONMENTAL NOTES
Status This little wren is fairly common throughout its range.
Feeding habits The wren moves rapidly and constantly in its search for tiny animals such as ants and spiders.
Predators As for the variegated wren (see above).
Reproduction As for the variegated wren.

SINGING HONEYEATER
Lichenostomus virescens

also found in the coastal areas of Western Australia, and is sometimes seen feeding in the mangrove swamps of the west coast. In the drier, arid outback it tends to feed on the nectar blossoms of one thicket and fly quickly to another.

IDENTIFICATION
Colour It has a bold black mask across the eyes and ears. Under the mask is a bright stripe of yellow, and its underside is striped with fawn-brown patches over a lighter colour.
Size Up to 22 cm long.
Distinguishing features Look for a bird that is the typical honeyeater shape, being slim, with a neat narrow head and long bill. If you are up and about early in the morning you might be lucky to hear the singing for which it is named.

LOCATION
The inland of mainland Australia to the coast of Western Australia.

HABITAT
Isolated scrubs and thickets in the drier areas, but also gardens and orchards. It is not just a bird of the arid inland, as it is

ENVIRONMENTAL NOTES
Status The singing honeyeater may not be

the most numerous honeyeater in Australia but you will find it over the greatest range.
Feeding habits It feeds on a wide variety of plants that supply nectar and fruit, including the fruit of cultivated orchards. Like all honeyeaters, it also feeds on insects, and this species feeds occasionally on the eggs and young of small birds like the zebra finch.
Predators Birds of prey and cats take the honeyeater.
Reproduction A frail cup of grass is slung from branches less than 4 m from the ground. In it are laid 2 or 3 light-fawn-coloured speckled eggs.

WHITE-PLUMED HONEYEATER
Lichenostomus penicillatus

LOCATION
Throughout Victoria and inland Australia, and the mid-coast of Western Australia. Except for Victoria, it is not found on the coast of eastern, northern or southern Australia.

HABITAT
Tends to be tied to the availability of water, although in the desert areas it is not always near watercourses. In many parts of its range you are likely to find it among the trees associated with inland waterways, particularly the river red gum. It is also a common bird of parks and gardens.

IDENTIFICATION.
Colour It is very close to the size of a canary, but its overall colour is grey rather than yellow. Up close you will see the white flash across its neck that gave its common name. The colour does change with locality, and you may notice that birds in the central and western outback have more yellow to their feathers.
Size Up to 17 cm long.
Distinguishing features You might be helped in your spotting of the bird by the aerial acrobats it occasionally performs. The male will fly high from the top of a tree or thicket, give a call described as 'chickowee', and then plummet back into cover. It is never still, but flicks around on branches and darts from place to place. In large groups it can be very aggressive towards other species of birds, and will actively and noisily drive them away from a feeding area. Mobs will even attack an animal as large as a marauding goanna.

ENVIRONMENTAL NOTES
Status Common throughout its range and where there are suitable food plants.
Feeding habits It takes a wide range of food, from blackberries to insects, a factor which allows it to live in a wide range of habitats.
Predators Cats and goannas prey on honeyeater species.
Reproduction As for the singing honeyeater (see above), but the nest can be up to 25 m from the ground.

SCRUBLAND AND SHRUBLAND

Reptiles and Amphibians

WATER-HOLDING FROG
Cyclorana platycephalus

LOCATION
Southern central Australia, from west of the Great Dividing Range in NSW and Queensland, right across to the coast of Western Australia.

HABITAT
Close to areas such as claypans and temporary creeks, where water is retained after the infrequent outback rains.

IDENTIFICATION
Colour Its olive-green colour is broken up with patches of a lighter green and brown.
Size Up to 6 cm long.
Distinguishing features It is probable that you will only see this fat, round, medium-sized frog, after heavy rain. As the water left from the rain dries up, the frog burrows deep down into the soil, using its shovel-shaped feet, and forming a little 'room' under the ground. It works on the inside walls of the room so that they do not let water out, and thus it retains water in its own system. The outer layer of its skin is not shed but remains around the frog like a plastic bag. Here it stays until the next big rain, which may be years.

ENVIRONMENTAL NOTES
Status There are several species of water-holding frogs in the outback and it is fairly common throughout its range.
Feeding habits During the rainy spells the frog must gorge on whatever small animal food is available to carry it over the next dry period.
Predators While out of its underground chamber it is food for waterbirds, as well as other birds of prey. I can find no record of predators digging it out, probably because the frogs dig down to about 1 m below the ground.
Reproduction The frog breeds during the short period that pools of water lie on the ground. When it rains it comes out of the hole it has dug in the ground and goes to where water has collected to mate, and for the female to lay eggs.

BEADED GECKO
Lucasium damaeum

LOCATION
Western NSW and Victoria, South Australia, and southeastern Western Australia.

HABITAT
Shrubby woodland in the drier areas, and under tussocky grasses. It lives in burrows

REPTILES AND AMPHIBIANS

in the ground, either ones it has dug itself, or ones left by insects, such as ants.

IDENTIFICATION
Colour Unlike most of its relatives you will be able to recognise this gecko by its colour. It is not the uniform grey with splotches like so many geckos, it is rusty reddish-brown with a creamy-fawn stripe down its back.
Size Up to 10 cm long.
Distinguishing features It is slimmer than most geckos, with a relatively long tail, and looks more 'lizard-like'.

ENVIRONMENTAL NOTES
Status This gecko is common throughout its range.
Feeding habits It is a night-time feeder, hunting over the ground for insects and other small animals that are its food.
Predators Any small lizard is prey for night-time hunters, and birds of prey such as owls catch them as they forage over the ground at night.
Reproduction A single egg is laid in leaf litter or a suitable crevice or crack.

EASTERN SPINY-TAILED GECKO
Diplodactylus intermedius

LOCATION
Southeastern Western Australia, southern South Australia and southwestern NSW.

HABITAT
This gecko is mainly found in the arid and semi-arid zones of its range. It lives in trees, shrubs and tussocky plants.

IDENTIFICATION
Colour It is greyish in colour, but its

Spiny-tailed Geckos Can Spurt Poison

If you find an eastern spiny-tailed gecko, do not be tempted to pick it up. Apart from the damage you do to the lizard if you handle it, it can also cause you extreme discomfort. Some of the lizards of this group can spurt a thick liquid from spikes in their tail. If you were to get this into an open wound or into your eyes, it would be very unpleasant.

SCRUBLAND AND SHRUBLAND

darker markings will help you identify it. They are scattered over its body in a fairly random fashion, although they form darker curved waves of colour down the sides of the body.

Size Up to 11 cm long. This gecko is small, like most of its relatives.

Distinguishing features The name comes from the small spines along the top of the tail, and you might find that in some individuals, dark markings form a series of bands all along the tail.

ENVIRONMENTAL NOTES

Status Common throughout its range, but note that its range is restricted to the very arid areas.

Feeding habits It feeds on insects and other small invertebrates.

Predators Any small lizard can be prey for larger carnivorous lizards, but this group is protected by the capacity to spurt out a noxious substance.

Reproduction A single egg is laid in leaf litter or a suitable crevice or crack.

THORNY DEVIL
Moloch horridus

dabbed with patches of red and black. The colours will not necessarily be the same each time you find it, as it is able to change the colour pigment concentrations in its skin to suit its surrounding, like many reptiles and amphibians.

Size It is only a small lizard, about 15 cm long from nose to tip of tail.

Distinguishing features Once seen, it is not forgotten. It is patterned and spiked in a wonderful manner. The whole of its body, including the head, is covered with the most fearsome array of spikes.

LOCATION
South Australia, southern Northern Territory, and central Western Australia to the coast.

HABITAT
From shrubland to desert.

IDENTIFICATION
Colour Its general colour is dark tan, banded with broad areas of yellow and

ENVIRONMENTAL NOTES

Status The thorny devil is fairly common in central and western Australia.

Feeding habits The thorny devil is the arch enemy of ants, which constitute the greater part of its diet. Someone who had a lot of patience counted a thorny devil eating almost 2000 ants in 1½ hours.

Predators Its camouflage colours and spiky appearance would protect the thorny devil from most predators.

Reproduction It lays up to 8 eggs in a burrow in the ground.

GIDGEE SKINK
Egernia stokesii

IDENTIFICATION
Colour Olive-brown to reddish brown on top and paler underneath.
Size Up to 25 cm long from head to tail.
Distinguishing features A guide to recognising it is its very short tail that has raised scales looking like spikes along the last section. It has a short rounded head, short legs and, except for the spiky tail, it has something of the shape of other skinks like the blue-tongued lizard.

It leaves little piles of faeces amongst its rocky home, in areas that are too dry and rocky for other animals to live, which may assist you in determining if it is present.

ENVIRONMENTAL NOTES
Status By the very nature of the arid habitat in which it lives it is not terribly common.
Feeding habits It feeds on insects.
Predators The barren and rocky nature of its habitat, along with the capacity to duck into rock crevices if danger threatens, protects the gidgee skink from most predators.
Reproduction It lays its eggs around and under rocks.

LOCATION
Northwestern NSW, South Australia, southwestern Queensland, southern Western Australia.

HABITAT
You will see the gidgee skink living in the rock crevices and ledges of rocky outcrops. Its name is linked to the gidgee tree *(Acacia cambagei)*, as it lives in the same habitat.

COMMON SCALY-FOOT
Pygopus lepidopodus

LOCATION
Southeastern and southern mainland Australia.

HABITAT
Under and among low shrubby bushes.

IDENTIFICATION
Colour The common scaly-foot comes in a range of colours, from grey through green to brown, occasionally with a pattern of blotches.
Size Up to 65 cm long from head to tail.

SCRUBLAND AND SHRUBLAND

Distinguishing features The common scaly-foot is in a group known as 'legless lizards'. It is not completely legless, as it has two tiny legs underneath its body at the back. But as these cannot be seen, it is more snake-like than lizard-like in appearance. Snakes typically have flattened heads, while the scaly-foot's head is more rounded.

ENVIRONMENTAL NOTES
Status This is a common reptile in the southeastern part of its range.
Feeding habits It feeds on invertebrates such as insects and spiders, and other reptiles.
Predators The scaly-foot is prey for a range of daytime hunting birds, including kookaburras and hawks. It is taken by reptiles larger than itself.
Reproduction It lays 4 eggs in amongst the litter of the scrubland floor.

Insects

ANT-LION (LACEWING LARVA)
Family Myrmeleontidae

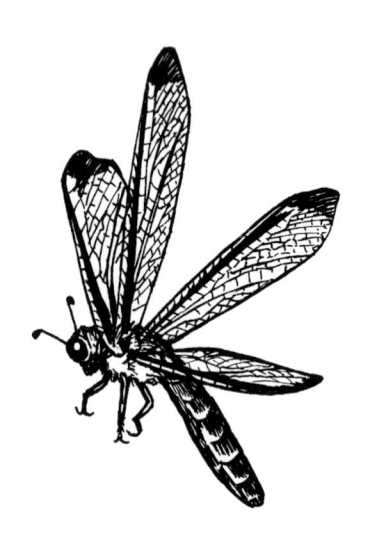

HABITAT
Dry, sandy soils in the open, or under rock overhangs and logs that protect the soil from direct falls of rain.

IDENTIFICATION
Size The larva is only a few millimetres long, living in a hole in the ground up to 5 cm across the rim.
Distinguishing features The ant-lion is the tiny larva of a fragile flying insect called a lacewing. The larva digs a tiny, beautifully sculpted, cone-shaped pit in dry soil and sand, and there can be many pits with larvae in a small area. At the bottom of the pit lurks the fierce-looking (under a microscope) larva. Not all ant-lion pits still contain a larva. If you wish to find whether anyone is at home, drop a tiny pebble, or twig, gently into the pit.

LOCATION
Throughout Australia.

INSECTS

If the ant-lion is still in residence it will eject the pebble out of the pit in one flick.

ENVIRONMENTAL NOTES
Status Very common.
Feeding habits It is equipped with a savage set of jaws. Any small insect, like an ant, that stumbles into a pit is trapped by the sloping, sliding walls of dry soil or sand. It slips down to the bottom of the pit where the hungry jaws of the ant-lion are waiting.
Predators Lizards relish the larvae, when they can get down to them.
Reproduction The lacewing lays individual eggs in dry soil.

Plants

BROAD-LEAF PARAKEELYA
Calandrinia balonensis

LOCATION
NSW, South Australia, Queensland, Northern Territory.

HABITAT
Soils that are a light mixture of sand and clay, on sand plains and sand dunes.

IDENTIFICATION
Colour It has soft, fleshy green foliage and reddish-purple flowers about 3 cm across.
Size The plant is only about 25 cm high but it may spread to cover a circular area of more than a metre.
Distinguishing features This group of plants is very similar to the 'pigfaces', a common plant grown in garden rockeries.

The way you recognise broad-leaf parakeelya immediately is by its clumpy appearance, the thick, bright-green leaves and the many purple flowers on short stems reaching up for the sun.

Parakeelya Stores Moisture

Plants that live in the arid outback have two main adaptations to survive the dry conditions. One is to have very dry, grey coloured leaves and stems, that contain and lose little moisture. The other is to store moisture in fleshy leaves, like parakeelya, and another fleshy outback plant called samphire (*Arthrocnemum* spp.)

ENVIRONMENTAL NOTES

Status This plant is common throughout its range. Its survival is helped by the fact that its fleshy leaves are a means of water storage. In very dry areas parakeelya is eaten by stock, and they do well on it. Parakeelya would be unable to survive sustained grazing.

Natural control agents Apart from the stock grazing, mentioned above, its fleshy leaves serve as a source of food and water for a range of insects.

Reproduction It flowers mainly in spring and the 1 mm wide seeds are held in a small capsule and locally dispersed to germinate.

YELLOW EVERLASTING
Helichrysum bracteatum

LOCATION
Throughout Australia.

HABITAT
It grows on a wide variety of soils, from sandy plains to rocky hillsides. In some areas it is very common amongst grey box woodland, and is often found in association with mallee.

IDENTIFICATION
Colour It has large, bright buttercup-yellow flowers, with russet orange centres, and the whole flower appears to glisten in the bright sun. The foliage is dark green.
Size Up to 80 cm tall.

Distinguishing features This is a flower that is commonly used for dried flower arrangements. It is one of a wide group called 'paper daisies' because of the papery appearance of the 'petals'. Like all of the daisies, the true flowers are in the mass in the centre, and the apparent petals are really modified leaves.

ENVIRONMENTAL NOTES
Status Very common from the better-watered areas through to the semi-arid portion of the outback.
Natural control agents Climatic conditions and leaf-eating insects.
Reproduction It flowers mainly in the spring to autumn and many tiny seeds are dispersed from the flower head.

PLANTS

JOCKEY'S CAP
Prostanthera striatiflora

purple stripes from the centre to the lip at the bottom.
Size The plant is up to 2 m tall and can be as wide across.
Distinguishing features The common name of this plant will lead you to identify the flowers first. The leaves are light green and lance-shaped, and they have a pleasant minty smell if crushed.

ENVIRONMENTAL NOTES
Status This plant is one of a very large group of the prostanthera or mint bushes. It grows in many different localities in Australia, but it is all characterised by the minty smell of the leaves. On the rocky slopes you are likely only to find scattered bushes.
Natural control agents The minty smell may serve as a deterrent to leaf-eating insects.
Reproduction It produces a mass of flowers in late winter to spring, to ensure that sufficient seed is produced to allow the growth of new plants in the harsh environment.

LOCATION
NSW, Queensland, South Australia, Western Australia, Northern Territory.

HABITAT
Rocky outcrops, ridges and hillsides. Mainly on shallow and rocky soils of hillsides, but also in red earth woodland areas.

IDENTIFICATION
Colour The flowers are white, bell-shaped, or like a jockey's cap if you have a good imagination, and have light-tan and

VELVET POTATO BUSH
Solanum ellipticum

LOCATION
NSW, Queensland, South Australia, Western Australia, Northern Territory.

HABITAT
A range of soils and vegetative types, from dry rocky hillsides to red sandy loam in scrubland and woodland.

IDENTIFICATION
Colour It has grey spreading stems and

oval-shaped leaves that are grey-blue. Like many of its relatives it has purple flowers with a yellow centre. It also bears a round greenish fruit, which is poisonous.
Size Up to 40 cm high. Fruit is about 2 cm in diameter.
Distinguishing features The flower and fruit are something of the shape and colouring of those grown on the cultivated potato.

ENVIRONMENTAL NOTES
Status The velvet potato bush is extremely dangerous to humans and livestock, very common, and therefore a pest.
Natural control agents The poisonous nature of the plant protects it from being eaten by insects or other animals.
Reproduction It flowers throughout the year and the seeds are carried in a fruit-like miniature green tomato.

Poisonous Solanum
This family of plants includes the cultivated potato, tomato, eggplant, capsicum and tobacco, but many of the plants in this family are very poisonous in the wild, including the deadly nightshades and wild tobaccos. Some of the wild species are used as food by the Aborigines who have knowledge of which plants to eat and which are dangerous.

STURT'S DESERT PEA
Clianthus formosus

plains to gibber covered ground. Often with scrubland plants like belah and mulga. Following a good winter rainfall, you may find scattered areas where the ground is carpeted with the red peaflower, particularly in those places where it is protected from grazing.

IDENTIFICATION
Colour The flower is a brilliant fire-engine red, shaped like a Disney cartoonist's flame devil, with a round, black knob in the centre.
Size This plant is a flat vine, growing up to 2 m wide.
Distinguishing features When Sturt's desert pea is in flower in winter and spring you will recognise it immediately. The bush it grows on is very unobtrusive, being a flat, sparse vine crawling along the ground, and you hardly notice it without the flowers.

LOCATION
NSW, South Australia, Western Australia, Northern Territory.

HABITAT
It can grow on a range of soils from sand

PLANTS

ENVIRONMENTAL NOTES
Status Depending on the season it may appear as scattered plants, or in thick clusters following winter rains. Sturt's desert pea is grown as a garden plant, but it takes an extremely clever gardener to duplicate the harsh soil and climate conditions of its natural environment. It is the floral emblem of South Australia.
Natural control agents Leaf-eating insects; sheep and farming have become unnatural control agents in some areas.
Reproduction The fruit is pod-shaped and contains many small seeds.

LOBED SPINIFEX
Triodia basedownii

Size It grows to about 45 cm high, and up to 1 m across the base of the tussock.
Distinguishing features Spinifex is a tussocky-shaped grass. You will recognise the older plants by the open centres left as they grow, creating a circular plant that can be up to 1 m across, and with little or nothing growing in the centre.

ENVIRONMENTAL NOTES
Status This is a common plant of the shrubland dune country, where very few other plants manage to keep a foothold. It is a dryland plant, adapted to long periods, often years, without rain.
One of its most important roles is as a home for small animals such as geckos and hopping mice. Some animal species are totally tied to the presence of spinifex and could not survive without it.
Natural control agents The climatic conditions are the major agents of control.
Reproduction The dry seeds are dispersed from the tall stems and carried or blown to a suitable site for germination.

LOCATION
Northwestern NSW, Queensland, South Australia, Western Australia, Northern Territory.

HABITAT
Sandy red earths or sand dunes.

IDENTIFICATION
Colour Straw-coloured to grey green.

FOXTAILS, PUSSY-TAILS AND RABBIT-TAILS
Ptilotus spp.

LOCATION
NSW, Queensland, Victoria, South Australia, Northern Territory.

HABITAT
Rocky ridges and slopes, as well as in sandy soils.

189

SCRUBLAND AND SHRUBLAND

IDENTIFICATION
Colour Varies according to the species, through purply white, to creamy-yellow, to yellowy-green.
Size Varies according to the species from 20 to 40 cm high. Some of the plants form bushes almost 1 m across and the flower heads vary in size from 2 cm to 22 cm.
Distinguishing features Foxtails, pussy-tails, rabbit-tails and long-tails all have a very similar appearance, with tufted heads on long stems.

The common characteristics to look for are reasonably long-stemmed plants, growing from a tuft in the centre. The flower heads look and feel like very soft fluffy bottlebrushes used to clean bottles.

ENVIRONMENTAL NOTES
Status The genus *Ptilotus* is very common throughout the semi-arid and arid zones.
Natural controls This wiry bush or scrubby grass is too tough for leaf-eating insects.
Reproduction It produces masses of tiny seeds.

SATINY BLUEBUSH
Maireana georgei

LOCATION
NSW, Western Australia, Queensland and South Australia in low rainfall areas.

HABITAT
Widely scattered through the scrubland and shrubland vegetation. Sands to sandy loams and also red earth.

IDENTIFICATION
Colour It has fleshy blue-grey leaves, yellow-orange flowers and reddish-yellow fruit.
Size It is a small shrub about 1 m high but often spreading over a wide area. The fruit is winged, and about 2 cm across.
Distinguishing features The bluebush

PLANTS

species has more than 50 representatives in Australia, and the satiny bluebush is fairly typical. When it is flowering and in fruit it will be easier for you to identify as it is very productive.

ENVIRONMENTAL NOTES
Status Bluebush species are common throughout the scrubland and shrubland.
Natural control agents The main controlling agent is climate.
Reproduction It may flower at any time of the year, but you are more likely to see it in the warmer months. Satiny bluebush produces so much seed that some of the older plants become broken down under the weight. This enables it to spread when conditions are ideal.

SPOTTED FUCHSIA
Eremophila maculata

IDENTIFICATION
Colour When the bush is in flower it is a bright spot in the outback, with the yellow-red flowers showing up against the dark green of the leaves.
Size Up to 1.5 m tall.
Distinguishing features The flowers are similar in shape to the garden variety of fuchsia. The native fuchsias, or eremophilas, are also called emu bushes because their flowers and succulent fruits are fed on by emus and other birds, like the mallee ringneck, that feed on the flowers in the early morning.

LOCATION
All mainland states.

HABITAT
It is generally found in areas where water lies after rain, such as on the contour of a rocky hillside, with a wide range of plants on clay soils.

ENVIRONMENTAL NOTES
Status This is a widespread plant throughout its range but it may appear as an individual plant or a thicket.
Natural control agents The availability of suitable sites controls the spread of this plant.
Reproduction Birds feeding on the succulent fruit help to spread the plant.

OLD MAN SALTBUSH
Atriplex nummularia

LOCATION
Mainland Australia in the low rainfall areas.

HABITAT
Mainly on clay soils in flat areas. Often found in flood plains, where the soil can vary from heavy grey clay to fine alluvial loam. It is also found in a variety of scrubland areas away from flood zones.

IDENTIFICATION
Colour Its overall colour is grey, although this gets shaded to a rusty orange when the plant is in flower.
Size It is up to 2 m high. It is often rounded in shape, thick, with brittle woody branches that can give the plant a ground cover of 4 or 5 m.
Distinguishing features You can distinguish old man saltbush when it is associated with other saltbush, or similar shrubs, by its size.

ENVIRONMENTAL NOTES
Status Old man saltbush is the largest and most widespread of all the saltbush, although it has been removed or severely damaged in some areas. Saltbush does contain salt, and this is one aspect that may make it palatable to stock. Often it is the only edible plant left in an area during harsh times, and sheep stay alive by feeding on it. Rabbits use the area under its shaggy, spreading branches as ideal places to dig warrens, and cattle bash it down as they feed on it. All in all, old man saltbush has a battle to survive.
Natural control agents Predominantly controlled by climate under natural conditions.
Reproduction Old man saltbush produces so many flowers as to change the colour of the plant. It flowers from spring to early summer.

MULGA
Acacia aneura

LOCATION
All mainland states except Victoria and Tasmania.

HABITAT
The red soil and rocky soils of the low rainfall areas.

IDENTIFICATION
Colour It has silvery grey-green leaves. The individual flower stems are a deep yellow. Although the flowers are not in the huge, golden clusters of wattles like the Cootamundra wattle *(Acacia baileyana)*, when in flower the mulga gives a

PLANTS

soft golden glow to its part of the outback.
Size It grows to less than 8 m high.
Distinguishing features The mulga is one of the wattle family, but it does not have the flower show of wattles of the higher rainfall areas. You will have to look for a plant that is bushy, thinly branched and grows in scattered clumps.

ENVIRONMENTAL NOTES
Status Mulga wood has a beautiful grain and it has been used for making small ornaments for many years. The Aboriginal people use its hard, strong wood for making boomerangs, and the European settlers used it for fenceposts and the foliage as fodder for their cattle.
Natural control agents As for other acacias, mulga is prone to attack by a range of insects or their larvae, that may completely defoliate the tree.

Reproduction It will flower at any time of the year following rain. Acacias have pod-shaped fruit containing many seeds, and these germinate very well under the right conditions, creating dense thickets of mulga.

MALLEE
Eucalyptus spp.

LOCATION
All the mainland states, in areas where the rainfall averages between 250 mm and 500 mm per year.

HABITAT
In poor soils, from sand plains and dunes, to the flat clay plains.

IDENTIFICATION
Colour Grey-green foliage, with the colour of the flowers depending on the species, from white through cream, yellow and red (the full range of eucalypt flower colours).
Size Mallee scrub is usually less than 8 m tall, and often is only about 4 m high.
Distinguishing features These eucalypts have many stems instead of the one trunk

seen on most 'gum trees': the plants springing up from the ground look like the ribs of a half-opened umbrella.

You will soon come to recognise the look of mallee forest, even though it may have many plants growing underneath in some areas, and be bare in others. The amount of undergrowth depends on the soil type and the amount of rainfall.

ENVIRONMENTAL NOTES

Status Although many mallee areas have been cleared for farming, it is still widespread in pockets, particularly in NSW, Victoria and South Australia.

Natural control agents As for other eucalypt species (see page 103).

Reproduction As for other eucalypt species.

Further Reading List

MAMMALS

FRITH, H.J., *Wildlife Conservation.* Angus and Robertson, Sydney, 1973.
RIDE, W.D.L. *Native Mammals of Australia.* Oxford University Press, Melbourne, 1970.
ROLLS, E.C., *They All Ran Wild.* Angus and Robertson, Sydney, 1969.
STRAHAN, R.(ed), *Complete Book of Australian Mammals.* Angus & Robertson, Sydney, 1983.

BIRDS

BLAKERS, M., S.J.J.F. DAVIES & P.N. REILLY. *The Atlas of Australian Birds.* Melbourne University Press, Melbourne, 1984.
PIZZEY, G. *A Field Guide to the Birds of Australia.* Collins, Sydney, 1980.
READER'S DIGEST. *Complete Book of Australian Birds.* Reader's Digest, Sydney, 1976.
SIMPSON, K. & N. DAY. *The Birds of Australia.* Melbourne University Press, Melbourne, 1984.

REPTILES AND AMPHIBIANS

COGGER, H.G. *Australian Reptiles in Colour.* A.H. & A.W. Reed, Sydney, 1967.
COGGER, H.G. *Reptiles and Amphibians of Australia.* A.H. & A.W. Reed, Sydney, 1975.
MCPHEE, D.R. *Snakes and Lizards of Australia.* Methuen, Sydney, 1979.
PINCHIN, R. *Frogs.* Hodder and Stoughton, Sydney, 1986.

FURTHER READING LIST

FISH

KOEHN, J.D. & W.G. O'CONNOR. *Biological Information for Management of Native Freshwater Fish in Victoria.* Victorian Government Printing Office, Melbourne, 1990.
LAKE, J.S. *Australian Freshwater Fishes.* Nelson, Melbourne, 1978.

INSECTS

CSIRO. *The Insects of Australia.* Melbourne University Press, Melbourne, 1970.
D'ABRERA, B. *Moths of Australia.* Lansdowne Press, Melbourne, 1974.
HEALY, A.C. SMITHERS. *Australian Insects in Colour.* A.H. & A.W. Reed, Sydney, 1971.
HUGHES, R.D. *Living Insects.* Collins, Sydney, 1974.

PLANTS

AULD, B.A. & R.W. MEDD. *Weeds.* Inkata Press, Melbourne, 1987.
BLOMBERY, A.M. *The Flowers of Central Australia.* Kangaroo Press, Sydney, 1989.
BROOKER, M.I.H. & D.A. KLEINIG. *Field Guide to Eucalypts.* Ikata Press, Melbourne, 1983.
CUNNINGHAM, G.M., W.E. MULHAM, P.L. MILTHORPE, J.H. LEIGH. *Plants of Western New South Wales.* NSW Government Printing Office, Sydney, 1981.
HALL, N., R.D. JOHNSTON & G.M. CHIPPENDALE. *Forest Trees of Australia.* Australian Government Publishing Service, Canberra, 1970.
WRIGLEY, J.W. & M. FAGG. *Australian Native Plants.* Collins, Sydney, 1980.

Index

Numbers in **bold** indicate the main entry for species that are mentioned several times in the text.

Abantiades spp., 141
Aborigines, 6, 41, 108, 110, 149, 192-3
Acacia, 32
  aneura, 192
  doratoxylon, 151
  pendula, 41
  stenophylla, 104
Acanthagenys rufogularis, 133
Acanthiza uropygialis, 136
Acanthophis antarcticus, 137
Acetosa vesicaria, 45
Amphibians, see frog, desert tree; frog, green tree; frog, water-holding
Amphibolurus barbatus, 29
Amyema spp., 150
Anas gibberifrons, 85
  superciliosa, 84
Anhinga melanogaster, 79
ant, bulldog, 142
ant-eater, spiny, 112
ant-lion, 184
Anthus novaeseelandiae, 24
Apis mellifera, 69
Aquila audax, 22
Ardea novaehollandiae, 81
Ardeotis australis, 167
Artamus cinereus, 135
Arthrocnemum spp., 185
Atriplex mummularia, 192
avocet, red-necked, 92
Azolla filiculoides, 109

babbler, white-browed, 173
Barnardius barnardi, 170
bat, 32
  Gould's wattled, 117
  lesser long-eared, 117
bee, honey, 69
bee-eater, rainbow, 170
beefwood, 149
beetle, scarab, 146
belah, 147
bellbird, crested, 129
berrigan, 152
Bidyanus bidyanus, 97
bilby, 14, 155
billy buttons, golden, 36
Birds
  Grassland, see pipit, Richard's;
  Honeyeaters, see honeyeater, spiny-cheeked;
    honeyeater, singing;
    honeyeater, white-plumed;
    miner, yellow-throated;
    mallee, malleefowl;
  Night, see boobook, southern; frogmouth,

tawny; nightjar, spotted;
Of Prey, see falcon, peregrine; kestrel, Australian; kestrel, nankeen; kite, black shouldered; eagle, wedge-tailed; falcon, black; falcon, brown; harrier, marsh; hawk, chicken; kite, black; kite, whistling
Open Country, see bee-eater, rainbow; bellbird, crested; budgerigar; bustard, Australian; chat, crimson; crow, little; dove diamond; emu; fairy-wren, white-winged; finch, zebra; kingfisher, red-backed; lapwing, banded; magpie-lark; martin, fairy; pigeon, crested; quail stubble; songlark, brown; thick-knee, bush
Parrot Family, see cockatiel; cockatoo pink; cockatoo, red-tailed black; cockatoo, sulphur-crested; corella, little; galah; parrot, Bourke's; parrot, red-rumped; ringneck, mallee
Water, see ibis, sacred; avocet, red-necked; coot, Eurasian; cormorant, little pied; darter; dotterel, red-kneed; duck, black; duck, maned; egret, great; grebe, hoary-headed; heron, white-faced; ibis, sacred; ibis, straw-necked; moorhen, dusky; native-hen, black-tailed; pelican, Australian; plover, black-fronted; spoonbill, royal; stilt, black-winged; swamphen, purple; swan, black
Woodland, see shrike-thrush, grey; babbler, white-browed; bronze-cuckoo, Horsfield's; bronzewing, common; butcherbird, pied; cuckoo shrike, black-faced; kookaburra, laughing; magpie, Australian; robin, red-capped; thornbill, chestnut-rumped; whistler, rufous;

woodswallow, black-faced; wren, variegated
bluebush, satiny, 190
boobialla, western, 70
boobook, southern, 123
box, bimble, 40
  black, 105
  grey, 146
  yellow, 145
Brachychiton populneus, 38
Brachycome spp., 37
bronze-cuckoo, Horsfield's, 121
• bronzewing, common, 126
brumby, 49
budgerigar, 168
Bufo marinus, 52
bulrush, 108
bunyip, 128
Burhinus magnirostris, 127
bushman's clock, 125
bustard, Australian, 167
butcherbird, 131, 140-41
  pied, **136**
butterbush, 152

Cacatua galerita, 122
  leadbeateri, 118
  roseicapilla, 26
  sanguinea, 123
Calandrinia balonensis, 185
Callitris columellaris, 41
Calyptorhynchus magnificus, 119
camel, 7, 163
camelus dromedarius, 163
cane-toad, 52
Canis familiaris, 162
Caprimulgus guttatus, 169
carp, common, 96, 99
Cassia artemisioides, 39
  spp., 172
  silver, 39
Casuarina, 120
  cristata, 147
caterpillar, bag-shelter moth, 41
  hairy, 121, 130
  procession, 31
catfish, 97
cat, feral, 7, 13-14, 24, **48**, 56-7, 62, 65-6, 75, 91-2, 113, 115-16, 118, 125, 127-8, 130, 160-62, 166, 169-70, 175-7, 179
cattle, 38
Cecropis ariel, 27
cedar, white, 69
Cercartetus concinnus, 160
Charadrius melanops, 86
chat, crimson, 175
Chelodina longicollis, 94

197

INDEX

chemicals, 35, 47
Chenonetta jubata, 60
Chenopodium nitrariaceum, 107
Cherax destructor, 101
 spp., 101
Chortoicetes terminifera, 33
Chrysococcyx basalis, 121
cicada, 131, **142**
Cinclorhamphus cruralis, 172
Circus aeruginosus, 91-2
Citrullus colocynthis, 43
 lanatus, 43
 spp., 43
Clianthus formosus, 188
Climacteris picumnus, 131
cockatiel, 25
cockatoo, Major Mitchell, 119
 pink, 103, **118**
 red-tailed black, 119
 sulphur-crested, 122
cod, Murray, 96, **98**, 101
Colluricincla harmonica, 134
Columbia livia, 55
cooba river, 104
coolibah, 104
coot, Eurasian, 91
Coptotermes spp., 34
Coracina novaehollandiae, 131
corella, little, 123
cormorant, little pied, 78
 pied, 78
Corvus bennetti, 60
Corvus coronoides, 60
Coturnix pectoralis, 56
Cracticus nigrogularis, 136
Craspedia chrysantha, 36
crayfish, 75, 99
 Murray River, **100**
crow, little, 60
crustaceans, yabbie, marron, gilgie, 101
cuckoo-shrike, black-faced, 131
cuckoo, 32
Cucumis myriocarpus, 43
cumbungi, 108
Cumumis spp., 43
curlew, 128
currawong (plant), 151
currawong (bird), 131
Cyclorana platycephalus, 180
Cygnus atratus, 82
Cyprinus carprio, 99

Dacelo novaeguineae, 125
daisy, 37
daisy, minnie, 37
damselfly, 102
darter, 79
Dasyurus maculatus, 113
death adder, common, 137
Demansia psammophis, 66
desert pea, Sturt's, 188
dingo, 16, 19, 49, 51-2, 114, 116, 159, **162**, 174
Diplodactylus intermedius, 181
 tessellatus, 64
Dodonaea spp., 35
 viscosa, 35
dog, domestic, 83, 85, 92, 114, 116
donkey, 7, **164**

dotterel, red-kneed, 89
dove, diamond, 165
dragon, bearded, 29
dragonfly, 102
Dromaius novaehollandiae, 18
dtella, tree, 140
duck, black, 84
 maned, 60
dunnart, fat-tailed, 156

eagle, 13, 15, 19, 51
 wedge-tailed, 12, **22**, 88, 159
echidna, short-beaked, 112
Echium plantagineum, 56
Egernia stokesii, 183
 striolata, 139
egret, great, 80
Egretta alba, 80
Elanus notatus, 20
emu, **18**, 51, 163, 191
Emydura macquarii, 95
Ephthianura tricolor, 175
Equus asinus, 164
 caballus, 49
Eremophila maculata, 191
Erythrogonys cinctus, 89
Euastacus armatus, 100
eucalypt, 7
 blossom, 53
Eucalyptus camaldulensis, 103
 largiflorens, 105
 melanophloia, 145
 melliodora, 145
 microcarpa, 146
 microtheca, 104
 populnea, 40
 sideroxylon, 144
 spp., 193
everlasting, yellow, 186

fairy-wren, white-winged, 177
Falco berigora, 21
 cenchroides, 23
 niger, 120
 peregrinus, 22
Falcon, 56-7, 64, 75, 123, 166, 170-1, 176
 black, **120**
 brown, **21**
 peregrine, **22**, 27, 61
Family Cicadidae, 142
 Myrmeleontidae, 184
 Tabanidae, 69
Felis catus, 48
feral cat, see 'cat'
fertiliser, 109
finch, zebra, 174
Fish, see carp, common; catfish; cod, Murray; crayfish, Murray River; perch, golden; perch, silver
Flindersia maculosa, 151
fly, bush, 68
flying-fox, little red, 53
fox, 13, 19, 33, 49-51, 54, 57, 61, 85, 90-2, 107, 114, 128, 159, 161-2, 166-8, 170, 174
foxtails, 189
frog, 50
 desert tree, 93

green tree, 61
 water-holding, 180
frogmouth, tawny, 124
fuchsia, spotted, 191
Fulica atra, 91

galah, 12, 22, **26**
Gallinula tenebrosa, 91
Gallinula ventralis, 90
Gastrimargus musicus, 32
gecko, beaded, 180
 eastern spiny-tailed, 181
 tesselated, 64
Gehyra variegata, 140
Geijera parviflora, 148
Geophila cuneata, 165
gilgie, 101
glider, feathertail, 113
goanna, 15, 19, 27, 31, 50, 54, 61, 67, 115, 119, 123, 126, 176, 179
 Gould's, **28**
goat, feral, 7, **165**
goosefoot, nitre, 107
Grallina cyanoleuca, 59
grass, kangaroo, 35
grasshopper, 21, 50, 168
grebe, Australasian, 77
 hoary-headed, 77
Grevillea juncifolia, 149
 spp., 149
 striata, 149
gum, river red, **103**, 115
Gymnorhina tibicen, 58

Haliastur sphenurus, 88
Halycon pyrrhopygiai, 174
hare, brown, 13
harrier, 57
hawk, 13, 15, 19, 27, 29, 31, 51, 56-7, 64, 67, 119, 123, 166, 170-1, 176, 184
 chicken, **21**
Helichrysum bracteatum, 186
heron, white-faced, 81
Himantopus himantopus, 93
Hirundo neoxena, 28
honeyeater, singing, 178
 spiny-cheeked, 133
 white-plumed, 179
Hop, domestic, 35
 wild, 45
hopbush, broad-leaf, 35
hopping-mouse, Mitchell's, 161
horse, 49
Hydromys chrysogaster, 75

ibis, sacred, 19, 83
 straw-necked, 19, 33
Ice Age, 6
Insects see ant, bulldog; cicada; damselfly, dragonfly; fly, bush; locust, yellow-winged; March-fly; meat-ant; moth, bag-shelter; moth, swift; termite
Iridomyrmex purpureus, 143
ironbark, mugga, 144
 silver-leaved, 145

198

INDEX

Jasus spp., 100
jockey's cap, 187
joey, 15-16

kangaroo, 6-7, 12, 36
  eastern grey, 15
  red, 17
  western grey, 16
kestrel, 176
  Australian, 20, 23
  nankeen, 24
Kinchega, 155
kingfisher, red-backed, 174
kite, black, 57
  black-shouldered, 20
  whistling, 88
koala, 115
kookaburra, laughing, 29-31, 63-4, 67, **125**, 140-41, 184
kurrajong, 38

lacewing, 184
Lake Eyre, 6, 73
lapwing, banded, 54
  masked, 54
Lasiorhinus krefftii, 157
  latifrons, 157
laughing jackass, 125
Leiolopisma guichenoti, 65
Leipoa ocellata, 166
leopardwood, 151
Leptocneira reducta, 70
Lepus capensis, 13
leveret, 13
lice, blood-sucking, 28
Lichenostomus penicillatus, 179
  virescens, 178
lignum, 91, **106**
Litoria caerulea, 61
  rubella, 93
Lizard, 163
  dragon, bearded, 29
  eastern blue-tongued, 65
  western blue-tongued, 65
lobster, salt-water, 100
locust, plague, 20, 24, 33
  yellow-winged, **32**
Lucasium damaeum, 180
Lysiana spp., 150

Maccullochella peeli, 98
Marcquaria ambigua, 96
Macquarie Marshes, 73
Macropus fuliginosus, 16
  giganteus, 15
  robustus, 159
  rufus, 17
Macrotis lagotis, 14, 155
magpie, Australian, 58, 141
magpie-lark, Australian, 59
Maireana georgei, 190
mallee, 154, **193**
malleefowl, 6, **166**
Malurus lamberti, 176
  leucopterus, 177
Mammals
  Marsupials, see bilby; dunnart, fat-tailed; glider, feathertail; kangaroo, eastern grey; kangaroo, red; kangaroo, western grey; koala; mouse, marsupial; planigale, narrow-nosed; possum, common brushtail; pygmy-possum, western; rock-wallaby, yellow-footed; wallaroo, common; wombat, hairy-nosed
  Monotremes, see echidna, short-beaked
  Placental, see bat, Gould's wattled; bat, lesser long-eared; mastiff-bat, little; hare; mouse, house; rabbit; camel; cat, feral; dingo; donkey; flying-fox, little red; fox; goat, feral; hopping-mouse, Mitchell's; horse; pig, feral; rat, plains; water-rat
mange, 50
Manorina flavigula, 132
Manorina melanocephala, 132
March-fly, 69
marron, 101
Marsilea drummondii, 107
martin, fairy, **27**, 32
mastiff-bat, little, 116
meat-ant, 143
Melia azedarach, 69
melon, camel, 43
  paddy, 43
  wild, 43
Melopsitacus undulatus, 168
Merops ornatus, 170
Milvus migrans, 57
miner, noisy, 132
  yellow-throated, 132
Minuria leptophylla, 37
mistletoe, 150
  yellow, 151
Moloch horridus, 182
monitor, lace, 138
Morelia spilotes, 62
Mormopterus planiceps, 116
moth, 124
  bag-shelter, 31
  swift, 141
  white cedar, 70
mouse, house, 20, **52**, 124
  marsupial, 33
mudlark, 59
Muehlenbeckia cunninghamii, 106
mulga, 192
Mus musculus, 25
Musca vetustissima, 68
myall, 41
Myoporum montanum, 70
Myrmecia spp., 142
Myrmecobius fasciatus, 34
myxomatosis, 14

nardoo, common, 107
Narran Lake, 84, 106
National Parks and Wildlife Service, 9
native hen, black-tailed, 90
Neophema bourkii, 171
nettle, 71
nightjar, spotted, 169
Ninox novaeseelandiae, 123
Notomys mitchelli, 161
Nullarbor Plain, 129
numbat, 34
Nyctophilus geoffroyi, 117
Nymphicus hollandicus, 25

Ochrogaster contraria, 31
Ocyphaps lophotes, 55
Order *Odonata*, 102
Oreoica gutturalis, 129
Ornithorhynchus anatinus, 113
Oryctolagus cuniculus, 14
owl, 65, 138, 156, 161, 181

Pachycephala rufiventris, 128
pan-pan-panella, 129
parakeelya, broad-leaf, 185
parrot, Bourke's, 171
  red-rumped, 26
Paterson's curse, 56
pea, Darling, 42
Pelecanus conspicillatus, 76
pelican, Australian, 76
pepper tree, 72
perch, golden, 96
  silver, 97
pesticide, 22
Petrogale xanthopus, 158
Petroica goodenovii, 130
Phalacrocorax melanoleucos, 78
  varius, 78
Phaps chalcoptera, 126
Phascolarctos cinereus, 115
pig, feral, **51**, 106
pigeon, crested, 55
  feral, 55
pigface, 185
pine, cypress, 39
  radiata, 42
  white cypress, 41
Pinus radiata, 42
pipit, Richard's, **24**, 33
Pittosporum phillyreoides, 152
plains rat, 161
Planigale tenuirostris, 156
planigale, narrow-nosed, 156
Plants, see azolla, red; belah; billy buttons, golden; bluebush, satiny; boobialla, western; box, bimble; box, black; box, grey; box, yellow; butterbush; cassia, silver; cedar, white; cooba, river; coolibah; cumbungi; currawong; daisy; daisy, minnie; desert pea, Sturt's; everlasting, yellow; foxtails, pussy-tails, rabbit-tails; fuchsia, spotted; goosefoot, nitre; grass, kangaroo; gum, river red; hop, wild; hopbush; ironbark mugga; jockey's cap; kurrajong; leopardwood; lignum; mallee; melon, wild; mistletoe; mulga;

199

INDEX

myall; nardoo, common; nettle; parakeelya, broad-leaf; pea, Darling; pepper tree; pine, white cypress; potato bush, velvet; quandong; saltbush, old man; spider-flower; spinifex, lobed; wilga
Platalea flavipes, 82
 regia, 81
platypus, 112
plover, black-fronted, 86
 spurwing, 54
Podargus strigoides, 124
Poephila guttata, 174
Poliocephalus poliocephalus, 77
Pomatostomus superciliosus, 173
Porphyrio porphyrio, 87
possum, common brushtail, 114
 potato bush, velvet, 187
Prostanthera striatiflora, 187
Psephotus haematonotus, 26
Pseudomys australis, 161
Pseudonaja nuchalis, 66
 textilis, 66
Pteropus scapulatus, 53
Ptilotus spp., 189
pussy tails, 189
pygmy-possum, western, 160
Pygopus lepidopodus, 183
python, carpet, 62
 diamond, 62

quail, stubble, 56
quandong, 148
quoll, spotted-tailed, 113

rabbit-tails, 189
rabbit, 7, 13- 14, 23, 36, 47, 50, 63
raven, Australian, 60
Recurvirostra novaehollandiae, 92
Reptiles, see death adder; dtella, tree; gecko, beaded; gecko, eastern spiny-tailed; gecko, tessellated; goanna, Gould's; lizard, western blue-tongued; monitor, lace; python, carpet; python, diamond; scaly-foot, common; shingle-back; skink, gidgee; skink, tree; snake, eastern brown; snake, myall; snake, western brown; snake, yellow-faced whip; thorny devil; tortoise, long-necked; turtle, Murray
ringneck, mallee, 170
robin, red-capped, 130
rock-wallaby, yellow-footed, 158
roly-poly, 44

safety when travelling, 8
Salsola kali, 44
saltbush, old man, 47, **192**
samphire, 185
Santalum acuminatum, 148
scaly-foot, common, 183
Schinus areira, 72
sea-eagle, white-bellied, 81, 88, 95-6
sheep, 35-6, 38, 163, 189, 192
shingle-back, 30
shrike-thrush, grey, 134
skink, common garden, 65
 gidgee, 183
 tree, 139
Sminthopsis crassicaudata, 156
snake, 6, 15, 50
 curl, 64
 eastern brown, 66
 myall, 63
 western brown, 66
 yellow-faced whip, 66
Solanum ellipticum, 187
songlark, brown, 172
spider-flower, 149
 honey-suckle, 149
spinifex, lobed, 189
spoonbill, royal, 81
 yellow-billed, 82
sporocarp, 108
starling, common, 132
stilt, black-winged, 93
stock routes, 11
Streptolia chinensis, 55
Sturnus vulgaris, 132
Sus scrofa, 51
Suta suta, 63
Swainsona spp., 42-3
swallow, welcome, 28
swamphen, purple, 87
swan, black, 82

table drain, 12
Tachybaptus novaehollandiae, 77
Tachyglossus aculeatus, 112
Tandanus tandanus, 97
teal, grey, 85
termite, 34
Themeda australis, 35
thick-knee, bush, 127
thornbill, chestnut-rumped, 136
thorny devil, 182
Threskiornis aethiopica, 83
 spinicollis, 19
Tiliqua occipitalis, 65
 scincoides, 65
tortoise, long-necked, 94
 snake-necked, 95
Trachydosaurus rugosus, 30
tree-creeper, brown, 131
Trichosurus vulpecula, 114
Triodia basedownia, 189
tumbleweed, 44
turtle, Murray, 95
turtle-dove, spotted, 55
Typha orientalis, 108

Urtica spp., 71

Vanellus miles, 54
 tricolor, 54
Varanus gouldii, 28
 varanus, 138
Vulpes vulpes, 49

wallaroo, common, 159
wasp, gall, 105
water-rat, **75**, 101, 103
watermelon, wild, 43
whistler, rufous, 128
wilga, 148
Willandra National Park, 25
willow, native, 105
wombat, 7, 163
 hairy-nosed, **157**
woodswallow, black-faced, 135
wren, variegated, 176

yabbie, 20, 96, **101**